BEYOND

THE MILITARY

JASON RONCORONI AND SHAUNA SPRINGER, PHD

BEYOND
THE MILITARY

A LEADER'S HANDBOOK
FOR WARRIOR REINTEGRATION

LIONCREST
PUBLISHING

BEYOND THE MILITARY
A Leader's Handbook for Warrior Reintegration

ISBN   978-1-5445-0557-2 *Paperback*
        978-1-5445-0568-8 *Ebook*

To the service members, veterans, and families who volunteered for military service, may you find your path to purpose and happiness beyond the military.

CONTENTS

ABOUT THIS HANDBOOK

We define the military profession through technical manuals, training circulars, publications, checklists, and guides that outline everything you have to do and precisely how you have to do it. We live and breathe by doctrine. Perhaps the most indispensable reference for operations and planning during my career was the *Staff Officer's Guide*—a handbook that combined doctrine, best practices, and techniques into one reference for military leaders. The *Staff Officer's Guide* provided the instructions for all things related to operations, planning, and mission command. It was among the most recognizable and indispensable resources for any tactical unit in the army.

The military has a manual for everything. Everything, that is, except for the hardest part of the military journey: *leaving. Beyond the Military: A Leader's Handbook for Warrior Reintegration* is meant to fill that void. This handbook serves as *your* indispensable guide to prepare you for military transition and civilian reintegration. Additionally, this handbook is written with the intimacy and tone of a coaching partnership and relationship counseling for your successful reintegration back into society. This is your guide to discover purpose and meaning for a more fulfilling life beyond the uniform.

WHO BENEFITS FROM THIS HANDBOOK?

This handbook will benefit service members of any rank transitioning from the military, but this was written specifically for more experienced and senior-level leaders. Based on my personal observations and experience through the transition and reintegration process, leaders with ten or more years of military service will benefit the most from this handbook within two years of their separation date (before or after). The *ideal candidate* is the leader who spent his or her formative years of adulthood serving in the military and is twelve months from separation or retirement. However, even those who have already been discharged from the military may substantially benefit from this content since making a successful transition and reintegration is a process—not a date on the calendar.

THE INTENT BEHIND *BEYOND THE MILITARY: A LEADER'S HANDBOOK FOR WARRIOR REINTEGRATION*

This handbook provides a mechanism to "look in" before you begin to "look out" for your next job after separation or retirement. The main purpose of this handbook is to uncover your unique identity story for the next chapter of your life. This handbook is a comprehensive, interactive resource that addresses the deeper psychological, cultural, and relational aspects of modern warrior reintegration. This handbook does not address the more recognizable tactics and practices involved in securing employment—topics that are the primary focus of existing "transition manuals." You won't learn how to update your résumé, translate your military skills, write a cover letter, or complete an online job application from this handbook. Instead, this handbook will help you through the more difficult introspective work that should occur before you start looking for the next job. This program was designed to facilitate personal growth so that you can discover your path for lifelong fulfillment—a more ambitious objective than simply finding a new job. Additionally, the contribution of Dr. Shauna Springer's expertise in the final section of this handbook offers critical insights for building and maintaining healthy, close relationships through military transition and beyond.

Every action in the military is grounded in the commander's Statement of Intent. Using the framework of Purpose, Method, and End State, here is the "intent" of this handbook:

PURPOSE

The purpose of this handbook is to create a strategy for civilian reintegration, continued growth, and lifelong success as a veteran leader in civilian society.

METHOD

This handbook is structured in three parts to address the key and essential tasks to solve the complex problem of military transition and civilian reintegration:

Part 1. The Threshold. Set the context for understanding military transition and define an Integrative Program of Transition to achieve higher and more sustainable levels of self-actualization through transition, reintegration, and beyond.

Part 2. The Military Transition and Reintegration Process. Discover and align your identity story with opportunities for lifelong growth and empowerment using existing doctrine as a template for creating a personalized solution to the complex problem of military transition and civilian reintegration.

Part 3. Culture and Relationships. Provide strategies to discover your new tribe and build healthy, meaningful relationships for continued growth and well-being as a veteran leader in society.

END STATE

The deliverables and intended outcomes of this handbook include the following:

1. Leaders recognize their authentic identity including their personal values (the WHO) and their unique purpose (the WHY), and they are prepared to pursue opportunities with the greatest potential for personal and professional fulfillment.

2. Leaders create an achievable and sustainable plan for integrative transition that optimizes whole health, socialization, cultural assimilation, economic stability, professional preparedness, and family adjustment in life beyond the military.

3. Military leaders and their families are inspired with the confidence to strengthen relationships and live a more empowering, joyful, and impactful life after military service.

We believe that military leaders are uniquely qualified to tackle some of the most complex and difficult challenges facing society today. This handbook seeks to align your passion and purpose to be a more impactful veteran leader in civilian society. The essential question this handbook seeks to answer is...

> *How can I create a life that honors who I am, allows me to make an impact doing things that I care deeply about, and strengthens my relationships in meaningful ways?*

THE STORY BEHIND THE HANDBOOK

Throughout my military career and beyond, I have been an avid student of leadership and the psychology of human behavior. I earned a master of science in industrial/organizational psychology and a master of business administration. My aviation career culminated in battalion-level command and included thirty-three months of combat service in some of the most dangerous regions of Afghanistan. When I retired, I spent some time working as a leader and strategic advisor for several nationally recognized nonprofit organizations that sought to improve the condition of wellness in the veteran community. I eventually became a Certified Professional Coach, Certified Authentic Leadership Coach, and credentialed coaching professional through the International Coach Federation.

Despite my extensive education and success through the military, I failed transition—not once, but twice. I left the military as a junior officer and landed in the wrong job. I was paid well, but I wasn't happy. My job lacked personal meaning. I didn't know my purpose. I didn't know who I was without the uniform. I felt lost both personally and professionally. After 9/11, I returned to active duty and served for another fifteen years. When I retired, I still didn't get transition right. My experiences, education, professional training, and the thousands of stories I've heard from veterans and their families informed the structure and content of this handbook. Stated another way, I want to provide everything that I wish I had for **either** of my transitions from the military.

On a personal note, my purpose is to ***inspire leaders to live meaningful lives in the service of others.*** My core belief is that the military experience is preparation for a more empowering and impactful opportunity in life beyond the military. Helping you find *your* purpose is one way that I fulfill *my* purpose. Given the deeper psychological, cultural, and relational approach of this handbook, I was excited when Dr. Shauna "Doc" Springer offered to leverage her more than twenty years of experience in working with veterans and their families to support this project. As a renowned expert in building and sustaining healthy relationships, her contribution is designed to help you forge stronger, healthier bonds with the people you care about most through transition and reintegration. Together, we share in the passion to help you discover *your* passion in life beyond the military.

Bearing that in mind, let's get started.

PART 1

THE THRESHOLD

Four or five moments...

There are only a handful of moments over the course of our lives that leave us forever changed. They define our path. They shape the person and leader that we will become. Getting married is one of these moments. Having children is another. For many of us, that first moment occurred at a young age. It happened shortly after we graduated from high school. It was the moment we drove through the front gate of that first military installation and reported for duty. It was the day we swore an oath to serve our country.

On that day, we crossed a threshold into an unknown world of adventure. Maybe you did it for the challenge. Maybe you did it for the college tuition. Maybe you did it just because—at the time—you didn't know what else to do. Whatever reason brought you to that moment, your life opened up to opportunities and experiences that made you a better version of yourself, and in the eyes of the nation you served, you became the hero.

After years or decades of service, you feel the impending approach of another one of these moments. It is the moment you decide to drive out that gate for the last time. It is when you remove the armor and put down the shield you've carried for so many years and return to the society you protected and defended. Every day in the service brings you one day closer to this moment: when you arrive at the threshold to life beyond the military. For all of us, leaving is a part of the journey.

Part 1 of this handbook serves as a guide to understanding that moment at the threshold between life in the military and life beyond the military. As you stand before the threshold, it is normal to hesitate. That is why Part 1 of this handbook examines whether or not it is time for you to leave. It also provides a context in which to understand transition from a psychological and even anthropological viewpoint. Finally, it defines a strategic approach to reintegration so that you can launch yourself into the next chapter of your life.

Every warrior will approach this moment, and what happens immediately before and after will shape your path in life beyond the military.

SHOULD I STAY OR SHOULD I GO?

This is perhaps the most frequently asked question at every juncture of the military journey. When you finished your initial service obligation, you asked yourself this question. When you received your most recent assignment orders, you probably asked this question. Each time the military wanted to uproot your family or send you on another deployment, you asked this question. The fact that you're reading this is probably a good indicator that you're asking yourself this question now. How do you know when the time is right to remove your body armor, unlace your boots, and remove the uniform that shaped your identity for most, if not all, of your adult life?

The first time that I left the army, I did so for all the wrong reasons. First, I worked for some toxic leaders. I assumed that what I had experienced in those first few years of service was the only possible outcome for every subsequent assignment of my career. Second, I thought that leaving the army would magically solve any and all problems in my personal life. Third, I did it for the money. Recruiters love hiring junior officers, and on the surface, my first job offer was for a lot more money than what I was making as a young captain in the army. I transitioned from the military for the wrong reasons, and as you might expect, my life didn't unfold in the ways I had hoped.

So, what are some of the right reasons for leaving the military? From my mistakes and the many conversations I've had with veterans across the country, I've discovered three signs that tell you when it's time to hang up the uniform. The first reason has to do with your health. The second concerns intentions: the distinction between what you *want* and what you think you might *need*. The last consideration is about your level of attachment to the uniform and your perceived sense of self-worth. Ultimately, these three reasons are related to your potential for continued growth over the course of your life.

REASON 1: CONTINUED SERVICE COMPROMISES YOUR HEALTH AND WELLNESS

This sounds obvious, but I'm not talking about the usual suspects for health and wellness.

Naturally, if you can no longer perform your duty because of an injury, combat action, or other significant change to your health, the military already has protocols to remove you from the line of duty. Since the wars in Afghanistan and Iraq began, we've developed more aggressive interventions to identify cases of traumatic brain injury (TBI), post-traumatic stress disorder (PTSD), and other issues related to a service member's state of emotional and mental wellness. Unfortunately, the cycle of deployments has created a revolving door between varying states of peace and war with unknown consequences to the long-term wellness of our military and veteran populations.

The hard truth is that we still don't know the enduring health implications of post-9/11 military service. The few studies that do exist suggest that the likelihood of succumbing to PTSD is three times more likely after the second deployment.[1] Unfortunately, we have men and women who have served in combat for as many as five or more deployments. Like it or not, this is the way of the future. We don't have a standard to recognize the limits of human endurance when it comes to combat deployments. We don't know when enough is enough. By default, we are learning as we go. It may be some time before we have proven treatment strategies for some of the more salient health conditions from repeated combat deployments.

The military may not recognize how many deployments are too many—but perhaps you might. Have the courage to be honest with yourself. The signs may be subtle, but both you and your family will notice the changes. You might feel detached from your partner. You might have chronic sleep issues. If you've already served on multiple combat deployments, you have to consider the impact of yet another deployment on the mental and emotional wellness of you and your family. This isn't a character issue. It is not a function of personal bravado. It is a matter of your physiology and psychology. Your health and wellness are the most important factors in the decision to leave the military, so have the courage to make the right choice before exceeding your limits.

REASON 2: THE THINGS YOU NEED REPLACE THE THINGS YOU WANT

When I was a lieutenant, I wanted to be a company commander. After company command, I was looking forward to battalion command. These positions were guideposts along my career, but I wasn't focused on any specific role, position, or job title. I truly believed in the work that I was doing. I was excited to serve. I didn't mind putting in the extra hours or

---

1. Anna Kline, Maria Falca-Dodson, Bradley Sussner, Donald S. Ciccone, Helena Chandler, Lanora Callahan, and Miklos Losonczy, "Effects of Repeated Deployment to Iraq and Afghanistan on the Health of New Jersey Army National Guard Troops: Implications for Military Readiness," *American Journal of Public Health* 100, no. 2 (February 2010), 276, https://doi.org/10.2105/ajph.2009.162925.

weekend time because I felt like I was making a difference. My intentions were growth related and based on my aspirations for personal achievement and organizational impact.

I was mindful not to overstay my welcome in the military. I didn't want to be that proverbial oxygen thief stuffed away in a corner office on a division-level staff. Sure, I would have been serving the institution that I loved, but honestly, I would have only been doing it for the paycheck, to pad my retirement pay, or to avoid my transition from the military. I would have been doing it for selfish reasons and not for the men and women with whom I served. When you focus on yourself, you behave contrary to the military values of selfless service and integrity. You start politicking assignment managers for easier jobs. You look for ways to get out of the tough assignments. It's hard to authentically serve others when you are too worried about serving yourself. I didn't want to be that guy. When I was no longer willing to run headstrong into the fray, I knew it was time for me to leave.

Scarcity and the inherent fear of transition encourage us to stay for the guaranteed paycheck and the incremental increase to our retirement pay. We compromise our future potential for a false sense of security today. The price you pay for that fear is the lost opportunity of doing something else that you might enjoy even more. The time spent getting another percentage point in retirement could be spent building an even better life after the military. Again, be honest with yourself. If you look at your career in terms of time-based benchmarks (needs) and not future opportunities (wants), maybe it is time to leave. The moment you feel like you can't walk away from the military might be the very moment that you should.

REASON 3: YOU CAN'T SEE YOURSELF IN SOMETHING OTHER THAN A MILITARY UNIFORM

The uniform is a responsibility, not a security blanket. Military leaders with more than ten years of service have had their formative years of adulthood shaped by the military culture. In his book, *Breaking the Habit of Being Yourself*, Dr. Joe Dispenza talks about the neurological pathways that are formed and reinforced through years of conditioning that results in a fully developed framework of behavior by the time we reach the age of thirty-five.[2] Through years or even decades of military service, we become attached to the uniform, but sometimes that attachment metastasizes into an unhealthy condition at the expense of our personal identity.

When you allow the uniform to define your state of being, you lose your sense of self and all of the compassion that goes with it. Your personal identity becomes an abstraction of the uniform. It infects every aspect of your life including your role as a spouse, parent, sibling,

---

2. Joe Dispenza, *Breaking the Habit of Being Yourself: How to Lose Your Mind and Create a New One* (Carlsbad, CA: Hay House, 2015), 61.

neighbor, and friend. You harden into the arbiter of standards who becomes increasingly disconnected from the very people you are charged to lead. You compel compliance based on rank and title, but fail to truly connect and inspire the men and women in your formation (or in your family). In short, you become the toxic leader. People avoid you because they believe you don't care, and truthfully, you don't. You focus so intently on the mission that you lose sight of the men and women who volunteered to stand alongside you to accomplish it.

With each passing year, you grow more distant from the people in your life. The more you "attach" to the abstract military identity, the less you feel "attached" to your family. The inevitable withdrawal you will suffer upon separation or retirement becomes cataclysmic. If you struggled to connect with men and women while wearing the uniform, imagine how much more difficult it will be to connect with men and women who *never* wore the uniform. The excavation necessary to rediscover your sense of purpose and personal set of values becomes a massive undertaking. ***Remember, the uniform doesn't make you great. You make the uniform great.*** When you fail to see that distinction, you may want to consider removing the source of that unhealthy attachment.

LIFE BEYOND THE MILITARY

Ultimately, the decision to leave the military should be based on the premise of personal growth. The first time that I left the military, I did so for the wrong reasons. I believed that the grass in the civilian world was greener than the shades of green on my camouflaged battle dress uniform. When I retired, things were different. Even though I was considered deployable by the standards of readiness at the time, three deployments and thirty-three months in combat were enough. Also, I had no desire for the best job at the next rank. Most importantly, I knew that I had another life beyond the military. I wanted to embrace the opportunity and potential for what happened next. When I realized that I couldn't grow on a path through the military, I knew it was time to find one beyond the military.

Once you fulfill your initial service obligation, you become a free agent. The needs of the military come first, but in today's military, we are all just volunteers. You set the terms. Our military represents the smallest percentage of the population while simultaneously supporting the longest period of global conflict in the history of our nation. This paradox requires the most capable leaders in terms of whole health, passion for service, and examples of personal inspiration. So when you ask the question, *Should I stay or should I go?* always remember that the best decision is one that serves both you and the military. May you have the wisdom to recognize when the moment is right and the courage to make the appropriate decision at that time.

UNDERSTANDING MILITARY TRANSITION AND CIVILIAN REINTEGRATION

I have a unique perspective on military transition because I did it twice. I also did it poorly, twice. The first time I left the military as a junior captain. I put my faith in a junior officer recruiting company to find the best job opportunity. By "best" I mean to say the option with the most prestigious title and highest-paying salary. They did. As I mentioned earlier, it was the wrong job for me. Less than a year after my separation from active duty, I was miserable. To make matters worse, I was laid off from that high-paying job during the economic downturn in 2001. It was a total disaster. My second transition was my retirement after twenty-one years of service. Once again, I ended up in the wrong job. Once again, I was unemployed. Once again, I was miserable.

By all measures of preparedness, I should have aced my transition to civilian life. As a captain and again as a lieutenant colonel, I landed a job months before I actually drove out the main gate for the last time. When I retired, I didn't have one, but *two* master's degrees. As a former battalion commander, I had an accomplished record of leadership and executive-level bona fides. As a recent MBA graduate, I also had the benefit of career services from a reputable university to help craft my résumé, write cover letters, and teach me the finer art of networking. So, what went wrong? The short answer is that I assumed that a great résumé was the first and most important step to a successful transition from the military. I thought transition was about finding a good job. I was wrong.

So, let's review: I was a West Point graduate, valedictorian of my MBA class, and former battalion commander who struggled during my transition to civilian life. Sometimes I think that the word *struggled* isn't strong enough. I was truly lost and didn't know what the hell I was doing. Civilian life was supposed to be easier than the military. I thought that I was just trying to find a new job, but *I was really trying to find a new life.* Let's explore the anthropology of warrior reintegration to better understand what it means on a deeper psychological and spiritual level to leave the military and return to society.

THE ANTHROPOLOGY OF WARRIOR REINTEGRATION

"Military Transition" is a contemporary label to describe a bureaucratic process. It changes the status of men and women from "service member" to "veteran." The modern program of transition was created during the drawdown of active duty forces at the conclusion of the Cold War.[3] Today, this program serves two purposes: (1) to determine a service member's qualification for compensation and ongoing benefits as a result of their military service, and (2) to mitigate the possibility and burden of unemployment compensation to the Department of Defense.

The Department of Defense pays the unemployment compensation for newly transitioned veterans who don't secure post-separation employment. Back in 2012, that bill approached nearly one billion dollars.[4] Once you recognize the purpose—the WHY—behind the transition assistance program, you quickly understand why so many veterans struggle to find a sense of passion and purpose when they depart active duty.

The process of returning warriors back to society existed long before the creation of federal institutions and government bureaucracies. Citizens from within the community embraced the responsibility to acknowledge and welcome warriors back into the social order. Through a combination of rituals and ceremonies, ordinary citizens of the tribe facilitated the healing and spiritual evolution necessary for successful integration back into civilian life. Unfortunately, the shrinking percentage of citizens with a firsthand appreciation of military service suggests that the veteran community has become estranged from our shared consciousness as a nation. Furthermore, our increasingly self-reliant culture fails to facilitate those connections necessary to nurture the deep psychological and spiritual needs of returning warriors.

These intrinsic needs are predicated on the universal principle of growth. The use of words like *separation* and *retirement* connotes a sense of finality, but the truth is that even the military leader who retires after twenty years of service still has the entire second half of life to continue leading others and serving society. We use the word *transition* to describe

---

3. U.S. Library of Congress, Congressional Research Service, *Military Transition Assistance Program (TAP): An Overview,* by Kristy N. Kamarck, IF10347 (July 12, 2018).
4. Gordon Lubold, "The Pentagon Spends $1 Billion a Year on Unemployment for Service Members; Mattis' Parting Shot; Pentagon Strictly Enforcing CODEL Travel; What Happened in Wardak?; What Happened to $60 Billion in Iraq?; and a Little More," *Foreign Policy,* March 6, 2013, https://foreignpolicy.com/2013/03/06/the-pentagon-spends-1-billion-a-year-on-unemployment-for-service -members-mattis-parting-shot-pentagon-strictly-enforcing-codel-travel-what-happened-in-wardak-what-happened-to-60-billio/.

a process without identifying the end state of that program. In other words, you know that you are leaving the military, but who are you going to be, what are going to do, and where are you transitioning to? Because we fail to establish the end state, we have no standard for assessing success or failure through the transition process.

Such an end state existed in primitive cultures. Warriors returned from the battlefield and ascended into leadership roles for the good of the tribe. They became the chieftains, wise elders, and leaders of the social order. They evolved into a higher state of consciousness and repurposed the wisdom and experience from their time as a warrior to improve the whole of society. They were not soldiers—or more appropriately warriors—for life. They became something more. The lesson we should apply from more primitive examples of reintegration is the imperative to repurpose our warriors along a path of continued growth to serve the long-term health and welfare of society as a whole.

Joseph Campbell developed a model of transition and growth independent of culture, religion, or ideology to describe the psychological and spiritual journey common among all warriors.[5] How we wage war may have evolved through history, but the warrior experience remains largely the same. Individuals from society are inspired to answer the call to service. They separate from the known world to become warriors and enter an unknown world of fantasy and adventure. In this unknown world, these warriors are free from the pretensions or constructs of civilized society. Rules from the conventional, ordinary world do not apply. They are taught to hunt, kill, and destroy their fellow man. When we answer our calling to protect and defend the social order, we immerse ourselves in the culture of warfare and expose our mind, body, and spirit to the extreme limits of humanity.

In this unknown world, warriors undergo a series of trials. You recognize these trials as deployments, military operations, and combat. Through these experiences, the psyche is assaulted by impulses from across the spectrum of our humanity. The full limit of emotions are experienced in the superlative, and many of the attributes and aspects of the self that warriors bring with them into this adventure will not survive the many challenges that they will face. The unknown world acts like a forge intended to burn away the old to make room for the new. War and the military experience forever changes the self. Homecoming rituals in primitive cultures were meant to shed the impurities from the battlefield so that war wouldn't infect regular society. Once cleansed, the warrior ascends into a higher state of being and is welcomed back into society.

The objective of this journey—the reward or the prize—is self-actualization. The Hero's

---

5. Joseph Campbell, *The Hero with a Thousand Faces*, 3rd ed. (Novato, CA: New World Library, 2008), 6.

Journey is a cycle of psychological and spiritual growth. Campbell refers to this process of spiritual evolution and personal transformation as an initiation.[6] In the spiritual context, initiation achieves a higher order of consciousness, a higher state of being. The warrior's return from the battlefield is not a redeployment in the conventional sense, but a return to ordinary civilization with the gifts of wisdom and experience gained from the journey. This is why the warriors ascended into leadership roles across primitive societies. Military heroes from the battlefield became ordinary heroes for society. The Hero's Journey outlines the path for a more empowering and impactful role beyond the warrior caste.

Joseph Campbell spoke about this cycle in the context of separation-initiation-return.[7] You may recognize this cycle as life-death-rebirth common across religious practices and instruments of faith throughout the world. The universal application of this construct is the reason why Joseph Campbell famously characterized this model, the Hero's Journey, as the *monomyth*.[8] In the context of the military, we separate from the innocence of the known world, endure the trials of military service, and return to society to serve humanity and ultimately improve the social order.

When you acknowledge the anthropology of the warrior caste against the broader context of the social structure, you begin to understand why statements like "manage expectations" or "take a step back" simply don't work. They never have. You also begin to appreciate why enabling behaviors through codependent relationships with government or nonprofit organizations doesn't just fail the service member, but they fail the whole of society. They are contrary to the imperative of growth practiced by civilizations since the dawn of warfare. The process of transition from the military is so much more than the screening process for entitlements or a job placement program.

Think back to the reasons why you joined the military in the first place. We had an inspiration, an intrinsic calling, to begin our military journey. We've all experienced things that have forever changed us. Perhaps there are some memories you would rather forget. The challenge is how to repurpose that experience into an empowering role when you return to society. Civilian reintegration is about the personal transformation necessary to satisfy the imperative for growth and our unique purpose in service to society.

It's time to move the proverbial goal posts. We frame a military career with the assumption that honorable separation or retirement is the goal, the end zone. But in the context of a

---

6. Ibid., 81–90.
7. Ibid., 28–29.
8. Ibid., 1.

person's life, it is only the halfway point. It is merely the fifty-yard line. You still have another half of the field to go before you actually finish the game. You can't do that as a member of the military, and you can't quit the game. So let's figure out who you were meant to become in order to make that happen. Completing your Hero's Journey is the deeper purpose of this handbook.

THE ART OF MILITARY TRANSITION

> *If you know the enemy and know yourself, you need not fear the result of a hundred battles. If you know yourself but not the enemy, for every victory gained you will also suffer a defeat. If you know neither the enemy nor yourself, you will succumb in every battle.*
>
> —SUN TZU, *THE ART OF WAR*

Since my very first lesson in military science, I learned the value of knowing yourself and knowing the enemy. Our experience in counterinsurgency warfare taught us to appreciate the complexity of the terrain (physical, social, cultural, etc.). See yourself, see the enemy, and see the terrain. A slightly different, more conventional interpretation of this ancient maxim is: *know yourself, know the players,* and *know the game.* My struggle through both transitions was because I violated this fundamental philosophy of the military art.

KNOW YOURSELF: I DIDN'T KNOW WHO I WAS

If you are like me, you joined the military at a relatively young age. My journey started just two weeks after my high school graduation. The military provided all the necessary guidance and direction. I didn't need to know my values. I didn't need to have a purpose. I internalized the Army Values, and the military culture defined my identity. It was easy while I was wearing the uniform. Once I took that uniform off, I didn't know who I was anymore.

The real me was buried underneath the cover and concealment of the military culture. I got used to the recognizable digital pattern of the army uniform. I was uncomfortable seeing myself in business casual. I felt guilty when I woke up after 7 a.m. Social conformity to the norms of army life was a powerful impulse. I was so used to being a soldier that I didn't know how to be anything else. I never looked inward to uncover the values that shaped my personal identity.

Because I didn't know my core values, I didn't know WHO I was. The first time that I left the military as a junior captain, my "high-paying job" was as an engineer. I had a degree in engineering, so finding an engineering job made the most sense at the time. I never considered things like "values." I couldn't tell you what my passion or purpose was. It didn't take long for me to realize that I didn't want to be an engineer, but I didn't know how to be anything else. I didn't know what I wanted. Because I didn't know WHO I was, I took a job based on WHAT I could do.

In addition to the WHO, I never defined my follow-on mission for life after the military. In other words, I didn't have a WHY. I'm sure there was a reason why I joined the army instead of going to college or getting a job like most of my friends from high school, but I never explored the underlying inspiration that led me to join the military in the first place. As I left the military, I thought that success was defined by a "good" job. I never developed a mission for my life. I never formulated a Statement of Intent. I realized only too late that without a sense of identity or purpose for my life beyond the military, my résumé wasn't worth the paper it was written on.

KNOW THE PLAYERS: I ASSUMED EVERYONE WAS ON MY SIDE

If you think the military is responsible for your transition, you are sorely mistaken. The military's job is to fight and win our nation's wars. The focus of our commanders is to ensure that the sons and daughters who volunteer for military service can fight, win, and return home safely to their families. You know how hard it is to get a unit ready for deployment. You know what's at stake. This might be hard to hear, but how you leave the military and what happens next in your life is your responsibility and yours alone. It's your life. How transition and reintegration set you up for success is entirely up to you.

Along those lines, you should carefully consider the interests of other players like recruiters and recruiting companies. Unless you are the one paying them to find you a job, that recruiter or company doesn't work for you. Furthermore, some recruiters may require you to sign a contract that limits your employment options. Understand that recruiters exist to barter your talent and potential to willing buyers. In many cases, the value of your compensation is reduced to pay for their services. In the recruiting and human resources sectors, you are a commodity bought and sold on the open market.

Lastly, I had no appreciation for what I was getting into when I started my new job. I thought I would show up in the corporate workplace the same way that I showed up for duty in a military unit. Same attitude. Same drive. I didn't take into account that the majority of people in the company simply didn't understand the military experience or culture. Consequently, they didn't understand me. It took some time before I realized that their lack of understanding wasn't a lack of appreciation or respect. They just didn't know any better.

I learned a valuable lesson from that experience. If you intend to show up with the intensity and mannerisms that helped you succeed as a leader in the military, you may be disappointed to discover that those approaches don't have the same effect in the civilian world. Culture matters. Nobody will follow a leader who is disconnected, aloof, or socially awkward. As part of your transition, you have to develop enough self-awareness to recognize the social and cultural blind spots that might impede your assimilation back into society. This, too, is your responsibility—and yours alone.

KNOW THE GAME: I THOUGHT TRANSITION WAS THE OBJECTIVE

The phrases "military transition" or "transition assistance" set the wrong premise. Leaving is easy. If you had more than one assignment location, you already know how to out-process an installation. What you are really trying to achieve is successful reintegration into civilian life. Transition is a shaping operation. **Reintegration is the decisive action**. The reason why so many veterans don't feel like they "fit" after leaving the military is because our civilian systems aren't calibrated for warrior reintegration. We've reduced the deeply emotional and psychological transformation from warrior to civilian into a job placement program. We don't optimize holistic wellness, nor do we address the social or cultural challenges of re-entering society. We shouldn't be surprised that so many veterans struggle in civilian life. Transition is easy. Civilian reintegration is hard, really hard.

Remember, you aren't just trying to find a new job. You are trying to discover a new life. Leaving the military is as much a deeply personal, social, and cultural endeavor as it is a professional one. Crafting your résumé is an important task, but before you do that, you need to think more strategically about your own program of personal transformation. **Know Yourself**, **Know the Players**, and **Know the Game**. Discover your values, uncover your purpose, and ignite your passion for an empowering life after military service. Understand the interests of all the stakeholders in the transition process, and focus on what you are truly trying to achieve: a successful reintegration into a healthy, happy, and empowering life filled with deep and meaningful relationships with those you love.

Leaving the military is not the end of anything. It is the natural progression into something better. Inspire, lead, achieve, and pursue the life you deserve as a result of your service and sacrifice. So, how do you plan and execute a deliberate process of personal transformation? How can you step into the civilian world with the confidence and wisdom to serve and improve our society as a veteran leader? The **Integrative Program of Transition** provides the answer to both of those questions.

THE INTEGRATIVE PROGRAM OF TRANSITION

The urgency for an Integrative Program of Transition in the military is analogous to what happened back in 2004 to create an integrative program for medicine. As it pertains to health, wellness, and the practice of medicine, we have come to accept healing as a function of body, mind, and spirit, but it wasn't always that way. Before concepts like "Whole Health" and "Patient-Centered Care" became the gold standard of healthcare, medicine was a practice defined and subsequently limited by diagnostics. When you were sick, you saw a doctor. That physician would assess your symptoms, determine a diagnosis, and prescribe a protocol for treatment. For the most part, this approach worked—until it didn't.

Against the backdrop of declining longevity and escalating healthcare costs, a group of visionaries across the field of medicine sought a different path for optimizing health and wellness. They set their intentions on a vision of proactive, preventive, and holistic healthcare. Their idea would eventually become known as the practice of Integrative Medicine, but there was significant resistance to this innovative approach from administrators and academics who sought to preserve and protect the status quo:

> In the 1980s and 1990s, physicians wishing to study integrative approaches to care within the academic arena were often told that it was a career killer; conventional medical journals refused to publish manuscripts covering topics such as acupuncture or mind-body medicine; researchers found it hard to secure grants to investigate the efficacy of integrative approaches; and providers across the country were discouraged—and sometimes even banned—from including in their practice medical interventions from any other culture as well as what were then nonmainstream approaches such as nutritional supplementation and mind-body practices.[9]

Medicine has come a long way since the end of the twentieth century, but it took a social movement of medical professionals, healthcare administrators, philanthropists, and academic visionaries to overcome the inertia from an entrenched mindset. This collaboration of cross-functional innovators became known as the Bravewell Collaborative. Today, dozens of integrative health centers partner with universities and medical facilities around the country, and holistic, patient-centered care has become *the* standard for the delivery of health services across the country.

Military transition is ripe for this type of disruption. The conventional practice of helping veterans find a job doesn't address the deeper cultural, social, and psychological challenges

---

9. Bonnie J. Horrigan, *The Bravewell Story: How a Small Community of Philanthropists Made a Big Difference in Healthcare* (McLean, VA: Academic Consortium for Integrative Medicine & Health, 2016), 8.

of civilian reintegration. It took nearly fifteen years for the groundswell to become mainstream for Integrative Medicine, but lucky for you, you don't have to wait that long. Because transition and reintegration are your responsibility, the Integrative Program of Transition outlined in this handbook is something that you can do for yourself.

Let's define an Integrative Program of Transition using what we know about the definition of Integrative Medicine. According to the Arizona Center for Integrative Medicine at the University of Arizona, "Integrative Medicine (IM) is healing-oriented medicine that takes account of the whole person, including all aspects of lifestyle. It emphasizes the therapeutic relationship between practitioner and patient, is informed by evidence, and makes use of all appropriate therapies."[10] If we applied that definition to the construct of military transition, then the **Integrative Program of Transition is a comprehensive approach to an individual's separation from military service that takes account of the whole person and includes all aspects of civilian reintegration. It emphasizes a holistic approach to personal and professional growth, is informed by evidence, and makes use of appropriate programs.**

Practically speaking, what should be included in this comprehensive program for transition and civilian reintegration? Well, for starters, it should address both the start point and end point for the process. This means that it should include all the factors related to transition (leaving the military) and reintegration (arriving back into society). Therefore, an Integrative Program of Transition must include optimizing whole health and wellness, socialization, cultural assimilation, economic stability, professional preparedness, and family adjustment. Each of these factors is an essential thread of continuity between the life of the service member in the military and life of the veteran beyond the military.

Let's consider each of these factors in more detail.

OPTIMIZING WHOLE HEALTH

Let's begin the conversation with the most important factors: holistic health, wellness, and resilience. Whole health includes the physical, mental, spiritual, and emotional aspects of personal wellness (see **Table 1.1. Activities That Contribute to Whole Health**).

Medical assessments during the clearing process are not intended to optimize your health and wellness. They are intended to treat any existing medical problems. Optimizing your health and wellness is something you have to accept responsibility for and do for yourself.

---

10. "Arizona Center for Integrative Medicine," What Is Integrative Medicine?: Andrew Weil Center for Integrative Medicine, accessed July 21, 2019, https://integrativemedicine.arizona.edu/about/definition.html.

Table 1.1 Activities That Contribute to Whole Health includes the physical, emotional, mental, and spiritual domains for holistic wellness in life as a veteran. The following examples are not all-inclusive, but they are some things to consider as you transition from the military.

Potential Activities Related to Optimizing Whole Health and Wellness	
Physical Health	**Emotional Health**
• Complete Separation/Retirement Exam • Complete medical procedures (surgery, physical therapy, etc.) • Exercise routinely • Set ambitious goals for physical fitness (races, teams, activities) • Practice healthy nutrition • Allocate 8 hours of sleep a night • Maintain a healthy weight • Limit alcohol use and quit tobacco	• Attend Counseling and/or therapy for service related conditions • Become self-aware and intentional about your emotional responses • Take a vacation/travel • Explore a hobby • Participate in relationship programs and/or workshops • Journal (can also help mental & spiritual health) • Dedicate time for activities with friends and/or family
Mental Health	**Spiritual Health**
• Seek learning opportunities through education • Read for personal growth • Be creative and express your creativity • Participate in counseling or therapy • Practice mindfulness • Prioritize self-care • Learn how to meditate • Practice yoga	• Actively practice your faith • Participate in a retreat • Join a fellowship group • Ground yourself in a deeper sense of purpose • Practice affirmations and gratitude reflections • Pray • Actively participate in charitable causes

SOCIALIZATION

The military provides its own social network of like-minded individuals. When you step outside that insulated culture, you have to build new social networks. The socialization line of effort is about actively establishing new connections with a predominantly non-veteran society. It will require some time and effort before you can achieve the same level of social connection that you once enjoyed through the military.

Outside military housing and the communities adjacent to military bases, there is a good chance that your neighbors won't know the first thing about military service. They may have some preconceived notions about veterans in the same way that you might have preconceived notions about civilians. The most difficult aspect of socialization is releasing those judgments and having the courage to challenge stereotypes.

Like it or not, you are the minority. You are a stranger in a strange land. If you want your relationships to consist of more than the obligatory "thank you for your service," then *you* have to make the effort. If you don't, then chances are that the rest of society will just leave you well enough alone. As a veteran, you represent a disappearing breed across the national landscape. Take the initiative. You can start by introducing yourself to your neighbors. You can start by simply saying *"hello."*

Table 1.2 Activities That Contribute to Socialization. When you disconnect from the military, you need to set a deliberate intention to connect in civilian society.

Activities Related to Socialization
• Taking active measures to get to know the people and families in your neighborhood
• Building a network of acquaintances and friends who are not veterans and have little or no experience with the military
• Participating in community activities (holiday events, block parties, food drives, etc.)
• Meeting and getting to know small business owners in your community
• Participating in volunteer work with your children's school, sports, or other activities
• Joining non-veteran service organizations that serve the greater community
• Connecting with local Veteran Service Organizations
• Changing your global perspective by following local news and radio to get "plugged-in"

You can build new social networks through your neighborhood, community organizations, church and youth groups, volunteer opportunities, and veteran service organizations. As veterans, we have a responsibility to engage the greater civilian society that has become disconnected from the military experience. We owe it to those still forward deployed and for all of our brothers and sisters who never made it back home. We must actively participate in our communities. It doesn't make sense to be passive toward the very society we were willing to protect and defend with our lives. Take advantage of opportunities for active engagement.

You don't need to wear a uniform or boast of your military experience to start a conversation or make a new connection. You just need to show up.

CULTURAL ASSIMILATION

The military culture is deeply rooted in tradition. Some might call it old-fashioned. Others might consider it outdated and aloof. Leaving that culture and entering civilian society is like moving to a different country. You need to learn a new language, new customs, and probably need to update your wardrobe. The processes, procedures, and mannerisms that worked so well for you in a military unit may not have the same effect as you attempt to step into a new role, job, or position in society. As I mentioned before, culture matters.

Culture defines the explicit and implicit norms of an organization. Culture is not a tagline or a company logo. It is not a series of pictures with motivational phrases hanging on the wall. Culture is how the people in the organization behave when no one is watching. Culture is what happens on the production floor, in back office meetings, and through internal email communications. Culture describes the living essence of an organization.

Culture is the mechanism that guides the attitudes, behaviors, and beliefs of the people in an organization in the same way an individual's values and purpose (the WHO and the WHY) guide and influence the attitudes, behaviors, and beliefs of an individual. The benefit of understanding your WHO (your values) and your WHY (your purpose) is to align your intrinsic qualities with an external environment that allows you to accelerate toward your personal and professional objectives.

Imagine the potential of aligning your personal values with the shared values of a larger group or organization. You achieve a certain resonance. You feel a sense of purpose, inspiration, and satisfaction in the work you are doing. You feel like a part of something special. When these elements do not align—as in the case of being in a profession or with an organization that doesn't fit with your values or purpose—you feel dissonance. You sense a longing for something more because your intrinsic needs are not being met. In the simplest terms, alignment feels inspired and misalignment just feels wrong.

You have to recognize where you stand before you figure out where you fit in a new organization. It might be convenient to say that the military culture defined the man or woman you have become, but that is simply not the case. Because of your values and purpose, the military was a vehicle for self-actualization during the time you served. Your values and purpose endure beyond the uniform. You just need to find a new vehicle to express your values and fulfill your purpose.

Table 1.3 Activities Related to Cultural Assimilation are how we determine our "goodness of fit" in a new culture after military service.

Activities Related to Cultural Assimilation

- Understand your own Values (the WHO) and your sense of Purpose (the WHY) to recognize opportunities to lead and inspire others

- See your blind spots as you move between the military culture and the culture of a new organization

- Recognize the explicit and implicit norms of an organization - i.e. how do people behave when nobody is watching

- Improve self-awareness regarding your energy and/or emotional intelligence to appreciate how you "show-up" under normal circumstances and under duress

- Learn the language and customs of your new environment before you start making changes or exerting influence (adopt the beginner's mindset)

- Align the mission of possible employers with your own purpose statement (How does the mission of the organization resonate with you on a personal level?)

- Explore the qualities of the leadership and design within the organization to determine whether or not those qualities align with your intrinsic strengths and common factors for success

- Identify how your personal values align with the values of the people in the organization.

ECONOMIC STABILITY

The most common fear in the transition process concerns the uncertainty surrounding personal finances. The military has a program of benefits that includes healthcare, housing allowance, and other incentives that are tax-free. If you stay until retirement, you will receive a portion of your military pay and healthcare for you and your family. If you transition from the military before you are eligible for these benefits, how you prepare for transition and reintegration could significantly impact your quality of life through transition and beyond. This part of the Integrative Program of Transition is about finding the right opportunity for economic stability to achieve what you want in life.

When I left the army as a junior captain, I took a position that, on paper, was about 25 percent more than my pay in the military. However, once I accounted for state taxes, health insurance premiums, and moving to a new federal tax bracket, my take-home pay was actually 33 percent less than what I was making in the military! I didn't appreciate the financial implications and disparities between my benefits in the military and the benefits of my corporate job. I also made the mistake of failing to assess opportunities for career advancement before I took that job. Because the position I took had a slow growth trajectory, it would have been at least four years before I had the education and experience necessary to reach a level where my take-home pay matched what I was making in the military.

I think many of us default to finances when we think (or worry) about transition. Someone has to pay the bills. Our families have their own dreams and expectations. Our greatest fear is that we won't be able to afford them. However, when we frame transition through the lens of a salary, we run the risk of accepting a job (any job) to pay the bills at the expense of our potential for a better opportunity. We cash in on short-term solutions at the expense of long-term prosperity.

Table 1.4 Activities Related to Economic Stability. Too often we feel the urgency for securing the next paycheck at the expense of more empowering opportunities.

Activities Related to Economic Stability
• Recognize the state and local tax implications of your chosen domicile
• Determine the commensurate civilian pay required to match your military pay and benefits
• Develop a budget for the duration of transition (1 year before to 1 year after)
• Assess current financial obligations and resources necessary to offset those obligations
• Estimate the financial requirements necessary to bridge any employment gap
• Determine the level of wealth necessary to achieve the things you want in life
• Network with different veteran and non-veteran professionals across multiple segments to make informed decisions about employment opportunities
• Determine the cost of insurance (health and life) including supplemental insurance requirements

The question we should ask is: "How can I have it all—meaningful employment, sufficient pay, AND happiness?" We don't address this question because we're too busy analyzing starting salaries. Economic stability is about the long game and discovering solutions that don't rely on government entitlements. Set your intentions for higher levels of sustainable wealth AND personal fulfillment. Economic stability is about creating solutions through the transition process, over the first few years of income generation as a civilian, and toward a level of wealth that allows you to achieve the quality of life you want. This factor looks beyond the urgency of the paycheck in the moment to discover a sustainable solution for greater wealth generation and personal fulfillment over the duration of your life.

PROFESSIONAL PREPAREDNESS

Professional Preparedness is how most public, private, and nonprofit entities seek to support service members through the transition process. Many organizations sponsor programs that offer accreditation for military experience and technical training. Some examples include the Project Management Professional (PMP) certification for management professionals, Six Sigma certifications for quality assurance, and Aircraft and Powerplant (A&P) technical credentials for aircraft mechanics. Other programs provide career-related services to help service members translate military skills and experience into viable career opportunities.

Table 1.5 Activities Related to Professional Preparedness includes the tasks we typically associate with military transition.

Activities Associated with Professional Preparedness
• Translate military experience into commensurate civilian experience
• Network and mentorship with professionals across different business sectors.
• Create a resume and template for cover letters
• Update your wardrobe and home office
• Attend workshops for employment opportunities
• Understand Federal, State, and Local resources for launching your own business or becoming a franchise owner
• Recognize the benefits and constraints of continuing government employment through civil service
• Update your professional profile on social media platforms
• Rehearse interviews
• Make a personal investment in your professional growth
• Obtain civilian/professional accreditation for military training, education, and experience
• Explore the experience, training, and credentials for the ideal, future job
• Identify the long-range path for the job and lifestyle you want (the battalion level command equivalent goal for the future)

In the construct of an Integrative Program of Transition, Professional Preparedness is about bridging the gap to create a wider range of opportunities through transition and beyond. It expands the current process of finding the next job by exploring the ideal path for continued growth. It envisions the pinnacle of your achievement at the culmination of your professional life.

Your experience in the military provides the best example to explain this process. We know what a twenty-year career in the military looks like—even if you don't stay for the full twenty years. Our assignment managers and mentors taught us to be ever mindful of how the next assignment met the required benchmarks to continue our career progression. A demanding assignment may impact your family life in the short term, but it may also position you for greater options and better opportunities for the future. It was all about staying competitive and keeping to the path. As you become a veteran leader, you have to find a new path. Professional Preparedness is about creating that path for the most attractive and impactful opportunities beyond the military.

Professional Preparedness looks beyond the point of transition. It is about mapping your future to get the training and experience for what is still to come. This is your strategy for professional growth to achieve your legacy when you ultimately retire from the workforce altogether.

FAMILY ADJUSTMENT

I made many mistakes through both transitions from the military, but my greatest failure was my lack of appreciation for how leaving the military impacted my family. Army life is the only life my family had ever known, so leaving was much harder on them than I had anticipated. We focus so much on the challenges the veteran faces through transition that we don't recognize the effects it has on our families. Family was one of the main reasons why I decided to retire, but I was so consumed with what *I* was going through that I wasn't paying attention to what *they* were going through. Many of the strategies for managing relationships through transition and reintegration are included in Part 3 of this handbook.

The military community invests a tremendous amount of time and resources into families. Installation activities provide a forum for families to interact and socialize. Celebrations through military formals and other unit activities provide a sense of belonging and membership to an exclusive and prestigious culture. When you leave the military, there are no more readiness groups, military formals, or holiday events on post. You don't appreciate those social connections until they are gone. As for your family, they have a unique perspective and their own challenges in transition. You cannot assume that the support offered to you as the service member applies in the same way to the rest of your family.

Even though your family is used to relocating to different homes and communities through the military, the sudden departure from that lifestyle has its own consequences. For example, now that you aren't planning on moving every two to four years, your spouse may want to start a career of his or her own. Military spouses seeking employment after an extended absence are at a significant hiring disadvantage. In fact, the unemployment rate for military spouses is four times higher than the national unemployment rate.[11] Spouses bear many of the consequences of belonging to the military without the commensurate recognition or status given to the veteran. In many ways, our spouses get all the bad without any of the good.

Table 1.6 Activities Associated with Family Adjustment reminds us that our entire family is going through the transition process with us.

Activities Associated with Family Adjustment
• Register children for school and after school care
• Prioritize family activities or vacation time during transition/terminal leave
• Open communication and dialogue concerning the transition
• Update Resume and Career Search (spouse)
• Register kids for extracurricular activities
• Finding church, youth, and community groups for your family
• Explore neighborhoods to determine where you want to live
• Attend school and community events
• Volunteer for activities involving your children

Take a minute to consider the impact of transition on school-aged children. For the first time in their lives, they are in a school district where children of military parents are the exception

---

11. Brooke Goldberg, "Military Spouse Unemployment Rate at Least Four Times Higher Than National Average," *MOAA*, October 6, 2017, http://www.moaa.org/Content/Take-Action/On-Watch/Military-Spouse-Unemployment-Rate-at-Least-Four-Times-Higher -Than-National-Average.aspx.

instead of the norm. Many of their classmates have little or no appreciation of what it means to be in the military. I still remember when my kids came home from school and asked me if I had killed anyone in the war. That's an awkward situation for anyone's children. As veterans, we have to be receptive to how the transition and reintegration process impacts family members of all ages.

We are used to going where the military tells us to go, when they tell us to go there. Our families have adapted well to that lifestyle, but when we leave the military, we no longer live under that constraint. You get to make more choices. So does the rest of your family. We have more latitude to make our own decisions. Ensure that the "we" includes your family—the people most important to you.

An Integrative Program of Transition is a lifestyle approach toward a higher standard of civilian reintegration. This approach addresses the deeper psychological, cultural, and social aspects of transition for you and your entire family. The Integrative Program of Transition provides a template for you to seize the initiative and own your transition. Remember, your success and happiness is your responsibility.

THE IDENTITY CRISIS: REINTEGRATION FROM THE INSIDE-OUT

Now that you understand the model for the Integrative Program of Transition, it's time to dig a little deeper. Once you submit your request for resignation or retirement, the military institution will process you out of the service. You're going to leave. Along the way, transition programs will provide assistance for building a résumé, formatting cover letters, networking opportunities across different industries, and preparing for interviews. They may even connect you with career fairs, alumni groups, and nonprofit organizations to extend your reach. These programs are extremely valuable and important, but they won't resolve the identity crisis that comes from removing the uniform.

In order to resolve this identity crisis, reintegration is a process that must necessarily occur from the inside-out. How you think in your head and feel in your heart must evolve before you can connect on an emotional and energetic level to inspire others as a veteran leader in society. Use YOUR values and YOUR purpose to define YOUR path. Set your intention to create the life you want to live. Remember, the mission statement and commander's intent that you follow for the rest of your life can only come from YOU.

This inside-out process of reintegration is about seeing your attributes and qualities as a leader without the cover and concealment offered by the uniform. Once you are confident and assured in your identity, you won't think and feel like a service member. You begin to think and feel as YOU. This necessary recalibration helps to reframe your perspective to find the right role, position, or job in your next career. Once you resolve the inherent identity crisis that comes from leaving the military, you can step confidently into your authentic identity as the leader you were meant to be.

INTERNALIZE AND REPURPOSE

You can't separate or remove the military part of your identity. Those years are imprinted in the cross-section of your DNA. They are integrated into your character and personality. The military years are over, but they aren't going anywhere. The knowledge and experience you gained as a soldier molded you into the leader that you've become. Reintegration from the inside-out doesn't ignore, reject, or forget the military aspects of your identity. You can, however, reorient that energy and refocus your leadership qualities to succeed in a new environment and different culture outside the military.

As you imagine what happens next, embrace the opportunity to think and feel as YOU, the leader you were meant to be. Know the WHO and the WHY of your story. Understand how to repurpose your traits and attributes as a leader. Seize the opportunity to determine what happens next on YOUR terms. The cross-section of your life tells a great story, but now you have a chance to write an even better chapter about what happens next.

So, how do you do it? How can you leverage everything you've learned, experienced, and gained through your years of military service to develop a plan to resolve the identity crisis and step into the right opportunity that accomplishes your mission in life and achieves your intent? The answer to all those questions is the Military Transition and Reintegration Process.

PART 2

THE MILITARY TRANSITION AND REINTEGRATION PROCESS (MTRP)

INTRODUCTION TO THE PROCESS

An Integrative Program of Transition (the departure) and Reintegration from the Inside-Out (the arrival) describe a complete and comprehensive process of personal transformation from service member to veteran. Practically speaking, how can you apply this process to you as you stand before the threshold of leaving the military? Because transition is about moving from the familiar to the unfamiliar, why not go with what you know when it comes to finding solutions to military problems? Our problem-solving approach in the army is known as the Military Decision-Making Process (MDMP). As applied to the challenge of transition and reintegration, this approach becomes the Military Transition and Reintegration Process (MTRP). By mirroring the military approach to problem-solving, we apply a familiar and proven methodology to an unfamiliar and seemingly daunting endeavor (see **Figure 1**).

The MTRP reframes the Military Decision-Making Process for the most difficult and inevitable mission in the military: leaving. It works through the first six steps of the MDMP in a manner applicable to transition and reintegration. The MTRP leverages the skills and habits formed through the operations and planning process to help you step confidently into the uncertainty of what happens next. The self-awareness you gain through this process provides the foundation to create your personal solution to the problem of transition and reintegration.

Figure 1. MDMP and MTRP Crosswalk. The MTRP provides a structured problem-solving process for the challenge of transition and reintegration. Step 7.0 (Orders Production) of the MDMP is not applicable to the MTRP and not included in this crosswalk.

Military Decision Making Process[12] ⟶		Military Transition & Reintegration Process
ACTIVITY	STEP	ACTIVITY
Receive the Mission	1.0	Discover Your Purpose (Find the WHY)
Mission Analysis	2.0	Identity Analysis
Course of Action Development	3.0	Opportunity Development
Course of Action Analysis	4.0	Opportunity Alignment
Course of Action Comparison	5.0	Opportunity Comparison
Course of Action Approval	6.0	Opportunity Integration

THE ONE-THIRD RULE OF TRANSITION AND REINTEGRATION

How long it takes to complete this process depends, in part, on how much time you have. The operations process from the MDMP recognizes a One-Third:Two-Thirds rule for planning. This means that you take one-third of the available time for planning and give two-thirds of the remaining time for subordinate elements to engineer their plan. For example, if you were expected to execute a mission in 48 hours, you would take the first 16 hours to prepare and present your plan, and you would allow your subordinate elements the remaining 32 hours to complete their planning and preparation. The MTRP uses a **One-Third Rule of Transition and Reintegration** and divides the process into three distinct phases: MTRP, Transition, and Reintegration. Under ideal conditions, you would allow eighteen months to execute all three phases of this process.

The MTRP Phase involves the execution of all six steps of the MTRP. It focuses on your Identity Analysis and the subsequent research and development of future career opportunities. The Transition Phase includes all of the separation activities that occur while you're still in uniform. The final phase is the Reintegration Phase. It begins on your date of separation and extends for the first six months of your life as a veteran.

For a variety of reasons, you may not have a full year before separation or retirement to complete this process. Military transition is a process, not a date on the calendar. Time alone

---

12. Department of the Army, Headquarters, *Commander and Staff Organization and Operations* (Washington, D.C.: US Army, 2015), 9-3.

won't do it—it's about how intentional you are with the time you have. In practice, successful reintegration could take several months or even years depending on your time in service and the nature of that service. More deployments and time spent in combat will require more time for reintegration, but for the purposes of your transition journey, allocating the same amount of time for each of the three phases is a start.

Figure 2. The One-Third Rule of Transition and Reintegration Model. This model portrays the suggested timeline for a service member who begins the process one year from his or her separation date.

⅓ Rule of Transition and Reintegration		
MTRP Phase (First Third)	**Transition Phase (Middle Third)**	**Reintegration Phase (Final Third)**
Execute the Military Transition and Reintegration Process	Execute Transition from the Military	Execute Civilian Reintegration
Ideal Application of the ⅓ Rule of Transition and Reintegration		
12 Months Before Separation	6 Months Before Separation	6 Months After Separation

Ideally, you should allow six months to complete the MTRP Phase, but given that this phase provides the foundation for everything that happens next, it should be no shorter than three months. The three-month standard is based on scientific research that suggests the neurological foundation for new habits occurs between 18 and 254 days with a median of 66 days.[13] Allowing yourself three months for the necessary introspection and an additional three months to form healthy and empowering habits sets the psychological foundation for you to accelerate through transition and reintegration.

The MTRP and Reintegration Phase are additional steps that acknowledge the drastic shift in culture and change in lifestyle that occurs through transition and reintegration. Previous transition protocols recognize only the middle phase—the Transition Phase—and fail to acknowledge two critical facts: (1) self-discovery and identity evolution are essential to resolve the identity crisis that comes from removing the uniform, and (2) the decisive point of the entire transition journey occurs in a three- to six-month window after separation. This is when the honeymoon period and celebrations end and real life beyond the military begins.

---

13. Phillippa Lally, Cornelia H. M. Van Jaarsveld, Henry W. W. Potts, and Jane Wardle, "How Are Habits Formed: Modelling Habit Formation in the Real World," *European Journal of Social Psychology* 40, no. 6 (2009): 1002, https://doi:10.1002/ejsp.674.

Therefore, your best bet for achieving success as a veteran leader in society is incumbent on your completion of all three phases.

Completing all three phases is important for all transitioning service members and veterans, even if you have already separated from the military. Given the anthropology of the warrior caste, neglecting or ignoring a process for identity discovery and evolution to resolve the inherent identity crisis comes at your own peril. Furthermore, the lack of active engagement to follow-through at the most critical juncture of the reintegration process runs the risk of leaving you feeling incomplete and not fully connected back in civilian society. Without the successful completion of all three phases, you can only hope to stumble into your authentic identity story and achieve the meaningful connections that lead to a meaningful life by accident. Because we are talking about the second half of your life, the stakes are too great.

With that in mind, let's walk through the six steps of the MTRP.

DISCOVER YOUR PURPOSE: FIND THE WHY

The two most important days in your life are the day you are born and the day you find out why.

—MARK TWAIN

When you apply the operations process to military transition, you might notice that you don't have a higher headquarters. Other than the requirement to separate from the service, you are not "receiving" a mission from anyone. You and you alone write the mission statement for the next chapter of your life. It is a function of a higher calling. The one moral obligation we all share is to be the fullest expression of our values in the relentless pursuit of our purpose. You have spent the majority of your life working to accomplish military missions, and now it's time for you to identify ***your*** mission.

The innate abilities that define our character, personality, and strengths are the tools we use to accomplish our mission in life. Each of us is born with an intention that represents our unique value proposition to the rest of society. Your intrinsic drive, what Dr. Lissa Rankin refers to as your "inner pilot light," is the energy that fuels the journey to fulfill your purpose in life.[14] Living a life oriented toward this purpose that is aligned with your authentic identity is the best, and only, course of action to achieve happiness, fulfillment, and joy. Furthermore, because these are the distinctive qualities for your self-actualization, they represent your greatest potential to any employer for opportunities beyond the military.

Your sense of purpose is connected to a deeper form of motivation. From that place you receive orders and commands—those subconscious impulses that have inspired you to action throughout the course of your life. Your purpose provides the energy to influence your

---

14. Lissa Rankin, *The Anatomy of a Calling: A Road Map for Awakening to Your Life's Purpose* (Emmaus, PA: Rodale, 2015), 41–42.

behaviors, direct your actions, and guide your decisions. You have felt the intrinsic nature of your purpose throughout the duration of your life. On the day that you can identify and put that purpose into words, you've arrived at what Mark Twain describes as the second most important day of your life.

So, let's start at the beginning. The most important question to answer regarding what you might do when you leave the military is to identify the reasons why you signed up in the first place. Beneath the recruiting clichés and justifications we share with family and friends is the real reason why you opted to be among the diminishing minority of men and women who volunteer for military service. Those reasons why provide clues to discover your WHY and help reveal the path to fulfillment beyond the military.

The good news is that you've been executing this mission—your purpose—for most of your adult life. For many of us, the reason why we served for so long in the military was because it aligned to our sense of purpose. In other words, the military became the means for you to accomplish your personal mission. Now, you need another means to accomplish the mission, but before you do that, let's make sure you understand exactly what that mission is.

There are consequences to living life in a manner inconsistent with your purpose. The reason why so many veterans and non-veterans sleepwalk through life is because they've lost (or never identified) their sense of purpose. They spend their days reminiscing about the past because they don't know their mission for the future. They don't know their WHY. You don't have to look hard to find people shackled to activities they think will make them happy, but they never *feel* happy. What they feel is empty. They feel disconnected from themselves and everyone else. You can have the fancy titles, buy a big house, drive expensive cars, and party like a rockstar, but if you are not aligned to your purpose, no amount of wealth or material possessions can fill the emptiness in your heart.

EXERCISE 1.1 RE-CALL TO SERVICE

You've always had a passion to lead, even before you raised your right hand and swore an oath to serve in the military. It probably existed long before you graduated from high school. Where does this passion come from? Your follow-on mission will align with the same intrinsic impulses that inspired your initial call to service so many years ago. Before we step into that next opportunity in life *beyond* the military, let's reflect on the origin of the motivation that inspired our service *in* the military.

PART 1. SOURCES OF INSPIRATION

Someone or something inspired us to answer the call to service. If not to volunteer for service, then to stay as long as we did. You didn't have to sign up for the military, and with few exceptions, you've always had the freedom to leave. We all have certain people in our lives who inspired us to become a better version of ourselves. At some point, we were convinced that the best opportunity came through the military. It may have been a historical figure, teacher, coach, or someone in your family. In some cases, it may have been a fictional character from a movie. Someone unlocked that potential and forever changed you.

Sometimes it isn't a person but a particular event that moves us. I can remember the swell of patriotism when Team USA defeated the Soviet Union in the 1980 Olympic Games. I can also remember how moved I felt when President Reagan addressed the nation after American warplanes bombed Libya in 1986. I wanted to fly after I saw the movie *Top Gun*. Whether it was a person or an event, there were qualities of these interactions or experiences that guided you toward military service. Let's take inventory of these motivations and inspirations.

In the first part of this exercise, identify three role models, events, or a combination of the two that were sources of inspiration. Use the spaces to the right to provide up to three reasons why these people or events were significant sources of inspiration for your journey through the military.

Role Model or Event	3 Qualities of that Role Model or Event that Inspired You

PART 2. KEY FACTORS

Now, let's explore more directly the reasons why you joined the military. Let's look past the incentive programs and get after what truly compelled you to choose military service. What did you imagine you might accomplish? Perhaps you saw yourself standing on some distant battlefield leading men and women in combat. Maybe you pictured yourself flying a plane or helicopter through dangerous skies on a perilous mission.

Since the dawn of civilization, members of the social order have been called to service. How we receive and interpret that calling is dependent upon our unique set of personal values, intrinsic drives, and culture. There are certain factors from our past that influenced our decision to join the military. Perhaps serving in the military is a family tradition. Maybe you grew up near a military base. For me, almost everyone from my graduating class was going to Penn State, and I wanted something more than that. The idea of "something more" was what inspired me to apply to the service academies in the first place. Understanding these factors reveals the underlying influences leading up to that first day of basic training.

In the second part of this exercise, we want to focus on the factors that influenced our decision to serve in the military. Pick up to five factors that drove you toward a military path.

5 Factors that Influenced Your Decision to Serve in the Military	
FACTOR 1	
FACTOR 2	
FACTOR 3	
FACTOR 4	
FACTOR 5	

Let's explore the continuity between Parts 1 and 2 of this exercise. Your purpose, the WHY, is always at work. It was working before you ever knew that you had a purpose. It was influencing and guiding your behavior long before you joined the military. These people, experiences, and other factors that resonate with you on an intrinsic level provide meaningful indicators to reveal your identity. When combined with the most rewarding aspects of military service, you begin to understand why the military was such a good fit for you.

EXERCISE 1.2 IDENTIFY THE MOST REWARDING ASPECTS OF MILITARY SERVICE

Certain aspects of military service resonate with us more than others. I doubt that many of us would identify family separation as something we enjoyed during our time in the military. That said, there were aspects of our service that we found truly rewarding. Some examples might include travel, training, discipline, excitement, the people, leadership, opportunities, reputation, responsibility, esprit de corps, or a connection to something greater. As you reflect back on your time in service, identify five words (or short phrases) with accompanying descriptions that best capture the most rewarding aspects of your military service. For example, you might say that *The People* were a rewarding aspect for you. In the description, share what qualities or characteristics about *The People* were so rewarding to you.

Describe the 5 Most Rewarding Aspects of Military Service	
Aspect	Description

One interesting observation to note here is the difference between what we loved about the military and the criteria we use to find the next job after the military. More often than not, we don't identify things like compensation, location, or position as the most rewarding aspects of military service, but those tend to be factors we use to start looking for the next job. For the most part, the rewards of military service typically include personal relationships, transformative experiences, and challenging opportunities. See the disconnect?

It begs the question that if this list highlights the things we valued the most from our military experience, why do we use a different set of criteria when it comes to framing what we do next? When you juxtapose what you learned about yourself from the past three exercises against the current mindset of finding the next job, you may start to understand the reason why so many veterans find themselves in the wrong jobs. It happens because they were looking in all the wrong places.

EXERCISE 1.3 WRITING A PURPOSE STATEMENT—FIRST ATTEMPT

When it comes to writing your Purpose Statement, be mindful of these three qualities:

1. Authenticity: The Purpose Statement only has to have meaning to you. If you worry or wonder about how your Purpose Statement "sounds" to someone else, you're allowing the ego to challenge and compromise your authenticity.

2. All-Encompassing: Your Purpose Statement is universal. There are no alibis or caveats. This statement should apply regardless of the environment or situation. It is not a switch that you turn on or off when you go to work. It covers both your personal and professional life.

3. Emotive: When you do things consistent with your purpose, it doesn't feel like work. You feel energetic and alive. When you partake in activities or behaviors that are inconsistent with your purpose, it requires effort and consumes energy to overcome the natural flow of your intrinsic drive.

The Purpose Statement is similar to a mission statement that you would craft in the military with several key omissions. Military mission statements include the five Ws—who, what, where, when, and why. Your Purpose Statement always applies to you, independent of time or location, so we can exclude the who, when, and where. Therefore, your mission statement or purpose is just the what (action) and the why (impact).

For example:

ACTION	IMPACT
To inspire	Leaders to live more meaningful lives in the service of others.

Let's take a moment and consider three different possibilities for your Purpose Statement. Select a different action verb and impact for each verb. Keep in mind that this is just a starting point. You don't have to get it right on the first try. Your Purpose Statement may evolve as you progress through this handbook. Just as we revisit the mission statement again after the Mission Analysis step of the MDMP, you will have a chance to revisit your Purpose Statement again after Identity Analysis, the second step of the MTRP.

Possible Purpose Statements	
ACTION	IMPACT

IDENTITY ANALYSIS

If I were given one hour to save the planet, I would spend fifty-nine minutes defining the problem and one minute resolving it.

—ALBERT EINSTEIN

Mission Analysis is a phrase that conjures some unique—if not unpleasant—memories. As a process, Mission Analysis provides a means for military leaders to apply the scientific method to analyze a tactical problem. You might remember being held hostage by the chief of staff, executive officer, or operations officer while you and your colleagues tediously walked through the steps of this process. Although I disliked Mission Analysis as a junior staff officer, I learned to appreciate the value of it later in my career. By the time I became a battalion commander, I considered Mission Analysis indispensable to the development and execution of sound plans for high-risk operations.

In the construct of the MTRP, this process is called the *Identity Analysis*. It analyzes the problem of discovering your path for life beyond the military. A crosswalk between the steps of Mission Analysis and the steps of Identity Analysis are included in **Table 2.0. Mission Analysis vs. Identity Analysis Crosswalk.** The objective of the Identity Analysis is to uncover the details of the WHO and the WHY of your story to help write the next chapter of your life. Stated another way, this process is meant to determine who you want to be when you can't be the service member anymore. Therefore, the analysis is introspective. By understanding your values, intrinsic motivations, strengths, and what you really want, you can craft an authentic Purpose Statement and intent for what happens next.

Although the Identity Analysis is not a perfect reflection of the Mission Analysis, it provides a framework for understanding the process to uncover your unique and most authentic identity story. ***This is the most important and most critical step of the transition and reintegration process, and therefore, the Identity Analysis is the primary focus of this handbook.***

Table 2.0. Mission Analysis and Identity Analysis Crosswalk. The Identity Analysis mirrors this crucial step from the MDMP.

Mission Analysis[15]		Identity Analysis
Analyze the Higher Headquarters Order	2.1	Analyze the WHO
Perform Intelligence Preparation of the Battlefield (IPB)	2.2	Understand the Transition Environment
Specified, Implied, & Essential Tasks	2.3	Setting Intentions
Review Available Assets	2.4	Review Intrinsic Strengths
Determine Constraints	2.5	Determine Limiting and Empowering Beliefs
Identify Critical Facts and Assumptions	2.6	Identify Common Factors for Success
Begin Risk Management	2.7	MTRP Action Plan to Address the Greatest Risk in Military Transition
Determine Commander's Critical Information Requirements	2.8	Determine Family Information Requirements
Build Collection Plan	2.9	Build Your Networking Strategy
Plan use of Available Time	2.10	Develop the Transition and Reintegration Timeline
Write Restated Mission	2.11	Write Your Statement of Intent

2.1. ANALYZE THE WHO

Tell me who the hell are you?

—ROGER DALTRY, THE WHO

That question spoke to an entire generation of rock and roll fans. Perhaps the reference is a bit dated, but I'm certain you've heard some form of this question before. People you meet for the first time may want to know your story or something interesting about you. If you've already started networking or exploring job opportunities, you may have been asked to share or tell something about yourself. Although the wording or setting may vary, the intention is the same. The person asking the question is trying to make a connection. They want to know *who you are!*

If someone were to ask you that question now, how would you answer? Could you do it without talking about your profession? What if you couldn't discuss your education, position, job

---

15. Department of the Army, *Commander*, 9-7.

specialty, or your role in your family? Answers that rely on those factors are only deflections. They describe general things that you do, but they don't reveal who you really are.

There are thousands, if not millions, of people from around the world who share your various titles, but there is only one YOU. You have a unique identity story. It transcends the labels that describe your responsibilities, qualifications, or experience. So, in order to really get to know yourself, you have to dig a little deeper. You must be able to describe what you see after you remove the labels.

THE CONNECTION BETWEEN YOUR VALUES AND YOUR IDENTITY

Values are what remain when you peel off the labels. Values provide the key to understanding who you really are. They highlight the qualities, attributes, and traits that define your unique identity. The person that others see on the outside is shaped by your core values on the inside. *Who you are* is a combination of the values that influence what you think, how you feel, and what is most important to you in life. Consequently, if you don't know your values, you don't really know who you are.

Values are the vital ingredients that define your character and shape your personality. They are inherently powerful because you don't get to choose your values. You are born with them. They are revealed over the course of your life. They have a primal, subconscious quality and provide an authentic lens for how you view and experience the world. Values are the embers beneath the surface that provide the glow and energy to fuel the intrinsic drive along the path to realize your true purpose in life.

YOUR VALUES AT WORK

If you pay close enough attention, you just might notice when your values are at work. You feel drawn to situations and activities that align with your values. When you are expressing your values, you feel inspired. You feel resilient. You feel energized. Work requires less effort when you behave in a manner consistent with your values.

Conversely, you may also recognize when you are not in alignment with your values. You'll feel that dissonance in the form of stress on a mental, emotional, and even spiritual level. When you choose to live in a manner inconsistent with your values, you defy your authenticity. This most often occurs when the ego strives for social acceptance and external validation. You try to become someone you think you should be at the expense of who you were meant to be. You hide behind your reputation, titles, and the material abstractions for happiness. The price you pay for this charade is the true sense of joy that you were meant to experience in your life.

Figure 2.1. How Values Show Up. These are examples of how values work beneath the threshold of awareness to shape your identity.

How Certain Actions and Circumstances Can Reveal Our True Values
You tell a lie that haunts you. After several days, you come clean because you just can't live with yourself. **Honesty** may be one of your values.
You seem to work at your best when you are in an inclusive environment where everyone treats each other with dignity and respect. **Respect** may be one of your values.
Whenever you start something, you stay with it until it is finished. You make personal sacrifices to see the task through to completion. **Fortitude** might be a personal value.
You refuse to settle for the status quo. You are always seeking to make improvements and find a better way. **Innovation** might be a personal value.

Comparison Between Intentional and Fear Based Values
Honesty sounds like a strong value, but like all values, it can be **Intentional** or **Fear Based**. Let's consider the following comparison to highlight the difference between an **Intentional Value** and a **Fear Based Value**:
Example 1: Honesty as an **Intentional Value**:
You tell a lie. Not a big lie, but an untruth nonetheless. Once you tell that lie, you feel an overwhelming sense of guilt. These feelings burden your conscience. When you can't take it anymore, you come clean and tell the truth. The reason why you felt the stress from this behavior is because your action was inconsistent with a personal value.
Example 2: Honesty as a **Fear Based Value**:
A friend confides in you that his wife has been lying to him. She had an affair. Upon discovering the truth, he was completely devastated. He tells you that he feels utterly worthless, but more than that, he feels humiliated because he was the last one to know. He says that he won't tolerate another betrayal, and therefore, he commits to making honesty his most important value.
Notice in the first example that just because you identify honesty as a value, it doesn't mean you will always be honest. When you behave in a manner inconsistent with a core value, you will feel it. This dissonance manifests itself in the form of guilt or shame. You feel stress and even pain when you act in a manner contrary to your values. This is an indicator that Honesty is an **Intentional** value.
Now look at the second example. Just like the first example, pain is involved. The difference is in the sequencing. In this example, the pain comes first. Also, the cause of that pain was external. The husband didn't behave dishonestly. His wife did. He formed a personal value as a precaution to avoid future pain. The value was selected for self-preservation instead of self-expression. This is an example of a **Fear Based** value.

Your values are always at work, and only you can decide whether or not they are working with you or against you. Values are meant to be positive or intentional, but given your experiences, you may define your values as negative or fear based. If behaviors and beliefs are guided by the memories of negative events, you are allowing fear to define your state of being. Subconscious impulses invoke behaviors to avoid the possibility of future pain based on past suffering. These impulses are part of your survival instinct and shouldn't be confused with your values. Values are not restrictive or limiting. They reveal the path for purpose, passion, and empowerment.

WHY YOUR PERSONAL VALUES MATTER AS A LEADER

Conducting business may not be personal, but leadership most certainly is. Personal values matter as a leader for several reasons:

1. Values Provide Clarity. Values inform decisions and guide actions through periods of uncertainty. Information changes. Circumstances evolve. Leaders have to be comfortable making decisions and taking action when they lack perfect information. Focusing on values can help remove the fog of ambiguity to reveal a clear course of action.

2. Values Endure. Jobs, positions, or titles are temporary. These are artificial labels given to you. They can change in a moment. They can be taken away. Your values will always be with you. Nobody can take them from you. You get to decide whether or not to honor your core values in how you choose to live your life.

3. Values Inspire. Your values are yours for a reason. As the truest expression of who you are, values drive your passion. They are the mechanism to unleash your potential. They represent the distinction between the effort of "doing" and the joy of "being."

4. Values Instill Calm. Leaders need to be comfortable in uncomfortable situations. Being grounded in your values facilitates greater resilience. Honoring your values instead of an attachment to a specified outcome has a calming effect. People turn to leaders for confidence and encouragement during challenging times, and leaders turn to their values for guidance and assurance.

5. Values Express Authenticity. Values represent the core of your personal identity. When you understand your values and allow them to guide your actions, shape your beliefs, and inform your decisions, others will see you for who you truly are as a leader and, more importantly, as a human being. Your authenticity invites others to connect with you on a deeply personal level. This connection is necessary to forge trust and inspire others to achieve and surpass the limits of their own potential.

HOW CAN YOU DISCOVER YOUR VALUES?

Discovering your values requires honesty and self-awareness. It could take several days, months, or even years before you recognize your core values. Once you do, you have an opportunity to become more authentic as a leader. You will know who you are. You can make meaningful connections and harness your intrinsic drive to achieve your purpose in life.

As you begin this process of self-discovery, have patience. You probably won't get it right the first time. It is normal to make changes as you become more self-aware of what is most important to you. Introspection is not easy and not always straightforward. Here are some things to remember as you embark upon your journey of self-awareness:

Values Are Emotive. It should feel good when you read the words that you use to describe your values. Some of the most inspired, motivated, and accomplished moments of life happen when you choose to live as an expression of your values. Think about some of those times and consider what themes or words come to mind.

Values Reduce Stress. Stress, regret, shame, and guilt are byproducts of actions, behaviors, and decisions inconsistent with your values. Reflect on some of the more stressful periods of your life. What values do you believe were being challenged in those circumstances?

Values Are Personal. As you define your values, they should have meaning specific to you. The dictionary definition of the word or phrase doesn't matter. What someone else might think about your definition doesn't matter either. What matters is how a particular value works through you.

Values Are Nonjudgmental. Values are not "good" or "bad." They just "are." Sometimes we allow other people's expectations or interpretations of a desired self-image shape what we think our values should be. Unfortunately, we are not only being dishonest with ourselves, but because we are constructing a façade to hide our true identity, we are also being dishonest with everyone else.

When actions, behaviors, and beliefs align with your personal values, they emote a sense of motivation, inspiration, and positivity. You feel alive! When actions, behaviors, and beliefs are inconsistent with personal values, they create stress, drain personal energy, and harbor negative emotions like resentment, guilt, or shame. Imagine the possibility of living with positive intention. Imagine if you had the ability to channel your strongest source of energy to fuel your journey to achieve your purpose and realize your intent in life. This is what happens when you apply conscious intention behind your values.

Core values reveal your true identity. Your potential lies within that identity. As a leader, the "who" matters most. If you seek a life of purpose and fulfillment, "what" you do and "how" you choose to do it are just different ways and means to express the "who." As it pertains to leadership, the leader you always wanted to follow is right there inside of you. Your values reveal the path to become the leader you were always meant to be. Authentic leadership begins by knowing who the hell you are.

EXERCISE 2.1. VALUES ALGEBRA

The purpose of this exercise is to clarify your personal values. As you work through the next several pages, you may hear your ego suggest that you select certain words to convey a particular image that you think people want to see instead of who you really are. Silence the imposter and use this tool to create self-awareness for who you really are as a person and a leader.

Step 1. Explore Possible Values. Over the next several pages are 240 words that describe possible values. This list is not all-inclusive, but it provides a starting point. Review this list and consider which of these words "feels" most like you. Highlight at least five but no more than twenty-five. It may help to review the list in its entirety at least once before highlighting any of the words.

Abundance	Acceptance	Accountability	Achievement	Adaptability	Advancement
Adventure	Affection	Affluence	Agility	Ambition	Amusement
Appreciation	Altruism	Audacity	Authenticity	Authority	Autonomy
Balance	Beauty	Belonging	Benevolence	Boldness	Bravery
Brilliance	Calm	Candor	Care	Charity	Charm
Chastity	Cheerfulness	Citizenship	Clarity	Cleverness	Comfort
Commitment	Community	Compassion	Competence	Competition	Composure
Confidence	Conformity	Congruency	Connection	Conservation	Consistency
Conviction	Cooperation	Cordiality	Country	Courage	Creativity
Credibility	Cunning	Curiosity	Daring	Decisiveness	Decorum
Dedication	Dependability	Determination	Development	Devotion	Dexterity
Dignity	Diligence	Direction	Discovery	Discretion	Diversity
Dominance	Drive	Duty	Economy	Ecstasy	Efficiency
Elegance	Empathy	Empowerment	Endurance	Energy	Enjoyment

Enthusiasm	Equality	Excellence	Excitement	Exhilaration	Expediency
Expertise	Exploration	Extravagance	Extroversion	Exuberance	Faith
Fame	Family	Fascination	Ferocity	Fidelity	Firmness
Fitness	Flexibility	Fluency	Focus	Foresight	Fortitude
Frankness	Freedom	Friendship	Frugality	Fun	Gallantry
Generosity	Gentility	Goodness	Grace	Gratitude	Growth
Harmony	Health	Heart	Hedonism	Honesty	Honor
Hospitality	Humility	Humor	Impartiality	Improvement	Independence
Individuality	Ingenuity	Innovation	Insightfulness	Integrity	Intellect
Intensity	Intimacy	Introspection	Judiciousness	Justice	Kindness
Knowledge	Learning	Liberty	Liveliness	Logic	Loyalty
Majesty	Mastery	Moderation	Modesty	Nature	Nonconformity
Obedience	Open-minded	Openness	Optimism	Order	Organization
Originality	Passion	Patience	Peace	Perfection	Perkiness
Perseverance	Philanthropy	Piety	Pleasure	Poise	Polish
Potency	Practicality	Pragmatism	Precision	Preparedness	Pride
Privacy	Proactivity	Productivity	Prosperity	Prudence	Punctuality
Purity	Quality	Rationality	Reason	Resolution	Respect
Responsibility	Restraint	Results	Reverence	Rigor	Sacrifice
Sagacity	Sanguinity	Security	Selflessness	Serenity	Simplicity
Sincerity	Solidarity	Solitude	Soundness	Spirituality	Spontaneity
Stability	Stewardship	Strength	Success	Sustainability	Sympathy
Synergy	Teamwork	Temperance	Thrift	Tolerance	Toughness
Tradition	Tranquility	Trust	Understanding	Unity	Utility
Valor	Vigor	Vivacity	Warmth	Wealth	Willfulness
Wisdom	Wonder	Worthiness	Youthfulness	Zeal	Zest

Step 2. Group Like Terms. Once you've identified the words that resonate with you, it's time to group like terms. The purpose of this step is to cluster words that could be describing the same value. For example, you may have highlighted the following words:

Wisdom   Intellect   (Reason)   Soundness   Understanding   Knowledge

Here is another example of possible like terms...

Courage   Fortitude   Strength   Valor   (**Bravery**)   Adventure

In each of these examples, the six words have synonymous meanings, so pick the one that stands out the most to you. Your selection should BEST embody the shared meaning among the grouped terms. In this example, *Reason* was selected as the best among the words in the top row, and *Bravery* was selected as the best alternative from the bottom row. This step only applies if you have a cluster of two or more similar terms. You may not have identified any clusters of similar terms. If that is the case, each word stands on its own and you can move to Step 3.

Step 3. Establish the Order of Operations. Next, you want to prioritize these words by their level of importance. If you grouped words together in Step 2, ensure that you only use the term that best represents that group of words. In the current example, you would consider whether *Reason* or *Bravery* has a higher priority as a personal value. You may identify as many as ten or fifteen different values.

Rank your potential values in order of importance in the chart provided:

Ranking	Value	Ranking	Value
1		6	
2		7	
3		8	
4		9	
5		10	

Step 4. Define Your Values. In the final step of this exercise, you will define your values in your own words. You want to have definitions for at least the top five values on your list. If you have groups of words that are related, you may want to use some of those words in your definitions. For example:

Value	Definition
Reason	Apply _wisdom_ and _knowledge_ to arrive at sound conclusions
Bravery	Demonstrate _courage_ and _fortitude_ in the most difficult situations

Notice that each definition begins with an action or a state of being. Notice how the words *Wisdom* and *Knowledge* were used in the definition for *Reason*. Notice also how *Courage* and *Fortitude* were used in the definition of *Bravery*. A list of three to five values and definitions will look something like this:

Value	Definition
Authenticity	Have the Courage and Integrity to Show-Up
Innovation	Challenge the status-quo with creativity and ambition to make things better
Passion for Life	Feel Alive!
Faith	Let Go and Allow
Service to Others	Improve society one person at a time

As you build your list of values, remember that this is only a starting point. As you gain greater self-awareness, you may want to change some of your chosen values or definitions. You may want to journal about your values to better understand how they show up in your life. Input your top five values and definitions in the chart below:

Value	Definition

It may take days or even months to settle on the words and definitions that describe your values. Don't get discouraged if it takes longer than you might expect. Self-discovery doesn't come with an instruction manual or a time limit. Be open to reviewing and exploring your values. If you can exclaim "That's ME!" as you read the values and definitions for those words, then you'll know that you've captured the qualities, attributes, and characteristics that define WHO you are.

2.2 UNDERSTAND THE TRANSITION ENVIRONMENT

In the first step of the MTRP, we examined the WHO. This covered the "See Yourself" component of Sun Tzu's strategic guidance. In the next phase of the MTRP, we want to gather intelligence about the transition environment and uncover the obstacles to civilian reintegration. In other words, it's time to examine the terrain and the enemy.

The threats that linger across the transition environment are byproducts of the social and cultural evolution that occurred over the past century. There was a time when almost every household had at least one family member who served in the military. Whether it was a member of the immediate family, an uncle, or a distant cousin, the military experience touched ordinary citizens of this country in a very personal way. Today, veterans are a disappearing minority across the national landscape. Fewer civilians are connected to the real burdens and sacrifices of military service. Consequently, so much of today's society has no idea what it means to be a soldier.

Releasing your attachment to the warrior identity and stepping away from the military culture comes with some significant psychological challenges and implications. Your body and mind have adapted to the social and cultural norms of the military, but many of those habits are not attuned to the accepted norms of civilian society. Disconnecting from the safe, insulated culture in the military invites a very real and palpable fear into your consciousness. The uncertainty that accompanies the personal and professional adjustment to civilian life makes transition and reintegration the most challenging phase of the military journey.

2.2.1 THE PHYSIOLOGICAL IMPLICATIONS OF MILITARY SEPARATION

Why does everything feel so different once you leave the military? Personally, I thought that losing my government-issued phone would be a welcome change in my life, but the once familiar ringtones and message alerts were quickly replaced by an uncomfortable—and unsettling—silence. I realized that my phone wasn't just a way for people to get in touch with me, but it was also my way of staying connected with them. In the weeks that followed my retirement, a terrible sense of loneliness began to fill the void once occupied by the urgency of life shared through government-issued smartphones.

We cherish the camaraderie and our sense of belonging in the military. Despite the inherent hazards of the job, we feel comfortable within the ranks of our formations. Given the nature of our duty and the amount of time we spend together, the bonds among soldiers are stronger than those of any other team from any other profession. Stated another way, being a soldier means being a part of a family. When we separate from the military, we disconnect from that family. We feel the pain and grieve the loss associated with that disconnection. To understand the nature of that pain, we must understand the implications of military transition on a physiological level.

THE BIOCHEMICAL UNDERPINNINGS OF MILITARY TRANSITION

I didn't know the first thing about hormones, neurotransmitters, or biochemistry while I was in the military. This aspect of psychology wasn't part of my Professional Military Education. However, when I read Simon Sinek's best-selling book, *Leaders Eat Last*, I was intrigued by his discussion about the biochemical system of rewards and punishments that guides our behavior.[16] Sinek was exploring the relationship between organizational culture and individual biochemistry. Motivation and inspiration, two fundamental qualities of effective leadership, are grounded in this interdependent relationship.

Everything we feel has a biochemical signature. Human beings produce a series of chemicals called hormones that fuel the limbic system. According to Dr. Loretta Graziano Breuning, we have four chemicals in the brain that help us feel happy: dopamine, oxytocin, serotonin, and

---

16. Simon Sinek, *Leaders Eat Last* (New York: Portfolio Penguin, 2018), 45.

endorphins.[17] In the context of leadership, Sinek considers dopamine and endorphins the selfish chemicals that incentivize personal achievement while serotonin and oxytocin are the selfless chemicals that provide a shared sense of belonging and security.[18]

Dopamine is the feel-good that motivates and reinforces behavior.[19] It is the reward our brain provides the body for achieving a goal. When we finish a task, achieve a milestone, or accomplish an objective, the satisfaction we feel comes from dopamine. When you score well on a test, receive an award, or get a promotion, dopamine gives you a bump. It is our own way of compensating ourselves for a job well done.

The reason why dopamine is considered a selfish chemical is because only the individual reaps the reward from his or her achievement. With each hormonal push, our brain records the cause and effect to incentivize similar behavior in the future. Our brain creates a neural template to remember those activities that accompany the hit of dopamine.

Like dopamine, endorphins are considered a selfish hormone. Endorphins are often associated with the runner's high or the physical exertion from a hard workout.[20] We recognize the benefit of persevering through painful exercise because of what it provides to our strength, endurance, or overall fitness. Endorphins allow us to push through the pain to get the gain.

The military experience presents us with plenty of opportunities to overcome uncomfortable and even painful situations. In combat, we feel the rush of endorphins to push through stress, anxiety, and physical hardship. Every successful mission is rewarded with an intoxicating dose of dopamine. The euphoria we feel during military operations is a mix of these addictive chemicals coursing through our system.

Because military duty has a higher incidence of life and death situations, we experience a greater amplitude of chemicals designed to help us push through hardship and accomplish the mission under extreme duress. The "combat high" is so powerful and addictive that many service members and veterans seek to satisfy their cravings through high-risk behaviors and other unhealthy diversions when they come home. Long after we return from a deployment, we still crave the explosive cocktail of endorphins and dopamine.

---

17. Loretta Graziano. Breuning, *Meet Your Happy Chemicals: Dopamine, Endorphin, Oxytocin, Serotonin* (Inner Mammal Institute, 2012).
18. Sinek, *Leaders*, 46.
19. Kate Brophy, "What Is Dopamine? Understanding the 'Feel-Good Hormone'," *University Health News* (blog), October 18, 2018, https://universityhealthnews.com/daily/depression/what-is-dopamine-understanding-the-feel-good-hormone/.
20. Tom Scheve, "What Are Endorphins?" *HowStuffWorks* (blog), June 22, 2009, https://science.howstuffworks.com/life/inside-the-mind/emotions/endorphins2.htm.

The next two chemicals involve social interaction. Serotonin and oxytocin are related to our sense of security, purpose, belonging, trust, and camaraderie. They represent the biochemical foundation for the qualities we value most in the military culture. As the leadership chemical, serotonin gives us a feeling of pride and importance.[21] We are proud of our uniform, our unit, and our heritage. Rank offers recognizable status within the social order. We salute and receive the same courtesy when passing a fellow service member. We greet one another with call signs and unit mottos. We are proud representatives of the ideals of our nation. Military units leverage the benefits of serotonin to create a culture of mutual respect with a shared commitment to duty.

We refer to our units as a band of brothers and sisters because of our trust in one another. We have oxytocin to thank for that. Oxytocin has been shown to increase positive emotions, altruism, trust, and sociability.[22] Oxytocin gives us the sense of connection we feel among our fellow service members. Because the military culture encourages the steady release of oxytocin, the military unit feels like a family.

We learn to love the challenge of serving our country despite the life or death implications of the job. When our fight or flight survival mechanism is triggered, we feel a surge of energy from the epinephrine. Cortisol focuses our biological systems to respond to dangerous situations. We rely on endorphins to push through the adversity. Dopamine is the biochemical reward for mission accomplishment. Even though the circumstances may be life threatening, we take comfort in the serotonin that comes from the respect, belonging, and that sense of importance. The confidence and trust we feel toward our fellow soldier in that foxhole is a result of the oxytocin. The biochemistry of the military experience has a way of offsetting the stress associated with the very real dangers of military service.

MILITARY SEPARATION AND CHEMICAL WITHDRAWAL

Serving in the military provides a path to fulfill our purpose, but it also feels good. "Trust and purpose mutually reinforce each other, providing a mechanism for extended oxytocin release, which produces happiness."[23] One of the reasons we continue to volunteer for military service is because the culture provides a biochemical solution for happiness. This is the reason why breaking that connection is so difficult—and painful.

Once we leave the military, we remove ourselves from that culture of respect and trust. As we

---

21. Sinek, *Leaders*, 57.

22. Concordia University, "Oxytocin Helps People Feel More Extroverted: Study Finds People More Sociable, Open, Trusting after Taking Oxytocin," *ScienceDaily*, December 9, 2011, https://www.sciencedaily.com/releases/2011/12/111209123212.htm.

23. Paul J. Zak, "The Neuroscience of Trust," *Harvard Business Review*, January–February 2017, https://hbr.org/2017/01/the-neuroscience-of-trust.

face new challenges in the civilian world, the stress feels different. We realize rather quickly that we are no longer insulated and protected by the chemical resonance we enjoyed from the military culture. We discover just how strong our attachment was to the environment that supplied our fix of serotonin and oxytocin, and once we are disconnected from that environment, we feel the pain of withdrawal. Social disconnection triggers the same neural pathways in the brain that recognize physical pain.[24] In other words, it really hurts when we leave the military.

Our separation from the military culture removes us from the dealer that supplied and maintained our chemical addiction. Leaving the military disrupts our homeostasis, and our bodies need to establish a new baseline in civilian society. Stated another way, we must endure the pain of withdrawal. It's not our fault that the brain lights up with a flood of chemicals that accompany the military experience, so we are not "addicts" in the true sense, but we still feel the pain from psychological withdrawal when we discharge from the military nonetheless. Transition implicitly requires a form of recovery to establish a new normal, and like any psychological attachment, breaking an unhealthy habit requires new behaviors to replace the old.

2.2.2. BREAKING THE HABIT OF BEING A WARRIOR

Your conditioning began during basic training. Frequency and repetition were an integral part of your indoctrination. In the beginning, the stress from the military regimen was overwhelming. You learned the habits of the military culture not because you wanted to, but because you had to. The basic training cadre had a way of convincing you that your old way of being was insufficient for your new life in the military. This was your initiation to break the habit of being a civilian to form new habits in your life as a warrior.

Over time, you internalized these habits. What began as a struggle for survival became the accepted behaviors and routines that helped you succeed as a warrior and leader in the military. Looking back, it probably felt uncomfortable the first time you did a facing movement. Your first salute was probably not the best reflection of military courtesy. Over time, many of the behaviors that defined the military culture grew into subconscious routines that became as automatic as blinking your eyes. Our bodies and minds became attuned to the norms of the military way of life.

Even more difficult and complex tasks became routine through frequency and repetition. Military training and readiness rely on this form of conditioning. We practice and rehearse to

---

24. Naomi I. Eisenberger, "The Neural Bases of Social Pain," *Psychosomatic Medicine* 74, no. 2 (2012): 130-131, https://doi:10.1097/psy.0b013e3182464dd1.

make complex behaviors automatic. We remand many tasks to subconscious processing—or "muscle memory"—to allow space for the conscious mind to attend to the emerging details and demands of more urgent priorities. Being cool and collected under pressure is a quality that requires extensive practice.

One personal example I might offer to demonstrate this conditioning process is from my experience in helicopter flight training. I will never forget the first time that I was given the controls of an aircraft not in contact with the surface of the earth. Every control input felt forced and abrupt. When I tried to hover, the aircraft bucked like a bronco across the landing strip. After each day of training, I crawled out of the aircraft drenched in sweat. Over time, my once mechanical inputs to the flight controls became much smoother. I got better with practice (a lot of practice). Eventually, the seemingly impossible task of hovering a helicopter became routine. Despite all initial evidence suggesting otherwise, hovering eventually became something that required very little conscious effort.

The military also taught us a very structured approach to process information to solve problems. This methodology, the Military Decision-Making Process, was reinforced through practice and experience throughout our careers. Our immersion into this way of thinking framed our intuition. Over time, the approved method of solving military problems became the chosen method for solving any problem. We instinctively apply the steps to define the problem, go through Mission Analysis, develop courses of action, assess the risk, and come to a sound conclusion. Solving problems became almost like a stimulus-response reaction that required very little conscious thinking.

These methods of learning are the result of a physiological phenomenon called neuroplasticity. "The neurons that fire together, wire together" is a phrase often used to describe the neural hard-wiring that occurs through repeated exposure to stimulus or cognitive function.[25] Your brain becomes conditioned to certain stimulus or cognitive processing in the same way that your musculoskeletal system becomes conditioned from exercise. When you go to the gym and increase the frequency, duration, or effort of your workout, you condition the muscles in your body to grow stronger. The brain responds in a similar way to repeated exposure to the same stimuli and problem sets. Over time, the muscles of your body become sufficiently conditioned to perform exercise with less physical effort, and likewise, the brain requires less conscious effort to arrive at solutions to recognizable problem sets.

25. Christian Keysers and Valeria Gazzola, "Hebbian Learning and Predictive Mirror Neurons for Actions, Sensations and Emotions," *Philosophical Transactions of the Royal Society B: Biological Sciences* 369, no. 1644 (2014): 2, https://doi:10.1098 /rstb.2013.0175.

As we spend more time in the uniform, the norms of the military culture eventually become the lens through which we see the world. We become the embodiment of this culture through our attitudes, behaviors, and beliefs. The persona of the soldier becomes a part of our identity. Our subconscious problem-solving processes conform to the practice and nuance learned through the military. When we face a stressful event, we tend to fall back on old habits. For service members, that means falling into the military way of being. Our muscle memory conforms to the recognizable task, condition, and standard that served us so well for all those years in the military.

As we age, these subconscious routines begin to dominate how we behave and interact with the world around us. The longer we serve in the military, the more entrenched these habits become. In his book *Breaking the Habit of Being Yourself*, Joe Dispenza talks about the power of subconscious habits to guide our actions and influence our behaviors as we approach middle age:

> Psychologists tell us that by the time we're in our mid-thirties, our identity or personality will be completely formed. This means that for those of us over thirty-five, we have memorized a select set of behaviors, attitudes, beliefs, emotional reactions, habits, skills, associative memories, conditioned responses, and perceptions that are now subconsciously programmed within us. Those programs are running us, because the body has become the mind. This means that we will think the same thoughts, feel the same feelings, react in identical ways, behave in the same manner, believe the same dogmas, and perceive reality the same ways. About 95 percent of who we are by midlife is a series of subconscious programs that have become automatic.[26]

Consider the implications of that passage in the context of military transition. If you joined the military right out of high school and served for a decade or more, much of what comprises your personal identity was shaped by the military culture. If you remain in the military until retirement, your entire adult persona is connected to your identity as a warrior. Because the military culture is distinct from the norms of civilian society, **you** are distinct from norms of civilian society. In the same way that the military customs and traditions don't fit in regular society, you don't fit either. Reintegration requires you to apply the remaining 5 percent of conscious intention to overcome the other 95 percent of your warrior identity.

You may not notice this incongruence in the days leading up to your separation date. All the preparation leading up to your final departure will feel very familiar. After all, you've out-processed a unit before. Changing duty stations and moving your family is nothing new.

---

26. Dispenza, *Breaking*, 61-62.

You've started jobs in new positions for different organizations. On the surface, much of your transition will look and feel very familiar. It is normal to assume that this is just another move and fall back into old habits when you separate or retire from the military.

Unfortunately, the habits you've relied upon to change duty stations won't work when you change your status from service member to veteran. When you change installations, jobs, or duty positions within the military, you are not changing your identity as a military professional. You may have a new unit patch or rank on your shoulder, but you still wear the same uniform. The values underpinning your role or position remain the same. Your stature and place within the culture remains relatively intact. Although every unit has its own way of doing things, we can generally accept a common set of behaviors, values, and beliefs that are universally recognized across every branch of service and military installation. That continuity doesn't extend past the front gate when you leave the military. Civilian society has its own set of norms, practices, and routines. Your military routines are simply not calibrated for the nuances of civilian life.

There is no formal process for reintegrating warriors back into society in the same way that basic training initiates a high school graduate or young adult into the military. When you started your military journey, you endured a formative process of conditioning to prepare and indoctrinate you to the military way of life. You became the warrior. Unfortunately, a commensurate process doesn't exist to transform the warrior back into a civilian. Consequently, you carry all of your initial issues and habits formed from your time in service back with you into the civilian world.

Our initial reaction to new problems in the civilian world is to default to our old habits from the military. Particularly when we are under duress, we will subconsciously gravitate toward familiar routines. Only after we are in a new environment will we begin to recognize that we don't fit in that environment. Unfortunately, the warrior archetype—the military way of being—cannot coexist in the mundane of civilian society. The traditions, rules, and norms are both distinct and different.

In the first several months after you transition, you may begin to feel this dissonance in the form of mental, emotional, and even spiritual stress. Your survival mechanism will get triggered when you leave the military in the same way it was triggered when you joined the military. This time, you don't have the support of your squad or team. This time, you don't have a cadre to indoctrinate you into the norms of your new culture. This time, you are largely on your own.

Leaving the military means repurposing old habits to form new ones. We must necessarily rely on the other 5 percent of our conscious mind to overcome the inertia from 95 percent of our subconscious habits. Our biochemical addiction and psychological conditioning to the military culture turns the otherwise innocuous act of transition into a formidable undertaking. As we become more informed about the psychological factors that affect military transition, a growing body of research suggests that *transition stress*—not the more common and recognizable diagnosis of PTSD—is the culprit for many of the social, cultural, and emotional issues that lead to more debilitating conditions of mental illness in the veteran community.[27] In order to successfully reintegrate back into society, we must break the habit of being a warrior so that we can embrace our authentic identity and become something more in life after the military.

2.2.3 CONFRONTING THE F-WORD

The military has its own version of the F-word. Like the other word you might be thinking of, this F-word is considered an obscenity in our culture. It represents something that is not to be tolerated. If you used this F-word to describe a fellow service member, he or she would definitely be offended. It represents what lurks underneath our persona and warrior ethic. We don't like to talk about it, but we all know it's there.

This F-word is the source of your anxiety during military transition. It is the emotion that keeps you up at night thinking about who you are, where you might go, and what you might do when you can't be a warrior anymore. It's what you experience in the days following the career conference when nobody calls you for an interview. It's what you sense as your separation date looms near without any job offers. It's what you feel when you can't answer the question from family and friends about what you might do after you hang up the uniform. It warns you of what might happen if you don't play it safe. It shackles you to mediocrity. It's the voice inside your head that tells you to stop listening to your heart.

The last enemy you confront in your military journey is the one you face when you drive out the main gate for the last time. The F-word that haunts you during military transition is *FEAR*.

THE NATURE OF THE F-WORD

On a physiological level, fear is an emotion tied to our survival instinct. It operates on a subconscious level. No warrior wants to admit when he or she is afraid, but the body knows when we are scared before the mind does. The amygdala is the structure in the brain beneath the prefrontal cortex that screens incoming stimuli for potential threats. This includes new and

---

27. Meaghan C. Mobbs and George A. Bonanno, "Beyond War and PTSD: The Crucial Role of Transition Stress in the Lives of Military Veterans," *Clinical Psychology Review* 59 (2018): 137, https://doi:10.1016/j.cpr.2017.11.007.

unfamiliar circumstances—like almost everything you experience when leaving the military. When presented with a potential threat, the amygdala sends signals to release hormones that mobilize your sympathetic nervous system well before you analyze the nature or severity of the potential threat.

You recognize this heightened state of arousal as stress. A certain level of stress can raise your cognitive appraisal to motivate higher levels of performance. If we assess that we have the capability and capacity to overcome the threat, then we move past the initial, subconscious reaction into deliberate, conscious action. In many cases, we excel as we overcome the challenge. When the conditions or circumstances have a level of novelty, uncertainty, or ambiguity, it becomes more difficult to assess our capability and capacity to handle the situation. We begin to worry. As a precaution, we maintain that heightened state of arousal. We take inventory of our vulnerabilities. In other words, we feel anxious, and we become afraid.

Fear invokes scarcity. It forces us to play defense. When we become anxious, our perspective narrows. We focus on the minimum necessary for survival at the expense of everything else. We lose our connection to creativity, vision, inspiration, and even happiness. Fear focuses all of our intention on the need for survival. Fear is what entices you to settle in a job well beneath your potential. Fear is what keeps you from launching that business idea. Fear keeps you from writing that book. When you have a fear of failure, you take what you can get instead of reaching for what you might want. Unfortunately, the transition environment is overflowing with fear-based energy.

WHERE THE F-WORD LURKS IN THE TRANSITION ENVIRONMENT

From the perspective of the military institution, the fear of transition is one of the most effective tools used by leaders to meet retention objectives. We stir the uncertainty and self-doubt that comes from the thought of securing a well-paying job with commensurate benefits in the civilian world. We do this with the best of intentions. We believe that we are taking care of our people and helping them take care of their families. Because we never address any of their fears about transitioning to the civilian world directly, we create the perception that staying in the military is the best and most logical choice. Though it may be unintentional, we encourage service members to succumb to their fear. Unfortunately, the day comes when reenlistment or continued service is no longer an option. All the fears that have been neglected, ignored, and packed away wait patiently for that day of reckoning.

The society we hope to join offers its own brand of fear. The widening civil-military cultural gap contributes to the misunderstanding that feeds this fear. Because the veteran's résumé doesn't fit into the human resources template for talent management, hiring managers fear a lack of return on investment (ROI) for new veteran hires. Employers don't want to take the risk and empower veterans at a level commensurate to the level of authority and responsibility they once enjoyed in the military. Some may even be intimidated by the leadership bona fides of transitioning service members. Consequently, recruiters tell transitioning service members to manage expectations. Senior leaders are advised to take a step back. The fear of losing ROI against the backdrop of the hiring costs, lack of understanding about the military experience, and the cost of turnover cause many civilian employers to proceed with extreme caution in their veteran hiring strategies.

From the service member's perspective, we fear the loss of income, status, and connection. Because we fear the loss of compensation and benefits, we too often settle for the minimum in a job just so we can pay the bills. We scavenge for entitlements to fill the gaps. Because we lose the rank and title, we fear the loss of status. Because we lose the camaraderie and trusted relationships, we fear disconnection, but we also hesitate to make new connections with non-veterans for fear of rejection. Perhaps the greatest fear that service members face in transition is the fear of failure. When you think about it, the F-word has a way of F-ing up your entire transition and reintegration experience.

The closer you get to your separation or retirement date, the cycle of fear takes on a dynamism of its own. It erodes our confidence. It detracts from our sense of self-worth and personal value. It frames our approach to life beyond the military into a fight for survival. We bank and sacrifice our leave time so that we can maintain an income while searching for the next job. We scramble for accreditations and certifications to validate our experience. We strive for any chance to speak with company representatives to get our name "out there"—even when we have no real interest in working for that company. We can't seem to attend enough job fairs for fear that we might miss something.

As military leaders, we learn to manage risk in every aspect of our lives. We lean toward making the safe bet when it comes to leaving the military, but that also comes with a risk. In fact, the stakes are higher when we decide to play it safe. If we don't take risks, we may never be disappointed or disillusioned, but when we look back upon our lives, we may realize only too late that we have wasted our gifts.[28] We are conditioned to believe that success comes from eliminating risk, but therein lies the paradox. The best things in life come from taking a leap of faith into the life you want to live.

Fear thrives in the transition process. It is the greatest enemy you will face as you leave the military. You can ignore it, you can succumb to it, or you can confront it. You confront it by

---

28. Paulo Coelho, *By the River Piedra I Sat Down and Wept* (London: Thorsons, 2014), 7.

choosing faith. You can believe in yourself, your purpose, and your ability to create the life you want to live. You can get what you want. Settling is a choice. Transition isn't about what you do, it is about who you want to be. It is about how you choose to show up in life beyond the military.

EXAMPLE 2.2 COMMON FEARS LEADERS FACE WHEN LEAVING THE MILITARY

Here is an example of the more prevalent fears across each domain of the Integrative Program of Transition that leaders face through the transition and reintegration process:

Optimizing Whole Health: When I consider the aspects of my health (physical, mental, emotional, and spiritual), these are the things I fear the most

Now that I don't have to get up in the morning for physical training, I fear that I am going to get fat. Especially as I get older, it will be harder for me to stay in shape.

Socialization. When I consider my ability to make connections with people outside the military culture, these are the things I fear the most:

Without my friends and contacts through the military, who am I going to hang out with? Once I leave the military, I lose my friends. I don't even know how to talk to civilians let alone making friends with them.

Cultural Assimilation. When I consider the differences between the military and civilian culture, these are the things I fear the most:

The people I work with won't get me. I am afraid that my aggressive style won't mix well in the corporate sector, and I will drive people away.

Economic Stability: When I consider my ability to achieve wealth outside the predictability of my military pay, these are the things I fear the most:

I am not going to be able to pay my bills if I don't get a job right away.

Professional Preparedness: When I imagine the ideal job or role for my life beyond the military, these are the things I fear the most:

I fear that my experience simply doesn't translate into the civilian sector. I am not competitive for jobs at my level of experience.

Family Adjustment: When I consider the impact that transition could have on my entire family, these are the things I fear the most:

My wife and kids were used to having things in common with other military families. It provided their network of friends. How are they going to get along once we leave our established network?

EXERCISE 2.2. CALLING OUT THE FEAR

Now, it's your turn. It's time for you to show your courage to face the enemy. Using **Example 2.2. Common Fears Leaders Face When Leaving the Military** as a reference, identify up to three fears across the domains of Optimizing Whole Health, Socialization, Cultural Assimilation, Economic Stability, Professional Preparedness, and Family Adjustment. These fears will set the framework for future exercises in this handbook.

Optimizing Whole Health: When I consider the aspects of my health (physical, mental, emotional, and spiritual), these are the things I fear the most

Socialization. When I consider my ability to make connections with people outside the military culture, these are the things I fear the most:

Cultural Assimilation. When I consider the differences between the military and civilian culture, these are the things I fear the most:

Economic Stability: When I consider my ability to achieve wealth outside the predictability of my military pay, these are the things I fear the most:

Professional Preparedness: When I imagine the ideal job or role for my life beyond the military, these are the things I fear the most:

Family Adjustment: When I consider the impact that transition could have on my entire family, these are the things I fear the most:

2.3 SETTING INTENTIONS

One of the most important outcomes from the Mission Analysis is the list of specified, implied, and essential tasks that a unit must complete in order to accomplish its mission. Specified tasks are those requirements outlined in the order. They are easy to recognize because they are written in black and white. We find the implied tasks by reading between the lines and figuring out all the things we have to do in order to accomplish the specified tasks. From the specified and implied tasks, we determine the essential tasks. These are the most critical things we NEED to do in order to successfully complete the mission and achieve end state.

In the context of Mission Analysis, ESSENTIAL is synonymous with NEED. By definition, the word *need* means *to require (something) because it is essential or very important*. When you think about it, the only thing you really need to do in transition is leave the military. Your separation or retirement orders will outline the coordinating instructions and other specified tasks that support that requirement. We derive the implied tasks by reading between the lines and figuring out all the things we think we need to do in order to achieve what we would consider a "successful" transition.

When it comes to satisfying our needs, basic survival comes first. We worry about paying the bills. We worry about providing for our family. From there, we worry about social acceptance and belonging. Fear is what causes us to worry, and fear limits our focus. Because of the fear, we are tempted to defer, delay, or neglect opportunities to pursue our purpose, find happiness, and experience the joy that comes from doing the things we WANT to do in life after the military.

Beyond our basic, psychological, and social needs is self-actualization. *In transition and reintegration, your self-actualization IS the essential task.* Self-actualization includes the personal and professional fulfillment from realizing your purpose. It comes from doing the things you WANT to do in your life. Unfortunately, fear keeps you focused on all the things that you think you need to do in order to meet some abstract standard of success. Over time, you might forget about the things you WANT, or you may just stop looking for them. You become conditioned to treat the best emotions in life as something that must be earned. By the time you finally give yourself permission to experience that fulfillment, happiness, or joy that comes from self-actualization, those opportunities have passed you by.

The reason why so many veterans feel stuck in the space between life in the military and life beyond the military is because they never set their intentions to achieve anything more than the bare minimum. They focus on survival, and consequently, survival is all they get. If you set low enough expectations, you may not be disappointed, but don't be surprised if you're not very happy either. After all, how can you hope to recognize opportunities for personal growth and professional fulfillment if you never go looking for them?

Instead of focusing on fear-based needs, what if you shifted your intentions to the things you truly WANT in life beyond the military? What if you imagined what living *on purpose* looked like? To demonstrate the power of shifting your intentions, consider the following example: To graduate high school, you only NEED to pass. In most school districts, a 70 percent earns you a cap and gown. With the bare minimum, you will get your diploma, but you probably won't get accepted into a prestigious university. With a low "C" average, you might not get accepted into any university. If you want more choices and better options after high school, you have to set your intentions on a higher goal. Consequently, you work hard academically. You participate in school sports or other extracurricular activities. You set yourself up to stand out because of the things you want in life after high school. The motivation comes from the intrinsic desire for something more, and the feeling of achievement comes from meeting your potential.

This principle also applies to how to build and sustain healthy, committed relationships. As Dr. Springer will explain later in the handbook, the best relationships are ones that are created by two people who do not NEED each other but who WANT to commit to a life partnership together because of how it will enhance their individual and collective growth.

Targeting the WANT instead of the NEED requires a certain level of ambition, confidence, and determination. If you didn't already have these qualities, you would not have succeeded as a leader in the military. It's not in your nature to settle for the minimum, and yet so many veterans do just that when they allow fear to shape their transition. As we begin a new chapter in civilian society, we can scavenge for basic needs or we can set our intentions based on what we really WANT.

When you shift your intentions from NEED to WANT, it will feel differently. When you imagine the things you WANT, you recalibrate your body and mind on the positive instead of wallowing in the negative of fear-based energy. You have greater access to higher-order functions to create a wider array of possibilities. You leverage your creativity and imagination in powerful ways to find unique and unexpected solutions. In simple terms, you position yourself to discover opportunities for success instead of worrying about the FEAR of failure.

EXERCISE 2.3. SHIFTING INTENTIONS FROM NEED TO WANT

The purpose of this exercise is to move past the bare minimum from the fear-based NEED and explore opportunities for what you WANT in life beyond the military.

Step 1: Confront the FEAR. Take a look at the fears you identified in **Exercise 2.2. Calling Out the Fear**. You will want to reference those answers as a starting point.

Step 2: Recognize the NEED. Our survival instinct reacts to FEAR. As you consider how you mitigate risk and safeguard yourself from these fears, what are the things you think you NEED to do across each factor in the Integrative Program of Transition? Stated another way, how would you characterize the bare minimum for a successful transition and reintegration back into society?

Step 3: Identify the WANT. Now, let's shift your intentions. Let's imagine what self-actualization looks like in terms of optimizing health and wellness, socialization, cultural assimilation, professional preparedness, economic stability, and family adjustment. Let's set your most essential task to achieve your purpose and experience lifelong fulfillment, happiness, and joy. It's time to imagine the ideal scenario for life beyond the military. This comes from identifying the things you WANT.

The WANT should include and surpass everything embodied in your NEED. Think of it this way: If the NEED gets you to the first down marker, then the WANT is what gets you into the end zone. Here are some questions to challenge your higher intentions across each of the domains for the Integrative Program of Transition:

Optimizing Whole Health: We all need to maintain a healthy lifestyle, but how would you define your optimal condition of health for the next chapter of your life? What if you ran a marathon, joined a tennis club, took up swimming, began cycling, or became an outfielder on a community softball team? What if you learned how to meditate or practice yoga? What does connected to your spirituality mean?

Socialization: Reflect upon the social networks you developed in the military, and imagine what that might look like in your civilian community. What kinds of events or activities interest you? How can you become more involved in your community? How can you expand your personal relationships to include non-veterans?

Cultural Assimilation: How would you define your new tribe in life beyond the military? How might you plan on addressing your leadership blind spots? What would you imagine the perfect fit in a corporate culture looks like? How can you calibrate your military leadership qualities for a civilian leadership role?

Economic Stability: You NEED a job that pays the mortgage, but beyond that NEED for financial security is what you WANT for your quality of life. Perhaps you want to travel. Maybe you want a beach house. What would the ideal quality of life look like today?

Professional Preparedness: As you imagine your future leadership role in society, consider the commensurate accreditations, qualifications, and education necessary for that role. Perhaps you want a master's or doctoral degree. Maybe you want an internship to gain experience in different job opportunities. How are you preparing yourself to excel along your next career path? When you retire, what position, role, or level of responsibility do you hope to attain?

Family Adjustment: Imagine the ideal family dynamic in post-military life. Consider how you might spend holidays together. Maybe you spend Sunday dinners around the table. What five qualities would best describe your family life after military service?

EXAMPLE 2.3 SHIFTING INTENTIONS FROM NEED TO WANT

Using the earlier template from **Example 2.2. Common Fears Leaders Face When Leaving the Military**, notice how these examples of shifting intentions move well beyond the need and explore what you really want in life after the military.

Optimizing Whole Health: Considering the aspects of my health (physical, mental, emotional, and spiritual), here is how I confront the FEAR and shift from NEED to WANT		
FEAR	**NEED**	**WANT**
Now that I don't have to get up in the morning for physical training, I fear that I am going to get fat. Especially as I get older, it will be harder for me to stay in shape.	I need to eat healthy, and I need to join a gym. I need to make time for working out in my new schedule	I want to run another marathon, and I'd like to be at my ideal weight so that I have the energy to do the things I truly enjoy doing.

Socialization. When I consider my ability to make connections with people outside the military culture, here is how I confront the FEAR and shift from NEED to WANT

FEAR	NEED	WANT
Without my friends and contacts through the military, who am I going to hang out with? Once I leave the military, I lose my friends. I don't even know how to talk to civilian.	I need to meet new people. I need to stay in touch with the people I used to work with.	I want to attend social events and spend holidays with new friends. I'd love to have get-togethers with neighbors for sporting events or dinner parties.

Cultural Assimilation. When I consider the differences between the military and civilian culture, here is how I confront the FEAR and shift from NEED to WANT

FEAR	NEED	WANT
The people I work with won't get me. I am afraid that my aggressive style won't mix well in the corporate sector, and I will drive people away.	I need to be patient and learn to speak only when spoken to. I need to keep my opinions to myself.	I want to build meaningful mentor relationships and make the same impact as a veteran leader as I once made as a military leader

Economic Stability: When I consider my ability to achieve wealth outside the predictability of my military pay, here is how I confront the FEAR and shift from NEED to WANT

FEAR	NEED	WANT
I am not going to be able to pay my bills once I leave the security of military pay and benefits	I need to get a job as soon as possible - preferably during my terminal leave just to be safe.	I want to find meaningful work that allows me to pursue my purpose and gives me some extra money at the end of each month

Professional Preparedness: When I imagine the ideal job or role for my life beyond the military, here is how I confront the FEAR and shift from NEED to WANT		
FEAR	**NEED**	**WANT**
I fear that my experience simply doesn't translate into the civilian sector. I am not competitive for jobs at my level of experience.	I need to manage my expectations and take a step back	I want to grow in my next job. I want to repurpose my learning and experience into a more empowering role beyond the military

Family Adjustment: When I consider the impact that transition could have on my entire family, here is how I confront the FEAR and shift from NEED to WANT		
FEAR	**NEED**	**WANT**
My wife and kids were used to having things in common with other military families. It provided their network of friends. How are they going to get along once we leave our established network?	I need to provide as much stability for the family as possible and be patient with my wife and kids as they adjust to a new lifestyle	I want our family to grow into a community and pursue their own passions in this next chapter of our lives

Now it's your turn. Consider how what you want honors your values and aligns with your purpose. Over the next six pages, identify up to three FEARS, the associated NEED to address each FEAR, and the ideal outcome (what you WANT) across each of the factors of the Integrative Program of Transition:

Optimizing Whole Health. Considering the aspects of my health (physical, mental, emotional, and spiritual), here is how I confront the FEAR and shift from NEED to WANT		
FEAR	**NEED**	**WANT**

Socialization. When I consider my ability to make connections with people outside the military culture, here is how I confront the FEAR and shift from NEED to WANT

FEAR	NEED	WANT

Cultural Assimilation. When I consider the differences between the military and civilian culture, here is how I confront the FEAR and shift from NEED to WANT

FEAR	NEED	WANT

Economic Stability. When I consider my ability to achieve wealth outside the predictability of my military pay, here is how I confront the FEAR and shift from NEED to WANT

FEAR	NEED	WANT

Professional Preparedness. When I imagine the ideal job or role for my life beyond the military, here is how I confront the FEAR and shift from NEED to WANT

FEAR	NEED	WANT

Family Adjustment. When I consider the impact that transition could have on my entire family, here is how I confront the FEAR and shift from NEED to WANT

FEAR	NEED	WANT

2.4 INTRINSIC STRENGTHS

As a part of the Mission Analysis, we inventory our resources—or assets available—to solve the problem. When you transition from the military, your most notable assets are your intrinsic strengths. Intrinsic strengths are the strengths rooted in core values. More specifically, your intrinsic strengths represent a means to express your core values. As it pertains to your identity, your values reflect a state of being, and your intrinsic strengths represent the act of doing.

Intrinsic strengths are the traits, attributes, and behaviors that come naturally for you. They provide the competitive edge to enable your best performance. Outside observers consistently recognize these strengths as the value you add to the rest of the team. To a potential employer, they represent your unique value proposition. Studies demonstrate that activities that align with your intrinsic strengths improve productivity, citizenship behavior, satisfaction, positivity, and connection.[29] These are the default settings for how you interact with others, solve problems, and contribute to society.

Intrinsic strengths are *your* assets. They represent your signature capabilities and value added as a leader. For example, *innovation* might be one of your values. The intrinsic strength associated with that value might be *an ability to see new alternatives to difficult problems.* If *bravery* is one of your values, then a possible intrinsic strength might be your *ability to remain calm and perform well under pressure.* If *authenticity* is one of your values, then a possible intrinsic strength might be your *ability to build trusting relationships.* The value of *integrity* might be seen as *the ability to make tough decisions and always do the right thing.* Notice how an intrinsic strength can be described as an ability. They give you power to achieve. You can even think of your intrinsic strengths as your superpowers because that is exactly what they are!

EXERCISE 2.4 THE MILITARY LEADER INTRINSIC STRENGTHS FINDER

This exercise combines your self-awareness and experience to help reveal your intrinsic strengths.

STEP 1. MAKE A PERSONAL ASSESSMENT.

Think about the times in your career when you performed your best. One of the reasons why these memories are so vivid is not just because of the positive outcome, but it also felt good, too. Values have an emotive quality, and you feel that sense of motivation, inspiration, and

---

29. Shiri Lavy and Hadassah Littman-Ovadia, "My Better Self," *Journal of Career Development* 44, no. 2 (2016): 95, https://doi:10.1177/0894845316634056.

confidence that comes from performing at your best. Use the following chart to highlight situations and circumstances where you were truly at your best. Also, describe what you consider to be the strengths and abilities that you used to enable that success.

Example of Success	Words or phrases that best describe the strengths or abilities that helped you succeed

STEP 2. COLLECT CORROBORATING EVIDENCE.

To validate your intrinsic strengths, we will search for supporting evidence from your career in the military. You will need to reference your fitness, performance, or evaluation reports to complete this next step. For a more comprehensive view, you might want to include peer or subordinate evaluations as well. If intrinsic strengths represent your hidden superpowers, then we should find evidence of those abilities in the feedback and comments from your raters, peers, and subordinates.

You may discover through this exercise that you have relied upon the same abilities regardless of your role or assignment. This is normal. Intrinsic strengths are universal. Over the course of your career, you may have worked in operations, human resources, logistics, or intelligence. Additionally, your broadening assignments provided unique opportunities for personal development and self-discovery, but you'll find that your intrinsic strengths continued to help you lead and achieve in those roles as well. The same abilities tend to show up again and again regardless of the job, unit, or location.

EXAMPLE 2.4.1. UNCOVER YOUR INTRINSIC STRENGTHS

Take a look at the following example of actual rater and senior rater comments from an evaluation report. Notice how the comments in bold provide possible evidence of intrinsic strengths.

Rater Comments: *Major Jason Roncoroni is the number one major in this brigade and the finest Brigade Executive Officer I have observed in my career; a future Battalion Commander.* **He displays the judgment and maturity** *to execute at that level now. Jason is a natural leader who performs flawlessly at the tactical level while* **understanding operational and strategic considerations.** *Impossible to over-task, MAJ Roncoroni effectively and aggressively leads the brigade staff toward one objective—the combat readiness of all assigned units. In a period of incredible turbulence following redeployment, he has* **flawlessly managed** *the complex ARFORGEN requirements of this brigade, synchronizing the manning, training, and equipping aspects to perfection. The result is a Combat Aviation Brigade that is prepared to deploy to RC-South in Afghanistan. Jason is a gifted officer who has clearly* **mastered the full spectrum of aviation operations** *and has distinguished himself among his peers in every measurable area of our profession.*

Senior Rater Comments: *Exceptional performance by an exemplary officer. Major Jason Roncoroni is the best Brigade Executive Officer among the seven brigades attached to the 101st Airborne Division (Air Assault).* **His tactical competence and professional maturity** *far exceeds his peers. Jason* **meticulously planned, brilliantly synchronized, and expertly guided the staff** *through a rigorous ARFORGEN process ensuring the brigade had the necessary aircraft, equipment, personnel, and training support to best prepare the subordinate battalions for the rigors ahead. Jason has all the attributes to excel as a Battalion Commander. Absolute unlimited potential. Promote immediately below the zone to lieutenant colonel. He is my first choice to command an Assault Helicopter Battalion.*

As you read the comments of your evaluation reports, what words or phrases seem to appear again and again? How might you describe these qualities in your own terms? Sometimes, you may want to use the exact words and phrases used by others, but you might find it useful to make some inferences to translate these comments into your own words:

Meaningful Statements of Performance	Potential Intrinsic Strengths (Qualities and Attributes)
Rater Comment: Judgment and maturity Senior Rater Comment: Professional maturity	**Judgment** or **Maturity**
Rater Comment: Jason is a natural leader who performs flawlessly at the tactical level while understanding operational and strategic considerations.	**Clarity** or **Vision** - the ability to conceptualize complexity or uncertainty in the context of the big picture.
Rater Comment: In a period of incredible turbulence following redeployment, he has flawlessly managed the complex ARFORGEN requirements of this Brigade, synchronizing the manning, training, and equipping aspects to perfection. Senior Rater Comment: Jason meticulously planned, brilliantly synchronized, and expertly guided the staff through a rigorous ARFORGEN process ensuring the Brigade had the necessary aircraft, equipment, personnel and training support to best prepare the subordinate battalions for the rigors ahead.	**Synchronization, Collaboration**, and/or **Vision** - the ability to align competing tasks to achieve a specific result

Much like your values, how you define these qualities needs to have meaning to YOU. Frame the definitions in a manner that connects and resonates with you. These intrinsic strengths are universal, so consider how you would apply these qualities to a future situation or assignment.

Definitions of Potential Intrinsic Strengths

Judgment: The ability to make sound decisions with incomplete information.

Maturity: The ability to navigate challenging relationships and competing perspectives.

Vision: The ability to find creative solutions to complex problems.

Clarity: The ability to recognize opportunities in uncertain and unpredictable circumstances.

Synchronization: The ability to bring out the best qualities of individuals for a common goal.

Collaboration: The ability to influence and build relationships as a member of a team.

Repeat this process for each of the evaluation or feedback reports you received over the duration of your career. You may find it helpful to use a journal to capture your values, purpose, and intrinsic strengths for easy reference as you continue this process of self-discovery.

STEP 3. TALLY YOUR RESULTS.

Once you reviewed each of your evaluation reports, tally the results. The qualities that appear most frequently represent the intrinsic strengths that others see in you. Compare what you've discovered between how others see you with how you see yourself from **Step 1** of this exercise.

Take a moment to reflect on how you see yourself and the qualities that suggest the intrinsic strengths that others have seen in you. What stands out when you compare the two?

Intrinsic Strength from Evaluation Reports (Word or Phrase)	Number of Times Strength Was Referenced (Total From All Reports)	Was This a 'Strength' that I recognized in myself? (Yes or No)

STEP 4. CONNECT YOUR INTRINSIC STRENGTHS TO YOUR VALUES.

Every strength is rooted in a value, so what do these strengths tell you about your values? The last step of this exercise connects your core values (the state of being) to your intrinsic strengths (the act of doing).

Through this exercise, you may have uncovered a blind spot regarding how you show up in different situations. The good news moving forward is that you get to choose how you want to show up as a leader. You can intentionally apply any of these strengths to achieve what you want in life. The strengths that have enabled your success in the past are the assets to enable your success in the future.

EXAMPLE 2.4 STRENGTHS AND VALUES CROSSWALK

Take a look at this example of a crosswalk to understand how values fuel your intrinsic strengths.

Values: The State of Being		Intrinsic Strengths: The Act of Doing	
Value	**Definition**	**Strength**	**Description or Ability**
Innovation	Challenge the status-quo with my creativity and ambition to make things better	Vision	The ability to find creative solutions to complex problems
		Clarity	The ability to recognize opportunities in uncertain or unpredictable situations

Based on this example, you could conclude that because this individual values innovation, they have the ability to find creative solutions to complex problems and the ability to recognize opportunities in uncertain or unpredictable situations. Now, it's your turn. Use the following template to connect your values to your intrinsic strengths:

Values: The State of Being		Intrinsic Strengths: The Act of Doing	
Value	Definition	Strength	Description or Ability

2.5 LIMITING AND EMPOWERING BELIEFS

Up to this point, we've explored some of the anthropological, psychological, and even bio-chemical factors involved in military transition. We've conducted a preliminary analysis of your purpose (the WHY) and your values (the WHO). We've examined how to overcome the fear of military transition to move past what you think you might need to embrace what you truly want. We've even reviewed your intrinsic strengths, the hidden superpowers behind your success as a leader. Now it's time to unpack your perceptions and biases about what might happen next.

The next step in the Identity Analysis examines your beliefs about military transition and civilian reintegration. In the MDMP, this is the part of Mission Analysis that involves *identifying the constraints* for the mission. Constraints take the form of a requirement or prohibition. In the context of military operations, they limit a commander's options and freedom of action. In the context of your life, your perceptions and beliefs become their own control measures. Optimistic, pessimistic, good, or bad—psychologists have long recognized that beliefs have a way of channeling a person's behavior.[30] Consequently, they can either be restrictive or permissive depending on your point of view.

Beliefs have an emotive, visceral quality. What you believe about your country, culture, and the principles of governance probably had a lot to do with why you volunteered for military service in the first place. Our shared beliefs about duty, selfless service, honor, and the warrior ethos define our standards of behavior as service members. Your beliefs about family have everything to do with how you show up as a parent and a spouse. Beliefs shape our behaviors, inform our perspectives, and influence how we recognize opportunities. Therefore, your beliefs provide the lens through which you see limitations or opportunities in life after military service.

LIMITING BELIEFS: THE APPLICATION OF "NOT GOOD ENOUGH"

Limiting Beliefs represent a negative point of view. They narrow your perspective and options for life beyond the military. The core idea for any Limiting Belief is that you are simply "not good enough." The voice inside your head is typically responsible for many of the negative thoughts that become internalized into your belief structure. Your self-doubting ego provides the inner monologue that attempts to convince you of all the reasons why you can't be who you want to be or do the things you want to do. Limiting Beliefs are your personal constraints. The outcome from a Limiting Belief takes the form of a *requirement*, something you think you must do, or a *prohibition*, something you think you cannot do.

---

30. Christopher Peterson, *A Primer in Positive Psychology* (Oxford: Oxford Univ. Press, 2006), 118.

Limiting Beliefs that take the form of a requirement are based on poor assumptions or faulty logic. For example, when we believe that our military leadership is not good enough for civilian employment, we assume that we *must* attain a Project Management Professional (PMP) certification as validation for future employment. A PMP might improve your standing for certain job offerings, but many leaders invest the time and energy to get this credential without ever establishing whether or not it aligns with anything they might want to do in their follow-on career. They do it just to be safe. They do it because they assume that employers won't recognize the value of their experience or the quality of leadership. They worry that they are simply not good enough. Consequently, they strive to convince human resources specialists, hiring managers, and even themselves that their leadership is good enough for a management position in the civilian sector.

Prohibitions tell the story what you believe you cannot do. For example, you might decide that you can't start your own business because you don't have the education or business acumen to be successful. Again, this is an application of "not good enough." As a result of this Limiting Belief, you fail to recognize that franchise opportunities come with a full suite of training, support, and expertise for aspiring business owners. You never investigate the many nonprofit and mentor opportunities that could provide much of the on-the-job business training, best practices, and lessons learned to launch a successful business as an entrepreneur. You ignore, neglect, or otherwise dismiss possible solutions because of what you believe you cannot do.

Limiting Beliefs are the starting point down a path of self-pity that ends in scarcity and un-fulfilled potential. Along this downward spiral, you may become angry with recruiters, hiring managers, and employers. You may even lash out at the military and blame them for your lack of preparation. You assume a victim mindset. You begin to second-guess and even resent many of your decisions in the transition process. Negative thoughts become hardwired into negative habits and behaviors that further reinforce the idea that you are simply "not good enough," and your low self-esteem will infect every part of your life.

When you see yourself as lesser, the rest of the world begins to see you that way as well. You may eventually believe that you are not good enough to interact with non-veterans. You may believe that you are not good enough to fit into the culture of your new job. You might believe that you can't be as mentally, physically, or emotionally fit as you once were. You might even believe that you will never earn enough for the lifestyle you dreamed of, and instead, you'll settle for a meager job just to make ends meet. Limiting Beliefs are dream killers. In the military, you may have been the leader—the creator of amazing opportunities and spectacular achievements—but in the civilian world, you become a victim at the mercy of "not good enough."

EMPOWERING BELIEFS: SEE THE CHALLENGE AS AN OPPORTUNITY

If Limiting Beliefs operate like tunnel vision, then **Empowering Beliefs** function like a prism that expands your perspective. Empowering Beliefs interpret challenges as opportunities. They allow you to see a wider array of alternatives. Where Limiting Beliefs invoke a sense of scarcity, Empowering Beliefs recognize an abundance of options for higher levels of achievement and self-actualization. Limiting Beliefs protect you from the danger of losing, but Empowering Beliefs allow you to imagine the possibility of winning.

An Empowering Belief begins with an optimistic affirmation of personal faith. When the Limiting Belief tells you that you are not good enough, the Empowering Belief shouts back: "YES I AM!" Empowering Beliefs act like a coiled spring of personal inspiration. They provide the positive energy necessary to harness your purpose, values, and intrinsic strengths to find a way to get what you want. Here are some examples of affirmations that represent Empowering Beliefs:

- I believe that I can grow a successful business on my own.

- I believe that I can rise to a C-suite-level position.

- I believe that I can be a great example to my family and my community.

- I believe that I can make a greater impact as a civilian than I did through the military.

- I believe that I can distinguish myself as a leader regardless of my job title or position.

To embrace an Empowering Belief is to take a leap of faith. The little engine that could had to first believe that climbing the mountain was possible before he could do it. If you can't believe in yourself through transition and reintegration, don't expect anyone else to either.

As military leaders, we are predisposed to assess any and all situations from the standpoint of where or when the mission might fail. We become experts in risk management. Assuming the worst made us effective at managing complex and dangerous operations. As a result, our mental processes default to making the safest bet. We are calibrated toward the worrying, skepticism, and even cynicism that fuels Limiting Beliefs. We bring this approach with us when considering the uncertainty, ambiguity, and challenges inherent in the transition process. Consequently, we settle. Our Limiting Beliefs make us enter through the shallow end of the pool instead of the taking that dive into the deep end. Too often, the price we pay for our Limiting Beliefs includes both our potential and our happiness.

The good news is that Limiting Beliefs are not a life sentence. Just because you have them today, doesn't mean you will have them tomorrow. You have the power the challenge Limiting Beliefs and turn them into Empowering Beliefs. You can make the switch. Once you are aware that a particular belief is limiting, you can explore a broader array of facts, examine alternative outcomes, and question assumptions to transform what was previously considered a constraint into an opportunity. Let's explore the example of becoming an entrepreneur in greater detail:

EXAMPLE 2.5.1 ANALYZING AND REPURPOSING A LIMITING BELIEF

One of the more common Limiting Beliefs for many leaders concerns the idea of becoming an entrepreneur after transition or retirement from the military. All Limiting Beliefs begin with an initial thought about what you think you must do or can't do in life beyond the military.

Initial Perception or Thought for a Limiting Belief (Application of "not good enough")
I *can't* start my own business. I *don't* have the knowledge or business acumen to be a successful entrepreneur, and I *don't* have the money to launch a business. I *can't* wait to start earning a sustainable income because I have real bills to pay.

Most Limiting Beliefs are grounded in facts. That is what makes them so powerful—and dangerous. What makes them limiting is how we selectively attend only to the facts that confirm the negative point of view.

Facts that Support This Initial Position
20 percent of startups fail in the first year. Nearly 50 percent fail by the fifth year.[31]
You don't have a degree in business or any formal academic instruction in subjects like marketing, accounting, taxes, or business operations.
Starting a business isn't free. Many startup businesses require at least some seed capital.
Some references suggest that startups typically don't become profitable until after 2-3 years of operations.[32] Other sources suggest at least 4 years are necessary before a startup truly becomes profitable.[33]

Because we are attuned to the negative, we are predisposed to fill in any information gaps with negative assumptions or interpretations. These assumptions and interpretations further reinforce our initial bias and limit our options.

Assumptions and Interpretations that Support the Perception or Bias
There is a 50 percent chance that I will fail as an entrepreneur.
I won't know what to do or how to make sound decisions when it comes to the uncertainty and complexity of starting my own business.
Starting a small business requires startup funding, so I will have to liquidate my savings or incur debt to become an entrepreneur. I won't be profitable right away, so I am going to start off civilian life behind financially.
I am going to let my family down. I am going to fail to uphold my obligations as a provider and they will think less of me. I don't have the time (or knowledge) to build a business plan. I can't possibly build something from scratch. It will never work.
If I don't start updating my resume and networking NOW, I am going to miss out on opportunities to get a job. I need to spend my time getting the accreditations necessary to be more competitive in the civilian job market.

The conclusion from this line of thinking is that you are simply not good enough to launch a successful business enterprise as an entrepreneur. Once you have reinforced your selective

31. Chad Otar, "What Percentage Of Small Businesses Fail -- And How Can You Avoid Being One Of Them?" *Forbes*, October 25, 2018, https://www.forbes.com/sites/forbesfinancecouncil/2018/10/25/what-percentage-of-small-businesses-fail-and-how-can -you-avoid-being-one-of-them/#dc957b243b5f.

32. Ellis Davidson, "The Average Time to Reach Profitability in a Start Up Company," *The Houston Chronicle*, April 09, 2019, https://smallbusiness.chron.com/average-time-reach-profitability-start-up-company-2318.html.

33. Wil Schroter, "How Long Will It Take To Have a Successful Startup?" *Startups.com*, October 15, 2018, https://www.startups .com/library/expert-advice/how-long-will-it-take-for-my-startup-to-be-successful.

facts with these assumptions and interpretations, you become entrenched in your original position. On a subconscious level, you start to accept the assumptions and interpretations as facts. Your initial position becomes internalized with your belief structure. You don't just *think* you might fail as an entrepreneur. You truly *believe* you will fail. You believe that you are putting your family at a grave disadvantage by spending your time creating something from scratch instead of updating your résumé and looking for the next available job. Once you've accepted this belief, you will perceive any alternative scenario as a threat. The Limiting Belief of "not good enough" partners with your fear to remind you of everything you could lose at the expense of any opportunity to win.

Limiting Beliefs focus on the excuses for why you can't do something instead of finding ways that you can. Notice how we never considered the remote possibility that starting your own business might be the best option to align with your purpose. We didn't consider how strategic alliances might address any knowledge, training, or financial shortcomings. We didn't examine how your strengths best position you to be among the small business success stories. Once we settled on "not good enough," we found the necessary evidence to confirm that position. Once you start making decisions based on perceived inadequacies, then inadequate—or "not good enough"—is how you and the rest of the world will recognize your value in life beyond the military.

Limiting Beliefs erase the full menu of opportunities available to you. When considering your unique path for life beyond the military, your Limiting Beliefs act like road closures, stop signs, and detours that restrict your path well before you've even determined your destination. As a result, too many veterans settle for what they can get instead of reaching for what they really want. The reason why so many veterans never find that sense of happiness is because they never went looking for it.

Here's the good news: You can repurpose Limiting Beliefs into Empowering Beliefs. In order to do so, you must challenge the biases underpinning your Limiting Beliefs. Using the same example to become an entrepreneur, let's consider different points of view and insights to shift to a more empowering perspective.

Alternative Facts and Insights that Challenge A Limiting Belief

Almost half (49.7 percent) of World War 2 veterans became small business owners compared to less than 5 percent of Post-9/11 veterans, and small business owners contribute over $1 trillion to the U.S. economy.[34] The tradition of successful veteran small business owners has been a major factor in the growth and dominance of the U.S. economy.

Veteran small business owners are actually outperforming non-veteran business owners.[35]

As a military leader, you are an outlier. You have an exceptional record of performance and remarkable potential. Only a very small percentage of the population can do what you did.

Question: Given your experience, perseverance, fortitude, and leadership who else besides veterans are best prepared to thrive as small business owners?

Most of the jobs you had in the military came with little or no formal education or training to prepare you for that particular role, yet you still succeeded! Many government and nonprofit agencies offer workshops, seminars, and education programs to close the knowledge gaps regarding starting your own business.

Question: How could you build a bench of mentors and advisors to provide guidance and expertise to succeed?

Many grant programs exist for veterans seeking funding as entrepreneurs.[36]

Question: How might a business partner offset potential funding challenges?

Entrepreneurs typically early more than salaried employees over the course of their lifetime.[37]

Over a 5 to 10 year period, the potential growth trajectory for a successful new business far exceeds the steady slope of income from a salaried job.

Question: How does the steady income from the salaried job achieve the quality of life you desire over the course of 5 or 10 years?

Not all small businesses require a wealth of capital to get started. Depending on the industry and the market, a modest investment might be all that is necessary to establish a business entity and begin operations. It just requires some research to find out what is truly necessary.

Question: What personal investment are you willing to make to achieve the things you truly want in life beyond the military?

According to the Department of Labor, the Veteran Unemployment Rate in January, 2019 is less than 4 percent.[38] Veterans find jobs in Corporate America. Based on these numbers, you can always find a job, but you might not always have the opportunity to create something on your own.

Question: What if starting your own business works?

34. Kimberly Weisul, "Where Are All the Missing Veteran-Owned Businesses?" *Inc.*, October 03, 2016, https://www.inc.com/magazine/201610/kimberly-weisul/missing-veteran-owned-businesses.html.

35. Rusty Creed, "America's Veterans Thrive in the Small Business World," *USA Today*, October 23, 2017, https://www.usatoday.com/story/sponsor-story/allstate-small-business-barometer/2017/10/23/sponsor-storyallstate-small-business-barometer/106927826/.

36. The Startups Team, "Small Business Answer," Small Business Answer | *Startups.com*, accessed July 21, 2019, https://www.startups.com/library/expert-advice/business-grants-for-veterans.

37. Jessica Stillman, "Entrepreneurs Make More Over a Lifetime, Study Says," *Inc.*, October 15, 2015, https://www.inc.com/jessica-stillman/entrepreneurs-make-more-over-a-lifetime-study-says.html.

38. "Veterans' Employment and Training Services," United States Department of Labor, accessed February 26, 2019, https://www.dol.gov/vets/latest-numbers/.

Given these facts, you might transform that Limiting Belief into an Empowering Belief:

Empowering Belief

I believe that I have the leadership, perseverance, and problem solving skills to launch a successful business enterprise. I believe that I will be profitable in every aspect of my life while making an impact doing something I love.

Limiting Beliefs provide excuses to say NO. Empowering Beliefs find a way to say YES. The purpose of this example was not to convince you to become an entrepreneur. As with every meaningful endeavor, you have to want it. The point of this example was to show you how to reframe your perspective to a more optimistic point of view. It's the difference between viewing an option from what you can't do versus what you can. Why not approach life beyond the military with all options on the table so that you can make more informed decisions regarding the best opportunity for you to be successful, impactful, and happy?

In summary, beliefs are emotive. This is why they are so powerful. They circumvent the rational thought process of the mind and become a feeling that can either inhibit or inspire action. In the case of Limiting Beliefs, they channel our approach to life after the military based on the idea that we are "not good enough." On the other hand, Empowering Beliefs provide the accelerant that fuels our motivation. Understand that your belief structure shapes your identity story. You can define your potential through constraints, or you can repurpose Limiting Beliefs to allow inspiration to guide your life beyond the military. When given the choice, always choose inspiration.

EXERCISE 2.5 IDENTIFYING YOUR LIMITING AND EMPOWERING BELIEFS

The purpose of this exercise is to: (1) recognize your Limiting Beliefs, (2) reframe your Limiting Beliefs into Empowering Beliefs, and (3) acknowledge up to ten Empowering Beliefs that serve as your personal affirmations—or Foundation Beliefs—for life beyond the military.

Part 1. Identify and Repurpose Limiting Beliefs. In the first part of this exercise, identify and analyze your Limiting Beliefs using **Example 2.5.1. Analyzing and Repurposing a Limiting Belief** as a template. Feel free to use additional sheets of paper to capture the facts, assumptions, and interpretations regarding these beliefs. You may also want to ask a mentor, coach, friend, or family member to act as a devil's advocate to challenge your initial position with some questions and different perspectives for you to consider.

Part 2. Empowering Beliefs. Not every belief you hold is a Limiting Belief. You may already have strong affirmations of what is possible. In many cases, these are your personal mantras that fueled your perseverance and enabled your success throughout your life. Write these statements in the form "I believe..."

Part 3. Ten Foundation Beliefs about Life Beyond the Military. The point of this exercise is to identify and challenge your belief structure in a way that you can make deliberate choices about how you approach your transition and reintegration back into society. As the final step in this exercise, you want to acknowledge ten Empowering Beliefs that serve as Foundation Beliefs for your transition from the military and reintegration back into society. It may be any combination of repurposed Limiting Beliefs or pre-existing Empowering Beliefs. These ten statements become your affirmations and inspirations for life beyond the military. You may want to reference these statements as a part of your daily meditation, journaling, or reflection practice. This is how you set the foundation for what is possible in life beyond the military.

PART 1. Identify and Repurpose Limiting Beliefs (Limiting Belief Number 1)

Initial Perception or Thought for a Limiting Belief (Application of "Not Good Enough")

Selective Facts that Support This Initial Position

Assumptions and Interpretations that Support the Perception or Bias

Alternative Facts and Insights to Challenge A Limiting Belief

Repurposed Limiting Belief into an Empowering Belief ("I believe" affirmation)

PART 1. Identify and Repurpose Limiting Beliefs (Limiting Belief Number 2)

Initial Perception or Thought for a Limiting Belief (Application of "Not Good Enough")

Selective Facts that Support This Initial Position

Assumptions and Interpretations that Support the Perception or Bias

Alternative Facts and Insights to Challenge A Limiting Belief

Repurposed Limiting Belief into an Empowering Belief ("I believe" affirmation)

PART 1. Identify and Repurpose Limiting Beliefs (Limiting Belief Number 3)

Initial Perception or Thought for a Limiting Belief (Application of "Not Good Enough")

Selective Facts that Support This Initial Position

Assumptions and Interpretations that Support the Perception or Bias

Alternative Facts and Insights to Challenge A Limiting Belief

Repurposed Limiting Belief into an Empowering Belief ("I believe" affirmation)

PART 1. Identify and Repurpose Limiting Beliefs (Limiting Belief Number 4)

Initial Perception or Thought for a Limiting Belief (Application of "Not Good Enough")

Selective Facts that Support This Initial Position

Assumptions and Interpretations that Support the Perception or Bias

Alternative Facts and Insights to Challenge A Limiting Belief

Repurposed Limiting Belief into an Empowering Belief ("I believe" affirmation)

PART 1. Identify and Repurpose Limiting Beliefs (Limiting Belief Number 5)

Initial Perception or Thought for a Limiting Belief (Application of "Not Good Enough")

Selective Facts that Support This Initial Position

Assumptions and Interpretations that Support the Perception or Bias

Alternative Facts and Insights to Challenge A Limiting Belief

Repurposed Limiting Belief into an Empowering Belief ("I believe" affirmation)

PART 2. Empowering Beliefs (Statements of "I believe"):

Empowering Belief 1

Empowering Belief 2

Empowering Belief 3

Empowering Belief 4

Empowering Belief 5

PART 3. Your 10 Foundation Beliefs for Life Beyond the Military

2.6 IDENTIFY THE COMMON FACTORS

If you were asked to identify a particular time when you were at your best as a leader in the military, what memories come to mind? What were some of the conditions that allowed you to succeed? What made these moments special? What were some of the remarkable qualities about the people you worked with? What were your personal takeaways from that achievement? The common factors from the best memories of your past provide critical insight to the kinds of opportunities and circumstances for success and fulfillment in the future.

The Mission Analysis process requires us to identify Critical Facts and Assumptions that are both relevant and necessary to the planning process. In the MTRP, we want to gather facts about your most meaningful professional experiences in order to make some relevant assumptions about the kinds of opportunities and conditions that will lead to your success in the future. Because your intrinsic drive is constantly at work to express your values and pursue your purpose, understanding the common factors from when you were at your best may reveal those conditions to achieve self-actualization and professional fulfillment in life beyond the military.

EXERCISE 2.6. COMMON FACTORS AND TRANSITION ASSUMPTIONS

The purpose of this exercise is to recognize the common factors from your most meaningful professional experiences to uncover the underlying themes from when you loved what you were doing and were truly at your best. To complete this exercise, you will need to recall three positive, memorable experiences from your military career. We will examine each of these experiences based on factors related to the situation, the people involved, and your personal takeaways.

The factors in this exercise are not all-inclusive, but they provide a starting point to guide your thinking about the conditions and circumstances that contributed to your success. You may discover and wish to incorporate different factors as you reflect on your experiences, but for the time being, let's define the common factors based on elements of the situation, people, and personal takeaways to inform your search for the right opportunity.

Situation: Situation pertains to the factors related to your work environment. These factors include **Urgency**, **Group Dynamics**, **Work Schedule**, **Structure**, **Role**, and **Novelty**. Each factor has two words with definitions to describe how that factor relates to the situation. Reflect on your career experiences, and choose the one word that best describes the urgency, group dynamics, work schedule, structure, role, and novelty.

Table 2.6.1. Factors Related to the Situation of Your Most Memorable Career Experiences

How would you characterize the Situation in terms of **Urgency**?	Crisis	You were consistently 'on-call' for crisis/emergency situations with significant implications. Each day provided a new set of challenges and uncertainty.
	Routine	You had a steady routine, and your day typically had few - if any - surprises. Very low stress.
How would you characterize the Situation in terms of **Group Dynamics**?	Individual	You essentially locked yourself away from the rest of the world to discover a solution to the problem.
	Team Effort	You couldn't do this alone. The team was locked in a room and committed to solve the problem together.
How would you characterize the Situation in terms of **Work Schedule**?	Predictable	You could set your watch by the schedule of requirements in this job.
	Organic	Everything was event-driven. You could not predict what might happen from one moment to the next.
How would you describe the Situation in terms of **Structure**?	Low-Structure	You had a great deal of autonomy: You had plenty of latitude to do what you wanted and when you wanted to do it.
	High-Structure	Lots of rules, quality control measures, and standing operating procedures that required compliance.
How would you describe the Situation in terms of your **Role**?	Person In Charge	You were in command with complete authority and responsibility.
	Team Member	You were a key contributor, but you were not the final authority held responsible for the outcome.
How would you describe the Situation in terms of **Novelty**?	New	You had to leverage your creativity and innovation to find advanced solutions to complex problems.
	Familiar	You had a well-developed script from the past that you used to solve problems.

People: Sometimes it isn't the situation, but the people who inspire us to be the best version of ourselves. It could be the attributes of a leader that had an impact on you. Perhaps it was the culture of the organization that allowed you to thrive, or it could be other factors related to the qualities of your team that were particularly memorable. As you analyze each of your career experiences, identify the five words that BEST describe the leadership, culture, and team.

Table 2.6.2. Factors Related to the People of Your Most Memorable Career Experiences

Leadership	Consider the aspects of the leader's personality or attributes of his or her character that inspired you. *What 5 qualities would best describe the leader(s) at that time?*
Culture	You may prefer the airborne or special operations. You might remember a specific work culture that existed on your ship or in your motor pool. What about that specific culture resonated with you? *What 5 adjectives would you use to describe the culture?*
Team	Regarding the team, what did the people on that team have in common? What made this team special? *What 5 words best characterize the group of people you were working with at the time?*

Personal Takeaways: Regardless of the outcome, we all have our own reasons why some experiences are more meaningful than others. It could have been the significance of the mission—you enjoyed being on the big stage, having media reporters in your unit, or being part of a historic operation. It could have been the opportunity to create something new or make a lasting change. It could have been the difficulty of the task—the challenge to do something that others said couldn't be done. It might have been for personal growth—perhaps you came away from that particular experience as a better version of yourself. Maybe the experience itself left you with a greater sense of gratitude. What you most valued from the experience on a personal level reveals the kinds of opportunities that might inspire you in the future.

Table 2.6.3. Factors Related to the Outcomes and Objectives of Your Most Memorable Career Experiences

Significance	How would you describe the scope or implications of the outcome?
Change	Perhaps you were part of a team that created something meaningful. How did the outcome achieve lasting change? What about making something better has meaning to you?
Difficulty	How hard was it for you and the team to achieve this objective? Sometimes the most memorable wins are the ones that occur when everyone expects us to lose. Some people enjoy being the underdog and achieving what conventional wisdom suggests is not possible.
Growth	Beyond the achievement is the personal growth and development. Sometimes we reflect on the most difficult trials of our journey with fondness for how they enabled us to evolve and grow into better leaders. How have you overcome adversity to become a stronger leader? What did you learn about yourself through the experience?
Gratitude	For some experiences, we gain a sense of perspective and gratitude that comes well after the fact. For example, deployments remind us of the importance of our families and could even alter our sense of priorities in life.

Having defined the factors related to the Situation, People, and Personal Takeaways, here are the detailed steps to complete this exercise:

STEP 1. IDENTIFY THE FACTORS FROM THREE MEMORABLE EXPERIENCES

Example 2.6. Career Experience Factors illustrate how to complete the Common Factors template for each career experience. Following that example are blank templates for you to identify the factors from three of your most meaningful career experiences. At the top of each form, there is a space for the who, what, when, where, and why for that experience. Use the definitions provided in **Table 2.6.1** through **Table 2.6.3** to complete one template for each experience.

STEP 2. DRAW CONCLUSIONS FROM COMMON FACTORS

Compare the completed templates for each career experience. Capture the common themes based on what you learn from analyzing these three experiences. For example: If each career experience was characterized as a crisis, then you might conclude that you prefer to work in situations where a heightened sense of urgency exists. As you examined the qualities of leadership, culture, and team, you might notice the same words appearing again and again that could indicate the kind of people you want to work for, the environment you want to work in, and the people you want to work with. Finally, the personal value you take from these experiences could signal the kinds of opportunities that you will find most enjoyable and empowering. Use the form entitled **Themes from Memorable Career Experiences** to list your conclusions from this analysis. These conclusions become the facts concerning the situation, people, and takeaways that contributed to your success and sense of fulfillment.

STEP 3. MAKE TRANSITION ASSUMPTIONS

Finally, make relevant assumptions based on your conclusions. For example, if you conclude that you work best in environments with organic schedules, low structure, with a high level of novelty, you might assume that you don't want to target positions in government or at large corporations with entrenched bureaucracy. If you have great clarity regarding the kinds of people and culture, then you might make some assumptions regarding the value structure or kinds of leaders you want to work for. Remember that assumptions are subject to change as you continue to learn and grow through the transition process. These are your critical facts and assumptions to help you target opportunities based on what you did well and most enjoyed throughout your career.

EXAMPLE 2.6 CAREER EXPERIENCE FACTORS

Common Factors Exercise: Career Experience EXAMPLE	
Describe this experience in terms of who, what, where, when, and why	I served as the Brigade Executive Officer for the 101st Aviation Brigade during the preparation and deployment for the strategic surge into Kandahar, Afghanistan in 2010-11. My responsibility was to resource the brigade with the people and equipment for the most critical period of Operation Enduring Freedom.

Factors Related to the Situation (Circle the term that best applies)

Urgency		Group Dynamics		Schedule	
(Crisis)	Routine	(Team)	Individual	Predictable	(Organic)

Structure		Role		Novelty	
(Low Structure)	High Structure	(In-Charge)	Team Member	(New)	Familiar

Factors Related to the People (Input the 5 qualities, adjectives or words)

Leadership	Trustworthy, Competent, Visionary, Confident, Dependable
Culture	Selfless, Proud Heritage, Supportive, Dedicated, High Achievement
Team	Professional, Competent, Brave, Intelligent, Committed

Describe Your Personal Takeaways Based on these Factors

Significance	I coordinated with agencies around the army and around the world to make multi-million dollar decisions with real impact to the mission
Change	Empowered people instead of rank to achieve amazing outcomes with a significantly undermanned staff.
Difficulty	High difficulty. We had to compress an 18 month plan into 12 months at the most critical part in the war.
Growth	Learned to trust my intuition and ability to visualize outcomes well before they happened.
Gratitude	Appreciate the opportunity to serve with the best at the most critical junction in the war.

Common Factors Exercise: Career Experience #1

Describe this experience in terms of who, what, where, when, and why	

Factors Related to the Situation (Circle the term that best applies)

Urgency		Group Dynamics		Schedule	
Crisis	Routine	Team	Individual	Predictable	Organic
Structure		**Role**		**Novelty**	
Low Structure	High Structure	In-Charge	Team Member	New	Familiar

Factors Related to the People (Input the 5 qualities, adjectives or words)

Leadership	
Culture	
Team	

Describe Your Personal Takeaways Based on these Factors

Significance	
Change	
Difficulty	
Growth	
Gratitude	

Common Factors Exercise: Career Experience #2

Describe this experience in terms of who, what, where, when, and why	

Factors Related to the Situation (Circle the term that best applies)

Urgency		Group Dynamics		Schedule	
Crisis	Routine	Team	Individual	Predictable	Organic
Structure		Role		Novelty	
Low Structure	High Structure	In-Charge	Team Member	New	Familiar

Factors Related to the People (Input the 5 qualities, adjectives or words)

Leadership	
Culture	
Team	

Describe Your Personal Takeaways Based on these Factors

Significance	
Change	
Difficulty	
Growth	
Gratitude	

Common Factors Exercise: Career Experience #3

Describe this experience in terms of who, what, where, when, and why	

Factors Related to the Situation (Circle the term that best applies)

Urgency		Group Dynamics		Schedule	
Crisis	Routine	Team	Individual	Predictable	Organic

Structure		Role		Novelty	
Low Structure	High Structure	In-Charge	Team Member	New	Familiar

Factors Related to the People (Input the 5 qualities, adjectives or words)

Leadership	
Culture	
Team	

Describe Your Personal Takeaways Based on these Factors

Significance	
Change	
Difficulty	
Growth	
Gratitude	

Themes From Memorable Career Experiences

Situation: What 3 conclusions do you draw from the common factors and your analysis of the situation from your most meaningful career experiences?

People: What 3 conclusions do you draw from your common factors and analysis of the people from your most meaningful career experiences?

Personal Takeaways: What 3 conclusions do you draw from the common factors and analysis of the Personal Takeaways from your most meaningful career experiences?

Assumptions Based on Themes and Common Factors

Based on the themes from the common factors of my most successful, memorable, and enjoyable experiences, I make the following assumptions about what will lead to my enjoyment and success in life beyond the military:

2.7 MTRP ACTION PLAN TO ADDRESS THE GREATEST RISK IN MILITARY TRANSITION

The credit belongs to the man who is actually in the arena; whose face is marred by sweat and blood; who strives valiantly; who errs and comes short again and again because there is no effort without error and shortcoming; who knows the great enthusiasms, the great devotions, spends himself in a worthy cause; who at best knows in the end the triumph of high achievement; and who at worst, if he fails, at least fails while daring greatly, so that his place shall never be with those cold and timid souls who have never tasted victory or defeat.

—THEODORE ROOSEVELT

SHIFTING YOUR PERSPECTIVE FROM HAZARD TO OPPORTUNITY

A preliminary risk assessment is an integral—if not the most important—part of the Mission Analysis process. Risk management reveals how, where, when, or why a mission might fail. You've probably completed and approved hundreds of risk management worksheets throughout your military career. Frequency and repetition conditioned your intuition to instinctively recognize the points of friction and the necessary control measures to reduce the hazards for a given mission. Whether as part of a combat operation, routine training, or even in conjunction with the leave and pass policy, the ability to manage risk has become a core competency of military leadership.

The military's approach to risk management is protective and preventive. Consequently, you've been conditioned to approach every mission—including transition and reintegration—from the perspective of identifying hazards and implementing controls to guard against failure. As it applies to the next chapter of your life, preventing failure doesn't necessarily ensure success.

When you leave the military, the nature of risk changes. The potential consequences you face include things like unfulfilled potential, missed opportunities, lack of social connection, and a life devoid of purpose or meaning. Self-actualization is what's at stake when we transition from the military. Therefore, you must reframe your perspective about risk from a preventive approach that avoids failure to a proactive one that pursues opportunities toward success. For transition and reintegration, risk management is not about how we protect against losing, but how we take deliberate action to achieve the greatest win.

THE RISK OF VETERAN PURGATORY

Transition is like a bridge across the vast divide between two worlds. The first world is the military one you are leaving, and the second world represents your destination in civilian society. Crossing the divide between these two worlds is the most challenging mission you will face along your military journey. The risk in transition is that you leave the military but never find your place back into society. Consequently, you spend the second half of your life trapped between these two worlds.

In the divide between the military and civilian worlds is the negative space called Veteran Purgatory. It is a state of being where you don't belong to the military, but you don't feel like you belong anywhere else either. This is a crisis of identity: you have to know who you are to recognize where you belong. The veterans who don't recognize their identity without the uniform leave the military without a follow-on destination. These veterans become the lost souls condemned to this purgatory.

If you're paying attention, you might notice some of these veterans wandering about in civilian society. They are former service members sleepwalking their way through life. They lack excitement or inspiration. They don't impress you as glowing examples of leadership—military or otherwise. They are coworkers who show up, do their time, and collect their paycheck. You see their faces but don't know their names. They are the neighbors you hardly see and never get to know. They have become indistinguishable in society except for the fact that they carry the "veteran" label.

For these veterans, the fire that once burned inside their hearts began to smolder when they disconnected from the military. The passion that once fueled their drive to succeed and lead is gone. These leaders that stood out as the heroes of our nation have become lost faces in the crowd. The excitement, the inspiration, and the joy that was once so vivid fades into the daily struggle to climb out of bed in the morning. This is what it means to be lost in Veteran Purgatory, perhaps the most significant risk you face in military transition.

YOUR HERO'S JOURNEY: YOUR BRIDGE

There are several inevitable events of every military journey. You will leave. You will disconnect from the military culture. You will shed your identity as a soldier. You will stand before the threshold to return back to the known world and complete your Hero's Journey. You will be challenged to embrace your unique, most authentic identity story. This is the challenge we all face upon leaving the military, and mitigation requires that we bridge the gap to cross the threshold between these two worlds. It is important to remember that only *you* can create *your* path. Only *you* can build *your* bridge. You bear the responsibility to build the bridge from the life you had to the life you want.

Here's the good news: You have the entire second half of your life to look forward to. Embrace the possibilities before you. You get to choose what happens next. Imagine if all of the leadership challenges *in* the military were simply your preparation for a more impactful and empowering opportunity *beyond* the military. A better opportunity awaits, but you must assume personal responsibility for *your* transition and reintegration. *You* must build *your* bridge.

We've explored your values, purpose, intrinsic strengths, Empowering Beliefs, and the common factors that have led to your success in the past. You've looked past the fear and explored what you truly want for your life. You've gotten out of your head and listened to your heart. Let's take action and create a plan that builds that bridge to connect you to the best opportunity to dare greatly as a veteran leader in civilian society.

BUILDING YOUR BRIDGE: THE MTRP ACTION PLAN

You've already gathered the tools necessary to construct your bridge. Much of your work through this handbook was intended to gain self-awareness around your core identity (values and purpose), your hopes and desires (the things you WANT), your intrinsic strengths, and your beliefs in the possibility of what happens next. These are the elements of your authentic identity story.

The exercises up to this point were designed to frame your transition and reintegration from a perspective of optimism. Positivity and optimism are essential for creating your action plan for transition and reintegration. In the field of psychology, optimism is more than a flippant description of mood. It has been linked to problem-solving, success, social connection, and a healthy life.[39] The positive emotions that come from optimism have been shown to expand our cognitive and behavioral faculties.[40] Optimism is what allows us to access the creativity to build the bridge and the intrinsic motivation to cross over to the other side. It is how we imagine the possibility of winning instead of worrying about implementing controls to guard against losing.

Every bridge requires a start point and an end point. The start point is when you make the decision to leave the military. It occurs before you even submit your separation or retirement paperwork. The end point is defined by your intentions for what you want in life after the military. Those intentions represent your destination back in the civilian world.

The next step in constructing your bridge involves building the foundation. In the context

---

39. Peterson, *Primer*, 114.
40. Ibid., 58.

of civil engineering, the foundation is responsible for carrying and distributing the load. Here's the good news: You've already completed this task. Your foundation includes all the elements that comprise your core identity and define your authentic self. Your values, purpose, strengths, and belief structure are the intrinsic qualities that make you both unique and powerful in this world. Your authentic self *is* the foundation.

Besides a strong foundation, the spans and support structures allow you to get from one side to the other. In the case of your transition, you can think of the spans as your intermediate objectives that cover the distance over the divide. The support structures come from your cadre of coaches, mentors, colleagues, transition specialists, career advisors, partners, family, and friends who want to see you complete your journey and succeed on the other side.

Consider this plan a *dynamic* design. Although the end point and foundation may be relatively fixed, the path you take to get from one side to the other might not be. As you expand your awareness and knowledge of different opportunities, you want to allow some flexibility to change your path or direction as necessary. This is perfectly normal and expected. Any plan in the military doesn't survive past the line of departure, and the same holds true for your plan in transition. Life gets a vote. This is why optimism is so important: it keeps you open to opportunities as conditions change and circumstances evolve.

EXERCISE 2.7.1 MTRP ACTION PLAN: BUILDING YOUR BRIDGE

Let's design your bridge that crosses the divide back to civilian society. These are your action plans to achieve your intentions. Once complete, these plans serve as your personal operator's manual to outline a step-by-step process for how you will transition from the military and reintegrate back into society.

Given that you already have the end point and the foundation for your plan, you can complete your MTRP Action Plan through the following steps:

STEP 1. ESTABLISH THE BRIDGEHEAD

You've already set your intentions. This exercise will help you build a separate plan for each of your intentions (the things you WANT) across the Integrative Program of Transition.

STEP 2. SET YOUR SMART OBJECTIVES

As it pertains to setting your objectives to achieve your intentions, you want to imagine what it would be like to have accomplished your goals and work your way backward. This approach is similar to many of the planning techniques—such as air assault planning—used for military operations. The framework for setting benchmarks and intermediate objectives follows the SMART acronym for goal setting:

S – Specific – Be definitive about what you want to accomplish. Establish a standard. Know what success looks like.

M – Measurable – Have a means to quantify your progress. How will you track your progress, and more importantly, how will you know when you get there?

A – Achievable – Stay within your span of control. Focus on what YOU can do. Know the constraints and limitations that impact a specific objective. For example, you can't set a goal to attain a certification in one month if the program of accreditation takes three months.

R – Relevant – Ensure each intermediate objective is consistent with your foundation (your core identity) and your standard for success. If the action and objective don't move you closer to your intention (i.e., move you closer to the bridgehead on the other side) then how is that activity worth the time and effort? How is the intermediate objective relevant in the big picture?

T – Time-Based – Setting a completion or suspense date provides accountability and provides a means to synchronize the many competing activities through the transition and reintegration process.

STEP 3. ORIENT TO YOUR FOUNDATION

Each objective should move you closer to end state, and they should also honor your values, align to your purpose, utilize an intrinsic strength, or follow a belief. If your objectives are not consistent with your foundation, then you risk losing focus or motivation when contingencies arise. Transition is hard and setbacks are likely to occur. By connecting your activities to an intrinsic form of motivation, you inspire continued movement toward the objective.

STEP 4. POSITION YOUR SUPPORT

You own your transition, but that doesn't mean that you have to do it alone. As mentioned earlier, your support structure can include any one or combination of the following: professional coach, mentor, career services advisor, transition specialist, résumé writer, recruiter, colleague, partner, family, and/or friend. These individuals can provide expertise, guidance, and/or encouragement. They can also hold you accountable to do the things that you say you are going to do through the transition process.

Bear in mind that not everyone who starts this journey with you will be standing by your side when you finish. People from the military culture may not be with you in the civilian world, and some resources may not be accessible until you get to the civilian world. This is the reason why mapping out that support is so important. It will expose your gaps in coverage, and once aware of the gaps, you can develop strategies to cover them.

STEP 5. SEQUENCE AND TIMING

Consider the daunting challenge of achieving all of your objectives simultaneously. Furthermore, you need to recognize that military leaders don't transition in isolation. You probably won't have the luxury of absolving yourself from military duties while you partake in the activities designed to prepare you for life after the military. Competing personal and professional demands—such as a medical requirement or a command assignment—may require sequencing activities to achieve your intended outcomes.

You will have two different opportunities to synchronize your actions through the MTRP. The first occurs when you initially build your calendar for transition (**Section 2.10. Develop the Transition and Reintegration Timeline**). This provides a draft for how events will unfold to achieve your end state. You will have another opportunity to synchronize each opportunity in time and space during **PHASE 4: OPPORTUNITY ALIGNMENT.** For now, it is important to recognize your priorities, the limitations regarding your pace toward each intention, and where to enlist support along the way. An executable plan is one that is manageable, but also one that allows you to maintain your inspiration toward the life you want beyond the military.

STEP 6. PERIODIC REVIEW

Your action plan is *dynamic*. You want to retain the agility to seize opportunities and the flexibility to change direction as the circumstances evolve. Small adjustments could have second and third order effects to the larger transition and reintegration plan. Establishing a timeline for review is important to make these adjustments and update the overall plan. You may discover a different intention. You may further clarify your values. As you learn through this process, you may even select an alternative landing point in the civilian world. The transition process is one of growth, so give yourself the opportunity to evolve as you go along.

EXAMPLE 2.7.1 MTRP ACTION PLAN

An example of the MTRP Action Plan for the Socialization factor is provided in **Figure 2.7.1.** Here are some notes and considerations as you review this example and prepare an MTRP Action Plan for each of your intentions.

1. Although the objective of this exercise is to be as specific as possible with your benchmarks, identifying the month might be all the specificity you can provide at this point. The purpose of the periodic review is to refine each suspense to stay on track.

2. For each factor of the Integrative Program of Transition, you may rely on one particular value, strength, or belief. However, if you complete your plans and you haven't addressed one or more values, you may want to review your values or how you choose to honor those values through your intentions. Remember, this is a dynamic process. As you gain more awareness about how you want to execute your transition, you may want to revisit your purpose, values, or intentions as necessary.

3. Each one of these tasks may have implied tasks that accompany them. For example, the goal of calling four friends each month comes with the requirement to know the specific birthday and phone number for each of your friends. You want to be specific with your objectives, but be specific as it pertains to the big picture. Keep the plan manageable. Every excruciating detail may not be necessary.

4. As a backward planning tool, the top two functions in the example would occur last, and they would most closely align with the stated outcome of this intention.

For some hints or ideas on the different activities that support each factor for the Integrative Program of Transition, refer to Table 1.1 through 1.6 in **PART 1: THE THRESHOLD.**

Military Transition and Reintegration Process Action Plan (EXAMPLE)

STEP 1. SET THE INTENTION (From Exercise 2.3)

I want to attend social events and spend holidays with new friends. I'd love to have get-togethers with neighbors for sporting events or dinner parties.

STEP 2. Set SMART (Specific, Measurable, Achievable, Relevant, and Time-Based) Objectives (Input the suspense in the far right column - STEP 5).	STEP 3. Orient to the Foundation. What value, intrinsic strength, or belief does the goal connect with?	STEP 4. Position Your Support. Who will provide expertise, guidance, encouragement?	STEP 5. Timing. When will you achieve this objective?
Attend one local community activity, concert, theater event, or fair each quarter	Passion for Life	Jill (Spouse)	First quarter is October–December
Invite new neighbors (up to 2 houses down) over for a backyard "welcome and get to know you barbeque"	Passion for Life	Jill (Spouse)	21-Sep-19
Call at least 4 "soldier buddies" on their birthday each month as a 10 minute check-in to see how they are doing	Believe I can be an example,	Jill (Spouse)	Beginning after I sign out
Join PTA and participate in one volunteer event at the school semi-annually	Service to Others, Purpose Statement	Jill (Spouse), Aidan and Everett (Kids)	Aug. to Jan. & Jan to Jun
Join Team RWB and participate in a group running event twice a month. Make 3 new introductions at each event	Passion for Life, Belief in deeper connections	Doug (friend and contact at RWB)	Beginning in August after move-in
Sign up to be a volunteer coach for youth football	Passion for Life, Purpose Statement	Jill (Spouse), Everett	Registration and training complete by July
Join local chapter of the West Point Alumni Association, attend two events a year	Belief in deeper connections, Authenticity	Freddie – fellow classmate in the area	Before the end of the month

STEP 6. PERIODIC REVIEW: Record the date and initial each time that you review and update the plan.

DATE / INITIALS	DATE / INITIALS	DATE / INITIALS	DATE / INITIALS	DATE / INITIALS	DATE / INITIALS

Military Transition and Reintegration Process Action Plan

STEP 1. SET THE INTENTION (From Exercise 2.3)

STEP 2. Set SMART (Specific, Measurable, Achievable, Relevant, and Time-Based) Objectives (Input the suspense in the far right column - STEP 5).	STEP 3. Orient to the Foundation. What value, intrinsic strength, or belief does the goal connect with?	STEP 4. Position Your Support. Who will provide expertise, guidance, encouragement?	STEP 5. Timing. When will you achieve this objective?

STEP 6. PERIODIC REVIEW: Record the date and initial each time that you review and update the plan.

DATE / INITIALS	DATE / INITIALS	DATE / INITIALS	DATE / INITIALS	DATE / INITIALS	DATE / INITIALS

Military Transition and Reintegration Process Action Plan

STEP 1. SET THE INTENTION (From Exercise 2.3)

STEP 2. Set SMART (Specific, Measurable, Achievable, Relevant, and Time-Based) Objectives (Input the suspense in the far right column - STEP 5).	STEP 3. Orient to the Foundation. What value, intrinsic strength, or belief does the goal connect with?	STEP 4. Position Your Support. Who will provide expertise, guidance, encouragement?	STEP 5. Timing. When will you achieve this objective?

STEP 6. PERIODIC REVIEW: Record the date and initial each time that you review and update the plan.

DATE / INITIALS	DATE / INITIALS	DATE / INITIALS	DATE / INITIALS	DATE / INITIALS	DATE / INITIALS

Military Transition and Reintegration Process Action Plan

STEP 1. SET THE INTENTION (From Exercise 2.3)

STEP 2. Set SMART (Specific, Measurable, Achievable, Relevant, and Time-Based) Objectives (Input the suspense in the far right column - STEP 5).	**STEP 3. Orient to the Foundation.** What value, intrinsic strength, or belief does the goal connect with?	**STEP 4. Position Your Support.** Who will provide expertise, guidance, encouragement?	**STEP 5. Timing.** When will you achieve this objective?

STEP 6. PERIODIC REVIEW: Record the date and initial each time that you review and update the plan.

DATE / INITIALS	DATE / INITIALS	DATE / INITIALS	DATE / INITIALS	DATE / INITIALS	DATE / INITIALS

Military Transition and Reintegration Process Action Plan

STEP 1. SET THE INTENTION (From Exercise 2.3)

STEP 2. Set SMART (Specific, Measurable, Achievable, Relevant, and Time-Based) Objectives (Input the suspense in the far right column - STEP 5).	STEP 3. Orient to the Foundation. What value, intrinsic strength, or belief does the goal connect with?	STEP 4. Position Your Support. Who will provide expertise, guidance, encouragement?	STEP 5. Timing. When will you achieve this objective?

STEP 6. PERIODIC REVIEW: Record the date and initial each time that you review and update the plan.

DATE / INITIALS	DATE / INITIALS	DATE / INITIALS	DATE / INITIALS	DATE / INITIALS	DATE / INITIALS

Military Transition and Reintegration Process Action Plan

STEP 1. SET THE INTENTION (From Exercise 2.3)					

STEP 2. Set SMART (Specific, Measurable, Achievable, Relevant, and Time-Based) Objectives (Input the suspense in the far right column - STEP 5).		STEP 3. Orient to the Foundation. What value, intrinsic strength, or belief does the goal connect with?	STEP 4. Position Your Support. Who will provide expertise, guidance, encouragement?	STEP 5. Timing. When will you achieve this objective?

STEP 6. PERIODIC REVIEW: Record the date and initial each time that you review and update the plan.					
DATE / INITIALS	DATE / INITIALS	DATE / INITIALS	DATE / INITIALS	DATE / INITIALS	DATE / INITIALS

Military Transition and Reintegration Process Action Plan

STEP 1. SET THE INTENTION (From Exercise 2.3)

STEP 2. Set SMART (Specific, Measurable, Achievable, Relevant, and Time-Based) Objectives (Input the suspense in the far right column - STEP 5).	STEP 3. Orient to the Foundation. What value, intrinsic strength, or belief does the goal connect with?	STEP 4. Position Your Support. Who will provide expertise, guidance, encouragement?	STEP 5. Timing. When will you achieve this objective?

STEP 6. PERIODIC REVIEW: Record the date and initial each time that you review and update the plan.

DATE / INITIALS	DATE / INITIALS	DATE / INITIALS	DATE / INITIALS	DATE / INITIALS	DATE / INITIALS

Military Transition and Reintegration Process Action Plan

STEP 1. SET THE INTENTION (From Exercise 2.3)			

STEP 2. Set SMART (Specific, Measurable, Achievable, Relevant, and Time-Based) Objectives (Input the suspense in the far right column - STEP 5).	STEP 3. Orient to the Foundation. What value, intrinsic strength, or belief does the goal connect with?	STEP 4. Position Your Support. Who will provide expertise, guidance, encouragement?	STEP 5. Timing. When will you achieve this objective?

STEP 6. PERIODIC REVIEW: Record the date and initial each time that you review and update the plan.

DATE / INITIALS	DATE / INITIALS	DATE / INITIALS	DATE / INITIALS	DATE / INITIALS	DATE / INITIALS

Military Transition and Reintegration Process Action Plan

STEP 1. SET THE INTENTION (From Exercise 2.3)

STEP 2. Set SMART (Specific, Measurable, Achievable, Relevant, and Time-Based) Objectives (Input the suspense in the far right column - STEP 5).	STEP 3. Orient to the Foundation. What value, intrinsic strength, or belief does the goal connect with?	STEP 4. Position Your Support. Who will provide expertise, guidance, encouragement?	STEP 5. Timing. When will you achieve this objective?

STEP 6. PERIODIC REVIEW: Record the date and initial each time that you review and update the plan.

DATE / INITIALS	DATE / INITIALS	DATE / INITIALS	DATE / INITIALS	DATE / INITIALS	DATE / INITIALS

Military Transition and Reintegration Process Action Plan

STEP 1. SET THE INTENTION (From Exercise 2.3)

STEP 2. Set SMART (Specific, Measurable, Achievable, Relevant, and Time-Based) Objectives (Input the suspense in the far right column - STEP 5).	STEP 3. Orient to the Foundation. What value, intrinsic strength, or belief does the goal connect with?	STEP 4. Position Your Support. Who will provide expertise, guidance, encouragement?	STEP 5. Timing. When will you achieve this objective?

STEP 6. PERIODIC REVIEW: Record the date and initial each time that you review and update the plan.

DATE / INITIALS	DATE / INITIALS	DATE / INITIALS	DATE / INITIALS	DATE / INITIALS	DATE / INITIALS

2.8 DETERMINE FAMILY INFORMATION REQUIREMENTS (FIR)

A STRATEGY TO STRENGTHEN FAMILY TIES

Family—and the idea of being there for our families—is one of the main reasons why leaders and career soldiers choose to leave the military. Up to this point, much of this process focused on objectives and intentions from an individual perspective—more specifically, YOUR perspective. That was intentional. This entire process operates under the premise that the best approach for both you and your family is the one that prepares you to be the most authentic version of yourself in life after the military. Once you have an action plan with associated measures of accountability to achieve self-actualization, you are ready to invite the rest of your family into the process.

In military operations, the Commander's Critical Information Requirements (CCIR) describe the information that the commander deems essential to make decisions during the execution of the mission. As part of the MDMP, the staff proposes information requirements, and the commander reviews and updates them for the mission. For your transition and reintegration back into society, information requirements are not determined by a commander or a staff. They are determined by you and your family.

In the MTRP, the Family Information Requirements (FIR) provide an opportunity to include your family in the planning and decision-making process. It also allows you to see different perspectives of the transition process and acknowledge the concerns of your spouse, children, siblings, and/or parents. The stress associated with transition and reintegration can test the bonds of any family, and the FIR provides a way to recognize those challenges in a manner that allows you to strengthen those connections.

As you begin to explore what transition and reintegration means to the rest of your family, you might be surprised to discover some significant differences between what your family imagines might happen from what you imagine might happen. Your children may have expectations about your availability in daily household routines or your active involvement in school activities that might conflict with the travel requirements or work schedule of certain job opportunities. Likewise, your spouse might make assumptions about your ability to contribute to the household as he or she returns to school, opens a new business, or returns to the workforce. Approach this step in the MTRP with an open mind. Everyone in the household transitions when you leave the military, and therefore, everyone under your roof deserves to be heard on how that process of transition and reintegration unfolds.

Transition and reintegration is a transformational life event for everyone in your household. The accompanying stress from this process could galvanize and strengthen the bonds between the members of your family. Alternatively, it could create tensions that weaken your relationships. A prepared family—one that allows honest communication, demonstrates respect, and provides a means for mutual support—grows stronger through the stress of the transition and reintegration process. The purpose of this step in the MTRP is to create a common operating picture for the known and unknown challenges of transition and civilian reintegration.

BENEFITS OF DEVELOPING FAMILY INFORMATION REQUIREMENTS

It is normal for your family to approach transition like any other change in duty station or relocation experienced previously through the military. They've grown accustomed to a certain routine. At first, they may seem rather underwhelmed. After all, many of the concerns and questions they have will be the same ones they have had through every other military move—at least initially. The important distinction is that this is not a move *in* the military. It is a move *from* the military. Just as old routines and habits won't necessarily work for you, they also won't work for the members of your family. An open process that brings everyone together to address these issues is as important to the well-being of your family as the issues themselves.

There are several benefits from a deliberate process to develop information requirements for the entire family. First, you impress upon your family that this move is different. Second, you give them an opportunity to voice their concerns and ask questions. Different perspectives means different sources of stress, and you get to find out what's most important to them through this process. Third, you validate their concerns and solicit feedback that builds trust and promotes buy-in. Finally, you leverage the knowledge and insight from your most trusted allies in your life to refine and improve your action plans. Ultimately, you transform the plan from "me" to "we" to strengthen family ties through the life-altering event of military transition and civilian reintegration.

Family leadership is shared by the partners in a relationship. What follows is just one way—and certainly not the only way—to engage your family in a discussion that addresses everyone's issues. You have no military rank in your family, so keep that in mind as you work through **Exercise 2.8 Determine Family Information Requirements (FIR)**. It is important to remember that the primary objective is to maintain and strengthen the intimacy, trust, and personal connection through this process.

EXERCISE 2.8 DETERMINE FAMILY INFORMATION REQUIREMENTS (FIR)

STEPS FOR CREATING AND MAINTAINING FAMILY INFORMATION REQUIREMENTS

This six-step process is designed to create and manage your FIR for the transition and reintegration process.

STEP 1: SHARE YOUR PLAN

The combination of all the action plans you've developed is your operator's manual for the transition and reintegration process. The first step in developing FIR is to share and communicate those plans. Just as with any mission briefing, you will want to share the mission (your purpose) and your current vision of end state. How much detail you provide regarding the planning process to this point (fears, Limiting Beliefs, strengths, common factors, values) is entirely up to you and would likely depend on the ages of your family members.

You may want to have a family meeting to share the work you have done on your transition up to this point. Keep it brief and highlight the key dates and events. You don't want to overwhelm them, and you don't want to treat your family like a military staff. Give the executive summary of the plan, and state your intention to make it the family plan. Set the expectation that each person should review the plan and offer feedback from a personal perspective. Let them know that you will follow up with each of them individually to discuss the plan and hear their concerns in more detail.

STEP 2: CONDUCT A ONE-ON-ONE REVIEW

In the days following that first conversation, schedule some time to meet with each family member individually. A One-on-One Review serves two functions: (1) it provides you a brief back from each family member about the existing plan, and (2) it provides each family member time to share and discuss their personal and more private concerns directly with you. Your spouse will probably want to do this anyway, but depending on their ages, children might be more forthcoming without their siblings present. Take the time to ask questions about their expectations and vision for what happens next. Their feedback and input might just surprise you!

Depending on the size of your family, this step could take some time, but it is an exercise in building trust. Lines of communication go both ways. By acknowledging and validating the concerns of your family members, you demonstrate compassion for their transition journey. You demonstrate that their perspective, concerns, and opinions matter. Furthermore, your example sets a standard for honest dialogue that may prove particularly beneficial when unexpected challenges emerge.

STEP 3: WRITE YOUR FAMILY MISSION STATEMENT

You have a mission that honors your values and your purpose for life beyond the military, but it might also be valuable for your family to write a similar statement to guide and focus your shared efforts through transition and beyond. Of course it would be related to your purpose and intent, but remember, that is just *your* mission and intent. The goal of bringing your family onboard is to integrate your single vision into a common vision that includes everyone in what happens next.

In order to simplify your vision for the family, it might be best to combine the military statements of mission and intent into a single statement that defines the family mission. An enduring mission provides clarity of purpose and a foundation to ground the members of your family through the challenges of transition, reintegration, and beyond. An example of a family mission statement is included in **Figure 2.8.1.** These statements may include shared values, how you honor relationships, the impact your family wants to have in your community, or a combination of all three. Use a format that suits your family. It could take the form a conventional mission statement, a list, or a narrative.

Figure 2.8.1. Example of a Family Mission Statement

Family Mission Statement
The Roncoroni Family is truthful in what we say and do. We commit to be present in the moment to Encourage and Support each other no matter what – through good times and bad. We Respect the opinions and ideas of others and choose to express kindness to others. We always give our best effort in any endeavor to live, love, and change the world.

STEP 4: SOLICIT INPUT TO BUILD THE FIR LIST

After you've met with everyone individually, it's time to bring the family together. In structuring the family meeting, you probably want to set some ground rules to facilitate open dialogue and honest communication. Remember, the objective is active participation. Set the conditions for family members to be heard in a respectful manner. You want their buy-in. If you end up being the only person talking, then you're just developing *your* information requirements and not *their* information requirements. Outbursts, judgment, criticism, or outright dismissing someone's genuine concerns make it more difficult to solicit honest input and active participation.

As a technique, you may want to ask each person to share their top three concerns or questions with the rest of the family. If an individual concern has repercussions for the entire family, then it may warrant inclusion on the Family Information Requirements. You may want to group their comments under the appropriate factor from the Integrative Program of Transition. If nobody is talking, try some direct questioning. Asking open-ended questions—questions that start with the words "what," "how," "tell," or "describe"—might trigger more active dialogue. Naturally, some of their concerns will be individual in nature and some questions may already have answers. Not everything will make the final list of the FIR, but allow enough time for each family member to speak his or her truth (**Table 2.8.1. Examples of Family Information Requirements** provides some common questions that family members might ask regarding the transition process). Again, your goal is to strengthen your family and make everyone more resilient for the challenges that lie ahead.

Table 2.8.1. Example Family Information Requirements. These examples are based on real questions and concerns of a family retiring after twenty-one years of service in the army.

Possible Examples of Questions that Shape Your Family Information Requirements
How will taxes impact our family income and our retirement pay?
If the military isn't making us move, why can't we just stay here so I can be with my friends?
How will we start a conversation with our neighbors, the teachers at school, or other parents of the baseball team? I am afraid that without our military ties, we won't have anything in common with them.
Are we going to rent for a while to figure out where we are going to be or are we just going to buy a house?
How will we access healthcare, and what are the associated costs, if we don't live near a military base?
Will mom (or dad) have to leave again?
Will mom (or dad) go back to work? How will you find a job after an extended absence?
What are we planning to do with all that leave time we saved up (what does everyone want to do with that leave time)?
How long do we plan on being at the next location before we move again?
How will the roles in the household change?
Will we all move together or wait until I finish the school year?
How will the medical or other requirements adjust the timeline for separation?
When can I register for sports or other activities in the area?
What is their impression of military people? (Do they even like the military?)

STEP 5: DELEGATION AND ACCOUNTABILITY

When we develop the CCIR for a military mission, we assign collection assets to gather the information necessary to make the appropriate decision. Your collection assets are your family members. You don't have to assume responsibility for addressing all the issues or answering all the questions. Empowering the members of your family helps to make them part of the solution. This is one technique to create buy-in for transition and reintegration.

Accountability is imperative to make this process meaningful. Everyone must be willing to hold each other accountable to collect and share information. Assign and delegate tasks as a family, and set reasonable deadlines to complete the necessary research to answer the information requirement. The more responsibility you share in this process, the greater the buy-in. Offering a sense of control through such a stressful period can be both grounding and empowering through this challenging period of your lives.

STEP 6: FOLLOW-UP

Establish a schedule of in-progress reviews. Your entire family is executing the mission of transition and civilian reintegration, so create your own system and schedule for routine follow-ups. These reviews become a forum for sharing information as a family. Ideally, you could incorporate these reviews as part of your existing family routines. After all, this is your family, not a military unit. Honor your family traditions, or use this process as a call to action to begin a new one. You can have an agenda, but such formality is not necessary. You can meet in the living room or around the dining room table. The structure isn't as important as the event. You want to prioritize these gatherings and protect the time for the family to share information about what they have learned, what has changed, and what new issues have emerged in an honest, judgment-free environment.

You can also use this time to celebrate incremental wins. Recognize the contribution of each family member and provide a forum to capture new issues. Showing progress in your family's ability to resolve issues infuses a sense of positive momentum. The resulting trust and confidence that they feel will bring your family unit closer together.

Template for Developing and Executing Family Information Requirements

This template is a way to manage Family Information Requirements. The structure intends to capture requirements based on the six-step process outlined earlier. How you choose to manage the information most important to your family is entirely up to you. You can make a simple list on a sheet of paper or a dry erase board. You can record items in your notebook so that you have it handy during the many meetings and appointments you will attend through the transition process. You may want to share it electronically so you can track and share progress in real time. Use what works for you. The objective is to provide a means to facilitate active communication and meaningful dialogue. This template just provides one way for you to do that.

Keep the number of FIRs at a manageable level. Too many FIRs may be cumbersome or unwieldy. You don't want to give the impression that this challenge is insurmountable. As you consider the delegation and accountability for research, data collection, developing options, start slowly. Try not to give any one family member any more than three information requirements. You can delegate more as certain requirements are met or new issues emerge. You want your family to be encouraged by setting and achieving reasonable milestones.

Here are the detailed instructions for completing this template:

FAMILY INFORMATION REQUIREMENT NUMBER: Number each Family Information Requirement for easy reference.

INTEGRATIVE PROGRAM OF TRANSITION FACTOR: Each of these information requirements should be connected to one of the factors from the Integrative Program of Transition. Those factors include: Optimizing Whole Health, Socialization, Cultural Assimilation, Economic Stability, Professional Preparedness, and Family Adjustment.

CONCERN OR QUESTION: This is the concern and/or question that impacts the entire family.

DELEGATED TO: Input the name of the family member responsible for researching and developing solutions for this particular concern or question.

SUSPENSE: Input the agreed-upon date for when the family member must address the issue to the entire family.

DEVELOPMENTS: This is a space for you to take notes as you gain clarity about the particular issue or question. Remember, the nature of questions or concerns may evolve throughout the process.

OUTCOME AND WAY FORWARD: Input the solution and the next steps for implementation. Remember to cross reference what you learn with your MTRP Action Plans to turn the "me" of the plan into "we" for your family. Here is an example of what one information requirement might look like in this template.

FAMILY INFORMATION REQUIREMENT NUMBER:	I	INTEGRATIVE PROGRAM OF TRANSITION FACTOR:	Optimizing Whole Health

CONCERN OR QUESTION:		DELEGATED TO	SUSPENSE
When can Aidan register for club baseball next spring?		Aidan	Nov. 20

DEVELOPMENTS:

1. New bat requirements for travel leagues. Aidan needs a drop 5 BBCOR Certified bat – He doesn't currently have one. (July 24)

2. Registration for tryouts for the spring season is in October (August 2)

3. Aidan requires a sports physical (form provided through registration portal) (August 2)

4. County leagues don't require tryouts, and registration is in March for the spring season (August 8)

OUTCOME AND WAY FORWARD:

We can schedule a sports physical before we leave. We will get him registered and provide a copy of our lease to prove residence. We'll follow-up with the club president about equipment requirements when we get into town

Use your own format or the templates on the following pages to capture your Family Information Requirements (FIR) for the transition and reintegration process.

FAMILY INFORMATION REQUIREMENT NUMBER:		INTEGRATIVE PROGRAM OF TRANSITION FACTOR:	
CONCERN OR QUESTION:		**DELEGATED TO**	**SUSPENSE**
DEVELOPMENTS:			
OUTCOME AND WAY FORWARD:			

FAMILY INFORMATION REQUIREMENT NUMBER:		INTEGRATIVE PROGRAM OF TRANSITION FACTOR:	
CONCERN OR QUESTION:		**DELEGATED TO**	**SUSPENSE**
DEVELOPMENTS:			
OUTCOME AND WAY FORWARD:			

FAMILY INFORMATION REQUIREMENT NUMBER:		INTEGRATIVE PROGRAM OF TRANSITION FACTOR:		
CONCERN OR QUESTION:		**DELEGATED TO**		**SUSPENSE**
DEVELOPMENTS:				
OUTCOME AND WAY FORWARD:				

FAMILY INFORMATION REQUIREMENT NUMBER:		INTEGRATIVE PROGRAM OF TRANSITION FACTOR:		
CONCERN OR QUESTION:		**DELEGATED TO**		**SUSPENSE**
DEVELOPMENTS:				
OUTCOME AND WAY FORWARD:				

FAMILY INFORMATION REQUIREMENT NUMBER:		INTEGRATIVE PROGRAM OF TRANSITION FACTOR:	
CONCERN OR QUESTION:		**DELEGATED TO**	**SUSPENSE**
DEVELOPMENTS:			
OUTCOME AND WAY FORWARD:			

FAMILY INFORMATION REQUIREMENT NUMBER:		INTEGRATIVE PROGRAM OF TRANSITION FACTOR:	
CONCERN OR QUESTION:		**DELEGATED TO**	**SUSPENSE**
DEVELOPMENTS:			
OUTCOME AND WAY FORWARD:			

2.9 BUILD YOUR NETWORKING STRATEGY

All military operations are based on the premise that intelligence drives maneuver. Purposeful action comes from relevant and meaningful information—or *intelligence*. The same rules apply when you leave the military. That is to say, intelligence informs deliberate actions and sound decisions through the process of transition and reintegration. The means for collecting that intelligence is through a process called networking. Networking is how you gather relevant information and build meaningful relationships to help you discover the right opportunity when you separate or retire from the military.

Networking is perhaps one of the most important activities in the transition and reintegration process. In addition to providing valuable information to refine, shape, and develop your plan, networking can also lead to referrals, recommendations, and important introductions to help you discover those opportunities that best align with what you want for your life. Consider the following statistics:

- According to LinkedIn, 85 percent of all jobs are filled via networking.[41]

- Referred candidates are 55 percent faster to hire.[42]

- Referred employees have 46 percent retention rate after the first year.[43]

- Employee referrals have shown to provide 25 percent greater profit.[44]

The data suggests that the best way to get your foot in the door happens when someone you know turns the doorknob.

Consequently, networking has become a convenient buzzword for every transition advisor, human resources analyst, recruiter, and employment specialist across the military and career transition landscape. The rhetoric around the urgency to expand networks has surpassed hyperbole and landed firmly in hysteria. Networking has become the panacea for addressing any and all concerns for a successful transition from the military. Unfortunately, the endless cycle of vapid LinkedIn requests, ice-breaker conversations, and travel to yet another career

41. Lou Adler, "New Survey Reveals 85% of All Jobs Are Filled Via Networking," *LinkedIn*, February 29, 2016, https://www.linkedin.com/pulse/new-survey-reveals-85-all-jobs-filled-via-networking-lou-adler.
42. The HRT Features Desk, "3 Reasons Why Referrals Are the Way Forward for Recruitment in 2018," *HR Technologist*, January 26, 2018, https://www.hrtechnologist.com/articles/recruitment-onboarding/3-reasons-why-referrals-are-the-way-forward-for-recruitment-in-2018/.
43. David Galic, "Why You Should Be Using Employee Referrals to Find and Hire New Talent," *Humanity* (blog), August 15, 2017, https://www.humanity.com/blog/employee-referral-program-benefits.html.
44. Ibid.

conference can be mentally, emotionally, and even financially exhausting with little to show for your efforts. When you use a spamming approach to networking, you will be lucky to find any job, let alone the right one.

Absent a focused and deliberate collection plan, your networking process will be highly inefficient and largely ineffective. You may make a lot of connections, but those connections won't deliver value. They won't get you closer to your end state. Building relationships takes time and energy, so treat your networking strategy in the same way you would develop a collection plan for targeting. You want to gather relevant information that informs your actions and decision-making process. When conducting your "reconnaissance" to understand what might happen next in your life, perhaps it is best to apply the fundamentals to the networking process.

GAIN AND MAINTAIN CONTACT

Networking is about building relationships, and that takes time. The process of transforming a contact into a meaningful connection doesn't happen overnight. A profile of just five connections could prove more valuable than a profile of more than 2,000 connections if those five people can bring you closer to the opportunity that helps you achieve your mission and realize your intent. Remember, you don't get married after the first date, and chances are you won't get hired after the first conversation. If you want your network to deliver value, invest the time and energy into building meaningful relationships. Finally, remember that meaningful relationships are ones where all parties benefit. Recognize and offer value to the people you want to offer value back to you.

Step back and consider what it took for you to make a meaningful introduction or offer a persuasive recommendation for someone else. What did it take for you to go above and beyond on someone else's behalf? Chances are you've been on the receiving end of similar referrals or recommendations for various positions or assignments throughout your career. Think about what made a particular referral or recommendation memorable. Consider the qualities of those relationships. Set the conditions to achieve similar outcomes with the people you *gain contact* with through the transition process.

Be patient and maintain contact. Trust takes time. Depending on how well you've managed relationships up to this point, it could take months before you develop the network that moves you closer to the ideal opportunity in life beyond the military. Pushing too hard or moving too fast comes across as manipulative or, even worse, desperate. Nurture connections, turn them into meaningful relationships, and build a trusted alliance willing to fight alongside you in the battle to achieve your purpose and realize your intent.

ORIENT ON THE NETWORKING OBJECTIVES

The primary objectives of your networking plan are: (1) to address an information requirement or open issue from your MTRP Action Plans, (2) to provide clarity regarding a path toward a potential opportunity, or (3) to build a relationship for an impactful introduction or referral. The only other possible function of networking is to connect you with someone who can address one of the three primary networking objectives. Given the time and energy necessary to build a network of value, you want to orient your networking activities toward one of these objectives.

Each relationship should provide value. Stay focused on your purpose, intent, and your action plan. If the relationship is not addressing any of your information requirements directly, then perhaps you should consider how much time you want to invest in that relationship.

You may find some former military colleagues working in the corporate sector who offer the allure of helping you get hired at their company. Don't let the temptation of a quick-fix for finding employment distract you from your path. While this fellow veteran might be a valuable resource to expand your network, new hires rarely have the authority to make hiring decisions. Even with the best of intentions, these promises offer false hope that typically ends in disappointment and resentment. Understand the capabilities and limitations of the people in your network. See how they fit into the broader networking strategy to address an information requirement or open issue from MTRP Action Plans, provide clarity regarding your path toward a potential opportunity, or build a relationship for an impactful introduction or referral.

RETAIN FREEDOM OF MANEUVER

Transitioning military leaders tend to network with large corporations or other government agencies. We tend to gravitate toward these opportunities because these organizations advertise positions online and actively attend hiring conferences. Working for a large corporation or within the civil service are just two of many different opportunities that exist. Entrepreneurship, franchising, small business, and nonprofit organizations are some others. Diversify your networking efforts to retain your freedom of maneuver. Explore different market sectors and different business entities. Keep an open mind as you widen the aperture to discover the right opportunity.

Be cautious of stakeholders that don't honor your interests as their number one priority. Some recruiters and headhunters may require a contractual agreement before you partner with them. Although these stakeholders may offer stronger assurance of employment, there is no guarantee that any opportunity they find will align with your values, your purpose, or what you really want for your life. After all, they don't work for you. They work for the companies that hire them. Fear of securing employment and a lack of self-confidence in navigating the job market are the reasons why many transitioning service members lock themselves into these kinds of arrangements. If you surrender your freedom of maneuver, you may limit your options to honor your values, service your intent, and achieve what you want.

REPORT INFORMATION ACCURATELY AND TIMELY

The purpose of timely and accurate reporting is to promote clarity for informed decision making. The same holds true for your networking process, but instead of reporting information to promote awareness and understanding for a higher headquarters, you are gaining self-awareness and understanding to shape and direct your plan and your path. As a military leader, you know how to recognize decision points. You've been conditioned to make hard decisions. You will need these skills as you cross the line of departure along your bridge to make that journey into life beyond the military.

Track information as it becomes available. Use what you are learning to update and refine your plan. It is normal to reevaluate one or more of your action plans as new information becomes available or unexpected possibilities arise. You may need to change a timeline or suspense. You may need to update one or more of your intentions. Remember, this intelligence can only drive maneuver if you actually apply what you're learning along the way.

DEVELOP THE SITUATION

The situation you are trying to develop involves how to apply your values, purpose, and intrinsic strengths in an opportunity that achieves what you want in life. Your conversations should involve active listening and meaningful questions that accomplish more than just a "yes" or "no" answer. If you are prepared for an informational interview or other networking engagement, you should have a list of prepared questions, and you should also trust your intuition and be open-minded to recognize opportunities to ask questions not included on that list. Don't be afraid to see where an unexpected turn in the conversation might take you, provided the discussion has the potential to offer some new insight to the networking objectives.

Two important qualities in the networking process include curiosity and open-mindedness. If you had all the answers, you wouldn't need to network in the first place. Making inquiries that start with words like "what," "how," "describe," "tell," "show," or "when" offer a wider range of answers than do questions that require a simple "yes" or "no" answer. Get comfortable with uncertainty and be open to the possibility that the best opportunity or question is the one that you haven't considered yet.

ENSURE MAXIMUM NETWORKING RESOURCES FORWARD

When it comes to building a network for career transition, you don't have to start from scratch. As you reflect on the many faces and names from your military career, you'll quickly realize that you already have a well-defined network of associates, colleagues, peers, mentors, and subordinates alike. *You have dozens if not hundreds of connections in your network already!* Be willing to reach out to the many people you've met and worked with throughout your career. They may prove to be your best advocates for communicating your brand, sharing your value proposition, and making powerful introductions to further expand your network.

Personal referrals and warm introductions help to expand the network that gets you hired. Think about how you respond to a referral from a trusted classmate, colleague, peer, or associate compared to the blind connection request through LinkedIn. Consider the difference between a personal introduction as opposed to the awkward exchange of business cards at some random hiring event. *Existing* connections provide the means to make *powerful* connections.

Don't be afraid to reconnect with a former colleague if you've lost touch. Life happens. More often than not, the people from your past will be thrilled to hear from you and more than happy to support your journey. I've never been turned away from an opportunity to reconnect with someone from my past nor have I turned anyone away who has reached out to me. Use the established network you already have before expending time and energy on cold calls, vapid connection requests, and crowded conferences to expand your network.

FINAL THOUGHTS ON NETWORKING

Networking is your reconnaissance for what happens next, so stick to the fundamentals. Networking isn't about making connections, it is about gaining and maintaining relationships through the transition process. If you don't orient your networking strategy to your intentions, the best opportunity can pass you by and you'd never know it. Diversify your networking portfolio and retain the flexibility to make decisions. Be vigilant and apply what you learn through the process to update your transition plan. Practice active listening and ask open-ended questions to gain a deeper understanding of different opportunities. Finally, use all the resources available in your network. You've been making connections throughout your military career, so use those connections!

You will revisit and utilize your Networking Collection Plan throughout the remaining steps of the MTRP. In any military organization, the collection plan and targeting matrix are living documents. The same holds true for your Networking Collection Plan as part of the MTRP.

Your Networking Collection Plan will likely evolve as you work through **Step 3. Opportunity Development, Step 4. Opportunity Alignment**, and **Step 5. Opportunity Comparison.** As you review these sections, you may want to capture new questions and information requirements for your Networking Collection Plan.

Intelligence drives maneuver, but remember that the best laid plan is just that, a plan. Execution is more dynamic. Your execution will require discipline, vigilance, and a steady flow of relevant information to inform decisions and make adjustments as the situation dictates, but let's begin by building a framework for your Networking Collection Plan.

EXERCISE 2.9.1 DEVELOP YOUR NETWORKING COLLECTION PLAN

As part of the Identity Analysis phase of the MTRP, we build the initial structure of your Networking Collection Plan. This is a starting point for building relationships, conducting research, and creating leads for opportunities beyond the military. Success requires vigilance and discipline. Here is a three-step process to build your network collection plan:

STEP 1: DEVELOP THE NETWORKING CONTACT LIST

This is your targeting process to identify potential connections across six business entities—entrepreneurs, franchising, civil service, nonprofit organizations, small business, and large corporations. In keeping with the fundamentals, begin with existing connections from across your military career. Include your alma mater, professional colleagues, mentors, and friends from outside the military. Challenge yourself to include veterans and non-veterans alike. After all, the non-veterans have more experience and expertise when it comes to being a civilian. Absent an existing connection, you can start with the resources in **Table 2.9.1. Definitions and Resources for Networking across Different Business Entities.**

STEP 2: RESEARCH

You may not be familiar with one or more of the business entities in **Table 2.9.1**, and therefore, you will have to conduct your own research into these opportunities. You want to be somewhat prepared and informed before you start asking questions. If you spend a thirty-minute call asking superfluous questions, you have not only wasted your time, but you have also wasted the other person's time. They may be less agreeable to make an introduction or speak with you again. Remember that your objective is to build meaningful relationships. To do that, you need to ask meaningful questions. Invest some time to study and understand the opportunities from each of these business entities. You will have a chance to start your research and explore opportunities during subsequent steps of the MTRP.

STEP 3: DETERMINE YOUR INFORMATION REQUIREMENTS

As you conduct your research, you want to capture the questions and concerns that will become your information requirements for your collection plan. Use a conceptual, big-picture approach. You want to identify your information requirements as they relate to your values, purpose, intrinsic strengths, and intentions. The purpose of this collection plan is to determine which opportunities best align with what you want in life after the military. The particulars surrounding each job opportunity (salary, location, job title, etc.) will be addressed during subsequent phases of the MTRP.

Don't wait to get a completed plan before you begin execution. Trust your intuition. If you have some nagging questions, you are probably ready to begin executing your Networking Collection Plan. It is never too early to begin building the relationships that will influence and shape your ideal opportunity in life beyond the military.

DETAILED INSTRUCTIONS FOR COMPLETING THE NETWORKING COLLECTION PLAN

Now it's your turn to build your collection plan as part of the broader networking strategy to discover the right opportunity after military service.

Name and Position of Connection: In order to capture multiple perspectives, you want to network with multiple people at different levels (i.e., federal government, state government, local government) or different levels of experience. For example, you may want to include someone who is just beginning their journey in that business sector, someone who is approaching the middle of his or her career in that business sector (two to ten years), and someone who is a more senior leader within that particular sector. Consider the different answers you would receive about military service if your network included a lieutenant on his or her first assignment, a senior company-grade officer, and a field grade-level commander. Try and capture the same range of experience when you build your networking strategy.

Email Address: Self-Explanatory

Contact Number: Self-Explanatory

Number: Number each question for easy reference. Try to limit the number of questions that you ask during each networking engagement. This is relationship building, not an interrogation.

Table 2.9.1. Definitions and Resources for Networking across Different Business Entities.

Business Entity	Definition	Where to Look to Find More Information
Entrepreneur	Start-ups, new business owners, sole proprietors, and self-employed professionals	Bunker Labs (https://bunkerlabs.org)
		Boots to Business (https://sbavets.force.com/s/)
Franchising	"Franchising is a form of business by which the owner (franchisor) of a product, service or method obtains distribution through affiliated dealers (franchisees)."[45]	Veterans Franchise (https://www.veteransfranchise.com)
		Vet Fran (https://vetfran.org)
Civil Service	Employment as a member of the civil service and general schedule (GS) pay scale for professionals	Feds Hire Vets (https://www.fedshirevets.gov/)
		USAJOBS (https://www.usajobs.gov/)
Nonprofit	"These are groups that are tax-exempt under Internal Revenue Code Section 501(c)(3) as 'public charities' because they are formed to provide 'public benefit.' Community foundations are also part of this group."[46]	Veterans Advantage (https://www.veteransadvantage.com/giving-back/trusted-military-organizations-and-nonprofits)
		National Council of Nonprofits (https://www.councilofnonprofits.org/tools-resources/how-start-nonprofit)
Small Business	The classification of a small business depends on the industry, but small businesses typically have between 250 and 1500 employees and generate less revenue than large business.[47]	The Veteran Business Network (https://veteranbusinessnetwork.com)
		Veteran Owned Businesses Directory (https://www.veteranownedbusiness.com/166/networking-services)
Large Corporations	Large corporations include existing and aspiring Fortune 500 companies (top 500 companies based on revenue from the past three years)	American Corporate Partners (https://www.acp-usa.org/)
		Veterati (https://www.veterati.com/)

---

45. "Franchising," *Entrepreneur*, accessed May 24, 2019, https://www.entrepreneur.com/encyclopedia/franchising.

46. "What Is a 'Nonprofit'?" *National Council of Nonprofits*, April 15, 2019, accessed May 24, 2019, https://www.councilofnonprofits.org/what-is-a-nonprofit.

47. Georgia McIntyre, "What Is the SBA's Definition of Small Business (And Why)?" *Fundera* (blog), June 20, 2018, https://www.fundera.com/blog/sba-definition-of-small-business.

Question: Frame your concerns and issues in the form of an open-ended question. Avoid YES/NO answers. Use words like *explain*, *how*, *what*, *when*, *describe*, and *tell*.

Observations and Answers: This is the space to input your notes, insights, and answers from your research and conversations with your networking contacts. For each entry, you may want to include the date and source of the information.

Take a look at a completed information requirement in **Example 2.9.1**, and then use the subsequent templates on the following pages to start building your collection plan for each different type of opportunity (entrepreneurship, franchising, civil service, nonprofit organizations, small business, and large corporation).

EXAMPLE 2.9.1 EXAMPLE OF AN INFORMATION REQUIREMENT AS PART OF THE NETWORKING COLLECTION PLAN

NUMBER	QUESTION
12	*How were you able to pay your bills while you beginning a business as an entrepreneur?*

OBSERVATIONS AND ANSWERS
1. *John used savings to fund his initial startup costs and cover what wasn't being covered by his retirement. (John Smith / 12 Apr 17)*
2. *Jason's wife went back to work and the combination of his retirement and her full-time job covered their living expenses enough for him to start his own business (Jason R. / 31 May 17)*
3. *Steve suggested that I look up federal loans and grant opportunities for funding a small business that included my salary as the founder (Steve Goodman / 3 Jun 17)*
My notes:
1) Estimate new business will cost $20K in startup fees for the website, licensing, and training.
2) If Jill's job covers the bills, then we can fund the startup fee from our retirement savings (after all, why else is that money there?)

ENTREPRENEUR NETWORK COLLECTION PLAN

Name & Position of Connection	Email Address	Contact Number

NUMBER	QUESTION

OBSERVATIONS AND ANSWERS

NUMBER	QUESTION

OBSERVATIONS AND ANSWERS

ENTREPRENEUR NETWORK COLLECTION PLAN

NUMBER	QUESTION

OBSERVATIONS AND ANSWERS

NUMBER	QUESTION

OBSERVATIONS AND ANSWERS

NUMBER	QUESTION

OBSERVATIONS AND ANSWERS

FRANCHISING NETWORK COLLECTION PLAN

Name & Position of Connection	Email Address	Contact Number

NUMBER	QUESTION

OBSERVATIONS AND ANSWERS

NUMBER	QUESTION

OBSERVATIONS AND ANSWERS

FRANCHISING NETWORK COLLECTION PLAN

NUMBER	QUESTION
	OBSERVATIONS AND ANSWERS

NUMBER	QUESTION
	OBSERVATIONS AND ANSWERS

NUMBER	QUESTION
	OBSERVATIONS AND ANSWERS

CIVIL SERVICE NETWORK COLLECTION PLAN

Name & Position of Connection	Email Address	Contact Number

NUMBER	QUESTION

OBSERVATIONS AND ANSWERS

NUMBER	QUESTION

OBSERVATIONS AND ANSWERS

CIVIL SERVICE NETWORK COLLECTION PLAN

PAGE _____ OF _____

NUMBER	QUESTION

OBSERVATIONS AND ANSWERS

NUMBER	QUESTION

OBSERVATIONS AND ANSWERS

NUMBER	QUESTION

OBSERVATIONS AND ANSWERS

NONPROFIT NETWORK COLLECTION PLAN

Name & Position of Connection	Email Address	Contact Number

NUMBER	QUESTION

OBSERVATIONS AND ANSWERS

NUMBER	QUESTION

OBSERVATIONS AND ANSWERS

NUMBER	QUESTION

OBSERVATIONS AND ANSWERS

NUMBER	QUESTION

OBSERVATIONS AND ANSWERS

NUMBER	QUESTION

OBSERVATIONS AND ANSWERS

SMALL BUSINESS NETWORK COLLECTION PLAN

Name & Position of Connection	Email Address	Contact Number

NUMBER	QUESTION

OBSERVATIONS AND ANSWERS

NUMBER	QUESTION

OBSERVATIONS AND ANSWERS

SMALL BUSINESS NETWORK COLLECTION PLAN

PAGE _____ OF _____

NUMBER	QUESTION

OBSERVATIONS AND ANSWERS

NUMBER	QUESTION

OBSERVATIONS AND ANSWERS

NUMBER	QUESTION

OBSERVATIONS AND ANSWERS

LARGE CORPORATION NETWORK COLLECTION PLAN

Name & Position of Connection	Email Address	Contact Number

NUMBER	QUESTION

OBSERVATIONS AND ANSWERS

NUMBER	QUESTION

OBSERVATIONS AND ANSWERS

LARGE CORPORATION NETWORK COLLECTION PLAN	PAGE _____ OF _____

NUMBER | **QUESTION**

OBSERVATIONS AND ANSWERS

NUMBER | **QUESTION**

OBSERVATIONS AND ANSWERS

NUMBER | **QUESTION**

OBSERVATIONS AND ANSWERS

2.10 DEVELOP THE TRANSITION AND REINTEGRATION TIMELINE

The purpose of this step in the Identity Analysis is to build an initial timeline to frame requirements and sequence activities for your transition and reintegration. You will have an opportunity to shape your calendar of events and activities in more detail during the wargame process **(Step 4.2. Wargame).** For now, you want to capture known activities to create an initial schedule using the **One-Third Rule of Transition and Reintegration Model** (see **Figure 2** from the beginning of **Part 2** of this handbook).

EXERCISE 2.10 THE TRANSITION AND REINTEGRATION TIMELINE

You can complete your initial Transition and Reintegration Timeline in three simple steps:

1. Gather the Tools

2. Set the Left and Right Limits

3. Populate the Calendar

Let's explore each of these steps in more detail:

STEP 1. GATHER THE TOOLS

In order to build a useful timeline, you need a calendar. Depending on your preference, you can use a desktop or digital calendar that serves as your base document. The calendar that holds your Transition and Reintegration Timeline is a living document, and therefore, digital calendars are preferable because they are easier to edit. In order to set the limits and populate the calendar, you will also require the following:

Regarding your outstanding obligations to the military:

- Separation paperwork including specific dates and requirements for clearing activities

- Administrative duty requirements such as inventory schedules, evaluations, change of command activities, etc.

- Outstanding operational requirements such as deployment schedules, exercises, deployment reintegration requirements, etc.

- Terminal leave accruals and permissive TDY

- Schedule of any ongoing medical or wellness activities such as surgery, physical therapy, etc.

Regarding your obligations to your family:

- A list of relevant school activities to include graduations, school enrollment requirements, start and end dates for the school year, etc.

- Significant events such as weddings, reunions, anniversaries, and birthdays

- Schedule and relevant timelines for youth/collegiate activities including sports, performing arts, internships, etc.

- Spouse employment and activities schedule

- Major holidays, days off, and planned vacations

Regarding your responsibilities to yourself:

- MTRP Action Plans

- Networking Collection Plan

- Family Information Requirements

- Education and Accreditation Schedules (as necessary)

Once you have this information, you are ready to build the initial schedule for your Transition and Reintegration Timeline.

STEP 2. SET THE LEFT AND RIGHT LIMITS

The next step is to set the left and right limits. Regarding the left limit, the moment you opened this handbook was when you started the process. **Figure 2.10.1. Breakdown of Activities by Phase** provides a guideline for the activities and main effort of each phase. Ideally, you would allow eighteen months to complete the full process of transition and reintegration, but the key determinant in setting your left and right limits is the amount of time you have before your separation date. Absent any constraints, allow six months to complete the MTRP and six months to complete your transition, but remember that the One-Third Rule of Transition and Reintegration Model is just that, a model.

Not everyone will have twelve months' leeway before they separate or retire from the military. If you don't have that much time, you want to allow at least three months to complete the Identity Analysis portion of the MTRP. Discovering your identity as an authentic leader is the most important and overlooked aspect of transition from the military. It is a process that takes time, and you don't want to force it. You could complete the remaining steps of the MTRP (Steps 3 through 6) concurrently with other transition activities; but without question, your values, purpose, intentions, intrinsic strengths, and beliefs are essential to discover your most empowering life beyond the military.

When possible, you want to allocate three months to complete Steps 3 through 6 of the MTRP and refine opportunities based on what you learn through the networking process. Networking is not exclusive to any phase of the model or any particular window on the calendar. Building relationships through networking is a lifelong endeavor. The reason for setting aside time to research and develop opportunities is so that you don't feel the pressure or heightened sense of urgency of securing a paycheck as your separation date looms near.

Figure 2.10.1. Breakdown of Activities by Phase. This is a general guideline for planning across each phase in the One-Third Rule of Transition and Reintegration.

Breakdown of Activities by Phase in the ⅓ Rule of Transition and Reintegration Model			
Phase	**MTRP**	**Transition**	**Reintegration**
Main Effort	Step 1 & 2 of the MTRP (1st Half)	Transition and Separation Activities	Find and Develop Opportunity
	Step 3 thru 6 of the MTRP (2nd Half)		
Key Activities	Identity Analysis (1st Half	Separation / Retirement Physical	Execute Action Plans
	Opportunity Assessment (2nd Half)	Transition Leave/ Permissive TDY	Begin Next Opportunity
	Refine Action Plans	Final Clearance	Lead, Inspire, Achieve
		Execute Action Plans	
	Networking and Relationship Building is ongoing through each phase and beyond		

The start date for the Transition (middle) Phase occurs when separation activities become your main priority. As a military leader, you will likely have competing obligations, but this phase is when you complete your transition or retirement physical and begin attending the mandatory activities for separation from the service. Your transition leave and any permissive TDY are also included in this phase. The end date for the Transition Phase is your separation date from the military.

The timeline for the Reintegration (final) Phase begins the day you officially separate from the military. As for the end date, you set that based on what you believe is necessary to achieve your desired state of being from your MTRP Action Plans. As mentioned earlier, a successful reintegration could take months or even years depending on the length and nature of your service. Be compassionate and stay focused on your desired state of being. The end point of the Reintegration Phase is event driven.

Given the impact of transition on a person's psychology, a shorter time for the MTRP and Transition Phase will likely require longer periods of time for the Reintegration Phase on the backside. The end date of the process is not when you start working in a new job, but the point in time when you believe that you will have achieved your new identity story—your ideal state of being as a veteran leader in society. Given the social and cultural challenges that accompany starting a new job, you may even want to establish that end point sometime after the first ninety days of new employment.

STEP 3. POPULATE THE CALENDAR

Once you've established a starting and ending point for each phase, it's time to populate the calendar. Go in order from the least flexible to the most flexible events. Start with your military requirements. Follow that up with family obligations. You have some latitude with how you rack and stack the activities associated with your MTRP Action Plans, so do those last.

This exercise will reveal just how much really happens during your transition and reintegration. You may notice how quickly the white space disappears over a twelve- to eighteen-month time period. This speaks to the inherent difficulty and overall gravity of this process. As you look at all the things you have to do in order to get what you want through your transition and reintegration, you quickly realize that successful execution requires your full attention.

This calendar is just a starting point. As you continue to network, you will refine your MTRP Action Plans. Life also gets a vote that will require you to adjust the calendar. As you gain clarity regarding the different opportunities available, you will likely add activities to position yourself for success. This is a normal part of the process. Plans don't survive crossing the line of departure. This is why leaders should always stay grounded in their overall Statement of Intent.

As the final step in the Identity Analysis process, let's take a look at your Statement of Intent for the life you want to create and the legacy you hope to leave.

2.11 WRITING YOUR STATEMENT OF INTENT

We've arrived at the end of the Identity Analysis portion of the MTRP. In the MDMP, the main outcome of Mission Analysis is the Restated Mission Statement. In the MTRP, the main outcome of Identity Analysis is to write YOUR Statement of Intent for the rest of your life. Take a moment and review how far you've come through the Identity Analysis portion of the MTRP (See **Figure 2.11.1**). You've completed a very deliberate process of self-discovery to resolve the identity crisis that comes from taking off the uniform, and now you're ready to write what happens next in your most authentic identity story.

It's hard to write your legacy. Each of these steps from the Identity Analysis informs your Statement of Intent and how you frame and assess opportunities moving forward to achieve that legacy. You've gone through this difficult process of self-discovery to help you put down on paper your Purpose, Method, and End State for the rest of your life. So, let's begin with the end in mind.

End State: The End State describes the *state of being* at the conclusion of operations. In a military context, the End State includes the status of the enemy (defeated, disrupted, destroyed, etc.), the status of the friendly forces (location, position, strength, etc.), and the condition of the terrain or environment (border established, elections complete, civil order restored, etc.).

As it pertains to the End State for the rest of your life, what we are talking about are those qualities that define *your ideal state of being*. The words you use to describe that state of being will shape and define your legacy. The power in this process is that you get to declare your own End State. Consider the ideal scenario for the rest of your life. If you believe that you have the power to create the future you want, then you are ready to step into this process and define your End State. If not, you may need to revisit **2.5 Limiting and Empowering Beliefs** and **2.7 MTRP Action Plan to Address the Greatest Risk of Military Transition** to identify any internal blocks to articulating your vision.

Figure 2.11.1 Steps and Intended Outcomes of the Identity Analysis Steps 1 through 10

Identity Analysis Step	Outcomes
Define the WHO	Determine Your Values
Understand the Transition Environment	1. Recognize the deep psychological and cultural implications of military transition 2. Call out the FEAR
Setting Intentions	1. Shift from a perspective of fear to a positive perspective of intention 2. Acknowledge what you WANT in life beyond the military
Intrinsic Strengths	Recognize the qualities and attributes that fueled your success as a leader in the military
Limiting and Empowering Beliefs	Challenge your belief system so you can widen the aperture of opportunities available in life beyond the military
Identify the Common Factors	Identify the common themes from conditions and circumstances that allowed you to succeed in the military
MTRP Action Plans to Address the Greatest Risk in Military Transition	Develop your operator's manual for transition and reintegration comprised of Action Plans for each intention (what you WANT) across each of the domains of the Integrative Program of Transition
Determine Family Information Requirements	1. Recognize the impact of military transition on the entire family 2. Establish a process for direct and active communication within the family through the transition process
Build Your Networking Strategy	1. Create a framework to gather and develop information for emerging opportunities 2. Address possible blind spots in understanding opportunities through the transition process
Develop the Transition and Reintegration Timeline	Develop a schedule for developing and executing your transition

Here are some important questions to consider as you craft your End State:

1. How do your values shape how you want to be remembered?

2. What words would you want to use to describe your enduring impact?

3. How do your intentions—what you WANT—frame the long-term objectives for your life?

4. What do your Intrinsic Strengths suggest about your potential impact?

5. If you were to see your Empowering Beliefs to their conclusion, what would the world look like?

6. What have you learned about how recurring themes for success throughout your career might foreshadow the enduring impact you will have from your legacy?

Method: When we talk about the method in the context of military orders, these are the key tasks that are deemed essential to achieve the desired End State. There is a direct correlation between accomplishing the key tasks and accomplishing End State. In other words, if the unit fails to achieve any of the key tasks, then the unit will fail to achieve the End State. Your Statement of Intent for the rest of your life is more aspirational, and the stakes are higher. We have but one life to live, so think about those key tasks to achieve everything you WANT in life.

When it comes to the Method, focus on your intentions. Reference **Exercise 2.3. Shifting Intentions from FEAR to WANT** and consider what it will take to shape the path that achieves your End State. Consider the different factors from the Integrative Program of Transition, but recognize that there is no universal template to identify your key tasks. Your journey is personal and unique.

Purpose: We have come full circle back to **Step 1. Discover Your Purpose** of the MTRP. You've completed the Identity Analysis to recognize and understand your WHY. Values inform your impact. When you consider your intrinsic strengths, consider the reasons why these qualities and attributes continued to show up throughout your career. Consider the themes behind your previous success and consider what that tells you about your potential and future impact.

Your purpose—the definitive statement of WHY—resides at the core of everything you have done and everything you intend to do. When you do things that align with your purpose, you feel inspired, empowered, and that sense of connection and importance in what you do. Even when the nation sends you to dangerous places to do difficult things, you go willingly because those activities are an expression of your purpose. Even difficult tasks feel right when they align with your purpose.

When you deviate from that glideslope, you feel that too. In your lifetime, you may attain great wealth. You may achieve tremendous stature. You may, in the eyes of people around you, appear to have everything and still feel like you have nothing at the same time. Regardless of the things you do, you will always feel the pull of that intrinsic energy that commands you to live on purpose. You will always come back to your WHY.

EXERCISE 2.11.1 WRITING YOUR COMMANDER'S INTENT

Let's write your Statement of Intent through a four-step process:

STEP 1. DEFINING YOUR END STATE

This exercise draws on every activity and portion of the MTRP that you have completed up to this point. You can define the End State by the different aspects of your life: Mission, Community, Family, Self.

Mission: When you consider your mission—your WHY—what words best describe your professional impact? How have you changed the world for the better? How have you made a difference?

Community: When you consider your friends, peers, colleagues, neighbors, and associates from throughout your life, what do you want to be remembered for? What is the memory you want to leave people with?

Family: What are the enduring themes you want to leave for the growth and prosperity of your family?

Self: What words define your ideal state of being? How do you become the best example you want to set for the rest of society?

Breaking down the End State by these different categories is just one way of completing this exercise. Use an approach that has meaning for you. Use the method that best establishes your destination for transition, reintegration, and beyond. The End State should connect everything that has happened up to this point in your life to that distant point on the horizon for everything that happens next.

Writing Your End State - Begin With the End in Mind. Describe how you want to define your impact or legacy	
Word(s)	Definition
	End State Regarding Your MISSION
	End State Regarding Your COMMUNITY
	End State Regarding Your FAMILY
	End State Regarding Your SELF

STEP 2. DETERMINE THE METHOD

The approach for determining those key tasks to achieve End State is based on what you WANT. The key is to identify those intentions that will help you realize your End State. A potential starting point is your WANT statements from the Integrative Program of Transition (**Step 2.3. Setting Intentions**). Another approach to the Method might involve your values, intrinsic strengths, and/or belief statements. This is your path—the HOW—to connect your Purpose (the WHY) to your End State (the WHAT). Use whatever format works to capture the most essential tasks.

Method: These are the essential tasks (the HOW) I will achieve my END STATE
Key Tasks

STEP 3. REWRITE YOUR PURPOSE STATEMENT

Since completing your first draft of a Purpose Statement (**Exercise 1.3. Writing a Purpose Statement—First Attempt**), you've undergone a deliberate process of Identity Analysis as part of the MTRP. Based on what you've discovered about yourself through this handbook, it is time to rewrite your unique Purpose Statement that is authentic, all encompassing, and emotive.

UPDATED Purpose Statement	
ACTION	**IMPACT**

STEP 4. PUTTING TOGETHER YOUR STATEMENT OF INTENT

Let's put it all together. Let's see what it looks like from beginning to end. As you complete this final step, consider what resonates with you most regarding your Statement of Intent. How does this statement reflect everything you've learned through the Identity Analysis as the embodiment of your true Purpose, Method, and End State?

Now that you've defined what success looks like, let's consider how this Statement of Intent might shape your transition and job search process. Now that you know who you want to be, you're ready to figure out what you might want to do.

MY STATEMENT OF INTENT

I, _____, assert the following **STATEMENT OF INTENT** for the life I want to create and the legacy I hope to leave:

PURPOSE - (the WHY)

METHOD - (the HOW)

END STATE (the WHAT)

OPPORTUNITY DEVELOPMENT

After analyzing the problem, it's time to come up with potential solutions. You remember this as Course of Action Development in the Operations Process of the MDMP. In the MTRP, it is called Opportunity Development, and the solution you are looking for is the one that allows you to realize your purpose, achieve your intent, and attain self-actualization in a meaningful life beyond the military.

This step of the MTRP frames your choices from the perspective of opportunities, not jobs. These are the potential paths you were initially exposed to in **Exercise 2.9.1. Developing Your Network Collection Plan**. Those six opportunities are as follows:

- Entrepreneurship

- Franchising

- Civil Service

- Nonprofit Employment

- Small Business

- Large Corporation

Entrepreneurship and Franchising are opportunities for you to become your own boss. These are **self-employment** options where you own the business. Civil Service includes employment in the **public** or **government sector**. Obviously, nonprofit employment describes employment opportunities in the **nonprofit sector**. The final two options, Small Business and Large Corporation, comprise **private sector** employment options. The Opportunity Development step of the MTRP provides a detailed approach to guide your research and challenge you to explore each career option with an open mind, curiosity, and optimism.

Each sector and employment option has its own distinctive benefits as well as some important considerations for success. The purpose of Step 3 is to explore the background, benefits, and challenges across multiple sectors and employment options. This step will require a combination of individual research and conversations with connections or mentors in your network. As you explore these opportunities, frame each option as if it was the only line of effort to realize your intentions for life beyond the military. In other words, treat each line of effort independently and as if no other options were available. Assume that you will execute each opportunity because you just might. By giving each opportunity the same level of attention, you open your mind to the possibility that the best option might be something you had never considered before.

3.1 ENTREPRENEURSHIP

BACKGROUND

An entrepreneur is someone who creates a business solution to address a problem or unfulfilled need in society.[48] Less than 5 percent of the current generation of veterans has launched a startup business—the lowest percentage for veterans of any wartime era.[49] After World War II, almost 50 percent of returning combat veterans started their own business, and again after the Korean War, nearly 40 percent of veterans returned from overseas to become business owners.[50] Much of the economic prosperity of the 1950s was generated by the ingenuity, courage, and fortitude of military leaders who became business leaders across society. The numbers suggest that today's veterans don't have the same entrepreneurial spirit to create their own opportunity by launching their own business.

DISTINCTIVE BENEFITS OF BECOMING AN ENTREPRENEUR

You Create Your Own Opportunity. Do what inspires you. Do what you love. Because you create your own opportunity, you can build a business that honors your values, aligns with your purpose, and capitalizes on your strengths. Creating your own opportunity is the most effective way to ensure that the path you take is one that best recognizes your authentic

---

48. Paula Fernandes, "What It Means to Be an Entrepreneur," *Business News Daily*, May 15, 2019, https://www.businessnewsdaily.com/7275-entrepreneurship-defined.html.
49. Weisel, "Where Are All."
50. Ibid.

identity story beyond the military. Furthermore, you get to leverage the full scope of your leadership and problem-solving abilities as an entrepreneur.

Personal and Professional Freedom. As your own boss, you have the greatest control over the vision, operations, and strategic direction of the business. While it's true that entrepreneurs work hard, you set your own schedule. You answer to no one other than yourself. You get to determine the priorities. You have the freedom to run the business where you want, when you want, and how you want.

The Stretch Opportunity for a Greater Reward. Entrepreneurship comes with risk, but it also comes with the prospect of a higher reward over the long term. The learning and personal development that comes with entrepreneurship positions you for continued success throughout the course of your professional life. Professionals with experience as entrepreneurs earn more than salaried employees over the course of a lifetime.[51] The return on your personal investment comes from the learning, experimentation, self-awareness, and professional growth from the startup experience.

IMPORTANT CONSIDERATIONS FOR SUCCESS

Business Acumen. Successful entrepreneurs require some skill and basic knowledge in the fields of marketing, sales, operations, and financing. If you don't have this knowledge, you need to be willing to learn it through your own self-development or with the assistance of a trusted mentor, partner, or business consultant. Having a great idea for a product or service isn't enough. You have to be able to bring that offering to your intended audience and successfully communicate its value to generate sales. You have to become familiar with business functions such as accounting, human resources, tax structure, and corporate governance. You have to recognize the difference between revenue and profit as well as the costs and benefits of different sources of capital for establishing or growing a business.

There are several strategies for aspiring entrepreneurs to develop their business acumen. First, you can go back to school to obtain a degree in business. This is perhaps the most thorough and also the most time-consuming approach. Second, you can leverage the many vetrepreneur workshops, resources, and organizations designed to communicate best practices, lessons learned, and available resources for starting your own business (See **Table 2.9.1. Definitions and Resources for Networking Across Different Business Entities**). Finally, you can reach out to a mentor to help guide you through the challenges of creating, funding, and running your own business.

---

51. Gustavo Manso, "Experimentation and the Returns to Entrepreneurship," (working paper, Haas School of Business, University of California at Berkeley, March 25, 2016), 19, https://dx.doi.org/10.2139/ssrn.2527034.

Alternative Sources of Income. The reason why fewer veterans embark upon the life of an entrepreneur is because other employment alternatives offer greater financial security in the short term. As an entrepreneur, you have to generate sales in order to draw a salary from your business. During the first ten-year period of the startup, entrepreneurs tend to make up to 35 percent less than they would have otherwise made in salaried jobs.[52] Working for someone else comes with a guaranteed paycheck. If you feel that fire to create your own business, the question you have to ask yourself is whether or not the opportunity cost of that 35 percent investment in the short term is worth the greater freedom and income potential over the long term.

Given the changes to your take-home pay after separation or retirement, you will likely need a supplemental source of income to sustain your family's quality of life. A spouse returning to work is one option. Withdrawing funds from your retirement or savings is another. The chance to step into something personally fulfilling for the second half of your life might be a worthwhile use of your savings. You could also find employment while developing a business concurrently, albeit at a slower pace than if you fully committed to the startup. If becoming an entrepreneur is the greatest opportunity for you to achieve your intent for life beyond the military, be open to different and creative paths to pursue your dream.

As a military leader, you have the most essential qualities necessary to succeed as an entrepreneur. Those qualities include self-discipline, integrity, persistence, a clear sense of direction, and decisiveness.[53] Sound familiar? Entrepreneurs take the leap of faith to create something from nothing because they believe that they can change the world. You already have the problem-solving and leadership necessary to succeed as an entrepreneur, but you have to decide whether or not you also have the passion and commitment to bring a business idea to life.

---

52. Noam Wasserman, *The Founder, S Dilemmas: Anticipating and Avoiding the Pitfalls That Can Sink a Startup* (Princeton: Princeton University Press, 2012), 18.
53. Brian Tracy, "5 Qualities Of Successful Entrepreneurs," *Entrepreneur*, October 05, 2016, https://www.entrepreneur.com /article/282962.

EXERCISE 3.1 IMAGINING YOUR OWN OPPORTUNITY

The purpose of this exercise is to imagine what kind of business you would create if you became an entrepreneur. For this exercise, imagine that you had no constraints or restrictions. You will have the chance to analyze and compare different options in later steps of the MTRP. For now, imagine what you would be doing if you were acting as your own boss, pursuing your true passion, and impacting society while at the same time earning a living.

Consider this a brainstorming session to identify the kinds of business ideas that really connect with your values, purpose, and strengths. What problem do you want your business to solve? How do you want to serve your community? Come up with three to five ideas about what you would want to do if money, time, and resources were not an issue. Consider the following example:

My Business Startup Ideas	
1	Professional coaching and consulting business that focused on the market of military leaders and veteran leaders in society. It would serve military retirees (nobody is focusing on this population of leaders at this time). I could leverage my experience in the military and education to help businesses optimize leadership of their veteran workforce.
2	Become a writer. Tell stories that combine story and human behavior to help leaders learn in a more impactful way.
3	A beachside restaurant and bar. Targeting middle aged clientele with a specialty menu. Inside portion would be open year-round and would cater to fine seafood dining. Too much of the beach scene caters to younger audiences – I want to create something for professionals to come together with live music, outdoor events, concerts, and activities that support the community. Be a place where 'everybody knows your name' at the beach.

Now, it's your turn. Use the space below to list some preliminary business startup ideas:

My Business Startup Ideas	
1	
2	
3	

In order to give you some idea of what it takes to develop a business plan, pick one idea from the above list that resonates with you the most. When you are ready to start building a plan, use the resources provided by the Small Business Administration (https://www.sba.gov/tools/business-plan/1). For now, consider how you might answer some of these conceptual questions that would inform the business plan:

BUSINESS PLAN CONCEPT QUESTIONS

ABOUT THE IDEA

What is the mission of the company?

What is the need you are addressing or value you are providing to society?

What makes your idea different from what is already out there?

ABOUT THE COMPANY OFFERING

How would you generate revenue? Who would you do business with (government, customers, other businesses, etc.)?

What is your value proposition, or why would people want to buy from you?

How much will it cost to get started and what are your potential sources of funding?

ABOUT THE MARKET

How would you describe your market (be as specific as possible)?

Given your description, how large is your potential market?

Where is your market located and how will you connect with them?

What advantage do you have over the competition?

ABOUT YOUR BUSINESS STRUCTURE

How would you envision the structure of your organization (nonprofit, corporation, self-employed, etc.)?

How many people are needed to get this enterprise started?

STATEMENT ABOUT POTENTIAL

Assuming you succeed, what does winning look like in 5 years?

Entrepreneurship is chasing a dream—more specifically, YOUR dream. Imagine what it would be like to create something that changes the world. That is the potential this opportunity offers you for the second half of your life.

3.2 FRANCHISING

BACKGROUND

A *franchisor* is a person or company who provides a license to a third party—or *franchisee*—for the purpose of conducting business under their name. The franchisor allows the franchisee to use the trademark and rights to products and services to operate a business in designated locations. According to the International Franchise Association, one of every seven franchises in America is owned by a veteran.[54] Franchise opportunities exist in "automotive, business services, commercial and residential services, lodging, personal services, quick service restaurants, real estate, retail food, retail products and services and table/full-service restaurants."[55] There is a good chance that many of the recognizable brands in your local community are franchises owned and operated by local business owners.

DISTINCTIVE BENEFITS OF OWNING A FRANCHISE

Franchise Leadership is Like Taking Command. In many ways, taking on a franchise is analogous to taking command of a platoon, company, battalion, or even a brigade. Like a military unit, the structure, mission, and function of the business are defined. Your job as the commander—or franchisee—is to create a successful enterprise in a specific location. Your job is to lead the workforce and improve the organization to achieve the mission of the business. Leaders who enjoy finding innovative solutions to structured problems with much of the autonomy they enjoyed as leaders in the military should seriously consider opportunities in franchise management.

Established Brand and Market. As a franchise owner, you work with an established product or service. If you want to be your own boss but don't want to launch a business from scratch, then the solution might be one that comes prepackaged with national brand recognition, advertising, and a pre-existing corporate strategy. Your future customers already know what you offer. Your job is to manage and lead the business (administration, labor, production, compliance, etc.) to achieve profitability in a location where, more than likely, a market already exists.

No Business Experience Necessary. Your ability to improvise, adapt, and overcome provide the means to succeed as a franchisee. Industry knowledge is not required. Business experience is not necessary. Furthermore, your success is integral to the success of the franchise model. In other words, your franchisor wants you to succeed. They want you to win. Many

54. Kimber Green, "Tips for Veterans Who Want to Be Franchise Owners," *US Veterans and Military Magazine*, May 11, 2018, https://www.usveteransmagazine.com/2018/05/tips-veterans-want-franchise-owners/.
55. Gordon Tredgold, "7 Things You Need to Know Before Becoming a Franchise Owner," *Entrepreneur*, November 22, 2017, https://www.entrepreneur.com/article/305010.

franchisors are willing to provide the training, education, mentors, and management support to help you achieve and sustain profitability. After all, the more profitable *you* are, the more profitable *they* are. What they want from you are the very things you are more than capable of providing: leadership, adaptability, and the ability to find creative solutions to complex problems.

IMPORTANT CONSIDERATIONS FOR SUCCESS

Startup Costs. Because franchisors own the product and the brand, they want potential business owners to have some skin in the game. Depending on the type of business, the startup costs for owning a franchise can range between $20,000 and $50,000.[56] These costs may cover licensing fees, training, and operating capital. Every franchise is different, and given the complexity of franchising agreements, you may consider making an additional investment to retain an attorney who specializes in franchise agreements before you enter into a contract.

Corporate and Brand Dependency. When you operate a franchise, you remain tethered to a corporate headquarters. Some franchise agreements may offer little room for creativity, ongoing royalty fees, and other restrictions and contractual obligations.[57] As a franchisee, you enter into a relationship with a corporate entity that ultimately has the final say in most of the strategic and many of the operational decisions that impact the business.

When you own a franchise, you also own the brand, which includes the good, the bad, and the ugly of everything that happens to that brand. You are not immune to national and even global public relations missteps and marketing challenges. For example, the double-digit decline in sales and expansion for Subway Foods from 2013 to 2017 was a result of public backlash from a foot-long sandwich that was actually only eleven inches long, coupled with the sexual assault scandal involving Jared Fogel, the international face of the company.[58] You don't have to control the size of the sandwich or know Jared personally to feel the consequences of these challenges to your bottom line.

EXERCISE 3.2 EXPLORING POTENTIAL FRANCHISE OPPORTUNITIES

When searching for the ideal unit to work for in the military, you research different organizations for an attractive mission, strong reputation for success, and proven leadership. The same follows when you explore potential opportunities in franchise management. Here

56. Don Daszkowski, "The Common Franchise Costs for Opening a New Location," *The Balance Small Business*, January 28, 2019, https://www.thebalancesmb.com/how-much-does-a-franchise-cost-1350463.

57. Jared Hecht, "The Pros And Cons Of Buying A Franchise," *Forbes*, February 27, 2019, https://www.forbes.com/sites/jaredhecht/2019/02/27/the-pros-and-cons-of-buying-a-franchise/#24f205311984

58. Josh Kosman, "Subway Scrambles to Understand Plunge in Sales," Business, *New York Post*, October 23, 2017, https://nypost.com/2017/10/22/subway-scrambles-to-understand-plunge-in-sales/.

are some suggestions to help you discover the goodness of fit when it comes to owning a franchise:

1. **Start with Products and Services You Use.** Go with what you know. You have to be comfortable and familiar with what you are selling. If you use the product or service on a regular basis, you will be more genuine and convincing when trying to sell that product or service. For example, if you don't eat fast food, then running a fast food franchise probably isn't for you. If you are an avid coffee drinker, then you might consider the potential of operating a coffee franchise.

2. **Investigate the Leadership and Values of the Corporate Headquarters.** Evaluate how well your values align with the shared values of the corporation. Understand what the founders and current leaders believe. Study the leadership and management philosophy of the organization and compare that with your own values, purpose, and Statement of Intent. Some franchise organizations are particularly active in various social and political spheres, so you want to ensure that these endeavors don't conflict with your established values or set of beliefs.

3. **Explore the Market Projections for Your Desired Location.** Understand how the business has performed during upward and downward trends in the economy. If the business represents a growing cultural trend, it might be worth looking into. If you identify a location where the population or market demographic is shrinking, you might want to consider an alternate location or a different franchise opportunity. Even though franchise opportunities come with a developed marketing strategy, it is still incumbent on you to ensure that the market exists in your desired location.

As you begin to explore franchise opportunities, leverage the resources available to veterans and spouses. The Small Business Administration has veteran-specific resources through the Office of Veteran Business Development and the Veterans Business Outreach Centers (www.sba.gov/offices/headquarters/ovbd/). Founded in 1991, VetFran (www.vetfran.com) is an organization whose mission is to connect veterans with franchising business ownership opportunities.[59] As it pertains to the initial capital investment necessary to purchase a franchise, many franchisors and lenders offer special incentives and rates for a veteran seeking to become a franchisee. Do the research to find the right opportunity for you. There are plenty of resources to help veterans determine whether or not owning a franchise offers the best opportunity in life beyond the military.

---

59. "About Us," *VetFran*, accessed July 21, 2019, https://www.vetfran.org/about-us/.

Complete the following steps as part of an initial search for potential franchising opportunities:

Step 1. Conduct an initial search for franchise opportunities on the International Franchise Association website (https://www.franchise.org/franchise-opportunities). As you narrow your search, reach out to your chamber of commerce and local business resources to determine whether or not your chosen community is an ideal location for that particular business.

Step 2. Conduct a deeper search of the company through their corporate website. Assess whether or not the values and mission of the company align with your mission and values. Furthermore, capture any issues regarding a possible agreement with that corporation. Some of these questions or factors could be related to profit sharing, licensing fees, startup costs, new construction, expansion, employment considerations, etc.

Step 3. Based on what you captured in **Step 2**, add the questions and concerns to your Networking Collection Plan. The company can probably connect you with a business owner to talk about owning a franchise. It is in their interests to find the right people to own and operate their franchise. Other franchise owners for the company act like sister units in the military: through strong relationships, you can build mechanisms for mutual support to achieve success.

Explore up to three franchise opportunities using the templates provided on the ensuing pages. Include the business name, industry, location, mission, and values of the corporate headquarters. As you conduct your research (Step 1 through 3 above), use the space provided to capture your questions or concerns and add those details to your Networking Collection Plan. Use the bottom of the page for any important insights or notes regarding the franchise opportunity.

Potential Franchise Opportunity Number One

Business Name / Industry / Location	Mission	Values

Specific Questions or Concerns Regarding this Particular Franchise (Input into the Collection Plan)
QUESTION OR CONCERN #1
QUESTION OR CONCERN #2
QUESTION OR CONCERN #3
QUESTION OR CONCERN #4

Notes and Comments about Franchise Opportunity

Potential Franchise Opportunity Number Two

Business Name / Industry / Location	Mission	Values

Specific Questions or Concerns Regarding this Particular Franchise (Input into the Collection Plan)

QUESTION OR CONCERN #1

QUESTION OR CONCERN #2

QUESTION OR CONCERN #3

QUESTION OR CONCERN #4

Notes and Comments about Franchise Opportunity

Potential Franchise Opportunity Number Three

Business Name / Industry / Location	Mission	Values

Specific Questions or Concerns Regarding this Particular Franchise (Input into the Collection Plan)

QUESTION OR CONCERN #1

QUESTION OR CONCERN #2

QUESTION OR CONCERN #3

QUESTION OR CONCERN #4

Notes and Comments about Franchise Opportunity

3.3 CIVIL SERVICE

BACKGROUND

Civil Service describes employment opportunities in the public sector, otherwise known as working for the government. Civil service, particularly at the federal level, has been a relatively safe landing place for veterans who represent nearly one-third of the total federal workforce.[60] However, it is important to recognize that civil service opportunities are not limited to federal employment. They also include opportunities at the state and local level. Civil service employees are compensated through public funding in the form of taxes, and therefore, they are accountable to elected officials in the administration and performance of their duties. Civil service opportunities span the entire spectrum of functions for a civilized society: labor, space exploration, scientific research, conservation, business and commerce, international relations, domestic relations, policy, education, defense, intelligence, infrastructure, health, housing, transportation, communication, law, ethics, environment, and human services are some of the publicly funded functions at the local, state, and federal level.

DISTINCTIVE BENEFITS OF CIVIL SERVICE EMPLOYMENT

Direct Application of Training, Skills, and Experience. Chances are that your military operating specialty has direct application to a commensurate position in the civil service. Security clearance and other forms of military training and experience make transitioning service members ideal candidates for many employment opportunities in the public sector—especially at the federal level. For many government agencies, you can find job descriptions that match your position and duty description from the military. You can find government job opportunities at the USAJOBS website (https://www.usajobs.gov). As you transition from military service into the civil service, you can continue to do many of the activities and functions you did in the military without having to wear the uniform.

Compensation and Benefits. Government jobs pay well. Few employers can match the healthcare, vacation, and retirement benefits of the military or civil service. Few civilian opportunities will offer scheduled raises and up to thirty days of paid time off a year. When it comes to retirement, the Civil Service Retirement System (CSRS) and Federal Employees Retirement System (FERS) have special provisions for increasing your retirement pay based on your years of military service. You may have to buy into these programs to combine your retirement, but the future annuity payments may prove to be a worthwhile investment. To determine how your military service contributes to your civil service retirement, you will want to consult with a human resources specialist from the prospective government agency (for more information go to https://www.fedshirevets.gov/veterans-council/agency-directory/).

---

60. "OPM Releases Veteran Employment Data," U.S. Office of Personnel Management, September 12, 2017, accessed May 28, 2019, https://www.opm.gov/news/releases/2017/09/opm-releases-veteran-employment-data/.

Ease of Cultural Assimilation. You may answer the call to service in the public sector in the same way you answered the call to service in the military. As a civil servant, you continue to serve the public welfare through a mission that resonates with your values and purpose in the same way the military did. Particularly at the federal level, civil service has many of the same protocols and workplace requirements of the military. These similarities, combined with the preponderance of veterans who comprise the workforce, would ease your assimilation into a new organizational culture. You can serve the public welfare in a mission that aligns with your purpose in a manner that requires minimal adjustment to a culture outside the military.

IMPORTANT CONSIDERATIONS FOR SUCCESS

Overcoming Bureaucracy. If you didn't enjoy the constraints of bureaucracy in the military, you won't find much relief in the civil service. The public sector is accountable to the taxpayer. Rules and regulations do exist, and they govern what and how business is done. Lasting change is possible, but it will likely require more time (a lot more time) than it would otherwise in the nonprofit or private sectors. Great ideas must be funneled through the systems and processes for implementation that could be very frustrating to the ambitious leader who craves autonomy, wants to implement creative innovations, or wishes to witness the direct impact of his or her actions.

Change is slow in the bureaucracy, and so, too, is the potential for career advancement. Just as in the military, tenure matters. Pay is standardized and somewhat stagnant depending on the political climate. Your prior service will likely give you a bump regarding your government service (GS) pay grade at the federal level, but you may lack the agency-specific experience to be competitive for emerging or more exciting opportunities. Your clock resets when you join the civil service, and you still have to put in your time.

Be aware of the conditions and restrictions that may apply to your employment in the public sector. When you are on transition leave, you are still technically a part of the military. There are restrictions to how you can represent other agencies while still a member of the active duty force. For Department of Defense positions, military retirees may incur a six-month mandatory waiting period prior to employment.[61] Do your research to understand how the rules and limitations apply to potential civil service opportunities.

Politics Matter. Military officers are different from appointed officials in the public sector. Appointed officials typically share the politics of and allegiance to an elected official. Their job is to develop the policy and enact the priorities that are consistent with the elected official's platform and initiatives. Military leaders are further removed from the particulars of policy initiatives.

---

61. "After You Go: Temporary Employment Restrictions," *Military.com*, accessed May 29, 2019, https://www.military.com/military -transition/employment-and-career-planning/employment-restrictions.html.

With the exception of routine functions or administrative jobs, your responsibilities could change drastically with the passing of political leadership from one elected official or party to another. You could get new leadership (including a new boss), new priorities based on changing agendas, and different levels of funding depending on budget constraints and funding priorities. You may have to relocate to a different department or assignment based on shifting agendas. Day-to-day operations could change almost overnight with the changing of the guard in political leadership.

EXERCISE 3.3 EXPLORING CIVIL SERVICE OPPORTUNITIES

The purpose of this exercise is to guide your research of potential civil service opportunities.

Name of the Organization or Agency: Self-Explanatory

Mission Statement: You want to understand the overall mission of the agency and also the mission for your targeted department or directorate within that agency (if known). Consider how your Purpose Statement aligns to the mission of the department or agency as a whole.

Organizational Values: Understand the core values of the agency in order to assess whether or not your personal values align with the agency's values.

Leader's Vision: The vision and direction of the agency or department is dependent on the vision and direction of the politically appointed leader in that position. In the military, the Secretary of Defense provides the overall guidance and strategy for operations and governance of each branch of service. Likewise, you will want to know the policy vision and direction that the appointed leader (or the elected official) has for the agency to determine whether or not that vision aligns with your vision.

Accomplishments: Coming from the military, you are used to being on a team with a strong reputation of success. If you are action oriented and want to see the impact of your work, research and understand the notable accomplishments from the past year for agencies you are interested in. If their performance record doesn't excite you, then consider how you can change that for the better or consider alternative agencies for employment.

Focus and Objectives: Every agency has strategic priorities and annual objectives. Take a look at the strategic focus and objectives for your agency or department. This will likely reveal the types of work you will be doing so that you can make an informed assessment of how you might spend your time as an employee of that agency.

Significant Challenges: Because the public sector is accountable to the taxpayer, any scandal or problems concerning productivity, operations, or culture become public problems. Research the criticism and negative press about the agency so that you understand what you are getting yourself into. Be fully aware of any public hearings involving possible governance or leadership issues.

Civil Service Opportunity Number One

NAME OF THE AGENCY	
MISSION STATEMENT:	
ORGANIZATIONAL VALUES:	
LEADER'S VISION:	
ACCOMPLISHMENTS:	
FOCUS AND OBJECTIVES:	
SIGNIFICANT CHALLENGES:	

Civil Service Opportunity Number Two

NAME OF THE AGENCY	

MISSION STATEMENT:

ORGANIZATIONAL VALUES:

LEADER'S VISION:

ACCOMPLISHMENTS:

FOCUS AND OBJECTIVES:

SIGNIFICANT CHALLENGES:

Civil Service Opportunity Number Three

NAME OF THE AGENCY	

MISSION STATEMENT:

ORGANIZATIONAL VALUES:

LEADER'S VISION:

ACCOMPLISHMENTS:

FOCUS AND OBJECTIVES:

SIGNIFICANT CHALLENGES:

3.4 NONPROFIT ORGANIZATIONS

BACKGROUND

Nonprofit organizations are tax-exempt entities under the 501(c)(3) designation from the Internal Revenue Service. Nonprofit organizations form a third sector of the economy apart from government (public) and for-profit (private) sectors as "an expression of private action for public good."[62] According to the National Council for Nonprofits, the 501(c)(3) offers income tax deductions for charitable donations over a wide variety of programs and services that include culture and humanities, education, animals, environment, human services, healthcare, international and foreign relations, programs for public or social welfare, and religion.[63] In 2015 alone, more than 1.5 million nonprofit organizations contributed almost $1 trillion to the US economy.[64] Between 2007 and 2016, nonprofits accounted for one in every ten jobs in the United States.[65] More importantly, the growth of nonprofit employment opportunities over that time was 16.7 percent—outpacing private sector job growth by almost four to one.[66]

DISTINCTIVE BENEFITS OF WORKING FOR A NONPROFIT

Direct Line between Personal Passion and Social Impact. By definition, nonprofit organizations exist to serve and improve society. Their objective is to achieve social impact—not profitability. Finding a nonprofit organization whose mission aligns with your passion and purpose provides a platform for you to continue a life of service to society. Under ideal conditions, nonprofit organizations harness the energy, ingenuity, and creativity of individuals and teams to discover enduring solutions to social problems without the bureaucracy or politics that encumber public institutions or the allure of profitability that distracts private companies.

Responsibility and Autonomy. Nonprofits typically offer leaders high levels of responsibility and autonomy. Most nonprofits don't have the revenue to sustain the payroll for a deep staff. Their success depends on your ingenuity and initiative. As a leader in a nonprofit organization, you become the shepherd for the cutting-edge solutions, new perspectives, and alternative approaches to conventional problems consistent with the mission of the organi-

---

62. Darian Rodriguez Heyman, *Nonprofit Management 101: A Complete and Practical Guide for Leaders and Professionals* (John Wiley & Sons, 2011), 6.
63. "What is a 'Nonprofit'?"
64. Brice McKeever, "The Nonprofit Sector in Brief 2018," *National Center for Charitable Statistics*, December 13, 2018, https://nccs .urban.org/publication/nonprofit-sector-brief-2018#highlights.
65. Lester M. Salamon and Chelsea L. Newhouse, *The 2019 Nonprofit Employment Report* (John Hopkins University: Center for Civil Society Studies, 2019), 3, http://ccss.jhu.edu/wp-content/uploads/downloads/2019/01/2019-NP-Employment-Report _FINAL_1.8.2019.pdf.
66. Ibid.,11.

zation. Many of the solutions for the more persistent problems across our society were first addressed through the nonprofit sector. Nonprofits put outside-the-box thinking into action.

Next Level Leadership Challenge. Most nonprofit organizations require active involvement from a combination of stakeholders that includes philanthropists, board members, volunteers, public institutions, private businesses, other nonprofit organizations, and the community at large. Not all of these stakeholders are on the same page. Getting everyone aligned and behind the cause presents a unique leadership challenge—one ideally suited for military leaders. Success requires all the best attributes of transformational leadership to include passion, charisma, exceptional communication skills, and, above all else, patience. Your ability to manage relationships and inspire cross-functional teams has prepared you for the leadership challenge of the nonprofit sector.

IMPORTANT CONSIDERATIONS FOR SUCCESS

Overworked and Undercompensated. Donors expect that most, if not all, of their contributions go directly to the mission of the nonprofit. Although this isn't practical, there is a natural downward pressure on salaries for management and administrative staff. In an effort to reduce costs, many nonprofits hesitate to hire the necessary administrative and support staff to keep the business running efficiently. Because the work still needs to be done, it falls to you, a member of your staff, or a volunteer that will probably occupy your time with necessary training and supervision. Many administrative and business functions are distributed among paid staff as additional duties, increasing the workload on the staff. These are some of the reasons why 50 percent of nonprofit employees suffer from burnout.[67]

As a leader in a nonprofit organization, you will wear many hats and operate outside your comfort zone, and chances are you won't be compensated accordingly for your efforts. If you have ambitious financial objectives and lavish intentions about your quality of life when you leave the military, you probably won't get there by working for a nonprofit. As a compensated employee, you will be expected to do more, and you will probably be paid less when compared to a commensurate position of responsibility and authority in the public or private sector. It all comes down to how much the cause is worth to you.

Measuring Impact. Measuring impact is one of the challenges many nonprofits face. It may be difficult for the organization to make the connection between donor investment, operations from that investment, and the intended outcome or social impact. This is particularly true for nonprofits attempting to address complex social issues. Many of the internal metrics used

---

67. Ben Paynter, "5 Ways Nonprofits Struggle (And How To Overcome Them)," *Fast Company*, April 03, 2018, https://www.fastcompany.com/40552662/5-ways-the-nonprofit-industry-is-failing-and-how-overcome-them.

by nonprofits may infer success without direct causality to the broader social objective the organization is trying to achieve. For example, an organization whose mission is to address veteran suicide may publish the number of clients they support, but how does the number of clients supported impact the suicide rate? Correlation is difficult to prove without a substantial investment into a lengthy, detailed study. Organizations may help on a microlevel without creating the change they seek on a macro level.

Proving social impact is imperative because third-party funding depends on it. Most grant applications require data and related analytics as part of the review and approval process. Furthermore, nonprofits can typically only carry two years of cash in reserve to cover expenses.[68] Therefore, fundraising is a continuous and essential function for everyone from board members down to volunteers to keep the project running. Without the ability to show measurable impact for the broader social issue, the organization is put in a precarious position for sustainability. Donors, foundations, and fundraisers want to know the impact of their investment toward the greater cause, or they will simply find a different place for their philanthropy. When it comes to revenue generation, just doing good isn't necessarily good enough.

EXERCISE 3.4 EXPLORING NONPROFIT OPPORTUNITIES

The purpose of this exercise is to increase your understanding of the mission impact, service operations, business operations, and culture for potential leadership opportunities in nonprofit organizations. This exercise will help you determine the credibility of a nonprofit's potential to achieve their mission and desired impact. This exercise will provide a chance to look beneath the surface of that initial infatuation to determine whether or not a particular nonprofit is the right opportunity for your personal and professional fulfillment.

PART 1. MISSION IMPACT

Most nonprofit organizations have ambitious and attractive mission statements. They believe in their cause, and they do a lot in the pursuit of that cause. Effort doesn't necessarily equal impact. For example, an organization may want to end suicide, but how do they measure that? How do they determine that their activities have influenced the social condition or made the desired change? As part of your assessment of nonprofit opportunities, you want to determine whether or not there is a valid, causal relationship between what the organization does, and the impact that organization has on the social issue. Later in the handbook, Dr. Springer shares that trust is a function of the alignment between what we say and what

---

68. "How Much Money Can a Nonprofit Have or Carry over from Year to Year?" *Nonprofit Expert*, July 17, 2017, accessed May 30, 2019, https://www.nonprofitexpert.com/money-carry-over/.

we do. In the same way, we can assess alignment to determine whether it is wise to pursue a potential opportunity in the nonprofit world.

The kinds of metrics that nonprofit organizations use will probably include a combination of quantitative and qualitative metrics. For example, an organization that supports veteran employment should be able to tell you how many veterans were hired as a result of their program, how long it takes to get a veteran hired, the turnover from job placement, etc. That organization will also likely have qualitative metrics in the form of testimonials and client feedback. The combination of these metrics reveals the impact that the organization is having on their intended mission.

PART 2. SERVICE OPERATIONS

There are two components to the operations for a nonprofit organization. The first concerns service delivery. In other words, *what does the nonprofit program actually do and how do those activities impact the mission?* Let's explore how nonprofit operations responsibly and effectively relate to the cause.

How a nonprofit executes its mission is as important as the mission itself. Many nonprofit organizations are born out of passion for a cause, but struggle to develop an effective method for supporting that cause. This is particularly true of nonprofit organizations in the human services industry. For example, an organization that boasts of alternative health treatments may claim that they have a cure, but the individuals making that claim may not be trained or qualified to make such an assessment or medical diagnosis. Lack of trained and qualified personnel to deliver treatments and assess outcomes may infringe upon ethical or legal issues depending on the nature of the services provided. You will want to examine how the organization is accredited, how the people are trained, and whether or not any third-party research exists to validate the effectiveness of the program. Here are some questions you might consider asking nonprofit organizations during your networking process:

1. How is your program accredited?

2. What studies have been done to validate your approach?

3. Where can I find the published data that specifically proves the effectiveness of your program?

4. What qualifies someone to deliver services for your organization?

5. What makes your organization or initiatives unique from other programs or approaches?

6. How do you validate the long-term outcomes of your program?

7. How do you manage quality control?

Strong passion doesn't equal effective execution. Absent a foundation of sound operations with repeatable outcomes, the organization may have plenty of dedicated people, but may not have an approach or process that yields any substantive progress to an enduring social problem.

PART 3. BUSINESS OPERATIONS

Nonprofit organizations are a different business entity, but they are business entities nonetheless. Besides the tax exclusion for 501(c)(3) organizations, the major differences between a nonprofit and for-profit business concern revenue generation and expense reporting. A basic understanding of the business operations is an important consideration to determine whether or not the cause represents a viable opportunity.

Before you assume a leadership role in a nonprofit, you want to understand how the organization funds its operations. The main reason why nonprofit organizations fail is because they run out of money. Revenue generation could include individual donations, events, social media fundraising, campaigns, direct marketing, endowments, private grants, public grants, and sponsorships. The preferred portfolio is a diversified one with multiple, sustainable streams of revenue.

Reliance on a single stream of funding for a majority of revenue could signal an organization at risk to sustain or continue operations. One good year with a powerful campaign doesn't mean the organization can count on that revenue in the future. Remember the ice bucket challenge or the twenty-two push-ups challenge? Those campaigns were successful, but they were also one-hit wonders. Know how much revenue is reasonably assured for the future and the organization's strategies to address any shortfalls. After all, their revenue-generation problems will become your revenue-generation problems should you decide to join their leadership team.

When it comes to expenses, nonprofit organizations report expenditures as Program costs, Management and General Expenses, and Fundraising Expenses on the IRS Form 990.[69]

---

69. Stephen Fishman, JD, "Reporting Nonprofit Operating Expenses," *Nolo*, accessed May 30, 2019, https://www.nolo.com /legal-encyclopedia/reporting-nonprofit-operating-expenses.html.

Program costs involve those activities that further the mission. Management and General Expenses are related to administration and overhead costs. Fundraising costs include the investment that the organization makes to generate more revenue. These are easy numbers to find because they are required entries in the nonprofit's tax returns (even though nonprofits are exempt from paying taxes, they are still required to file annually).

How the organization spends their money reveals the charitable ratios sought by donors before making a contribution. Most donors want 100 percent of their contribution to go toward the mission, and consequently, many organizations market their services using language that suggests "all" of the donations go toward the mission (i.e., the organization claims to put all the money toward the mission with no overhead). These claims are highly unlikely. A sound organization that is running efficiently requires overhead, and recent survey results suggest that nonprofits spend 36.9 cents on the dollar for overhead.[70] Responsible and transparent organizations will have the financials audited by a third party and publish their financial information on their website, so you should be able to review the associated ratios of a prospective nonprofit organization.

PART 4. ORGANIZATIONAL CULTURE

Every nonprofit organization functions differently. You want to know how engaged the board members are with the daily operations and appreciate the diverse expectations of different board members. A nonprofit that relies heavily on volunteers will have a transient and often volatile workforce. It will be harder to maintain quality control absent a thorough program of education and training. A small staff could indicate an organization that is overburdened. High levels of turnover could be an indication of poor leadership, poor administration, or a combination of the two.

Analyzing a nonprofit is imperative before you commit to joining the cause. The challenges that you identify through this analysis may reveal the reason why the organization wants to hire you in the first place, but you want to know that the organization has a feasible approach to their mission with a stable business foundation. Passion is not enough. The objective of this exercise is to determine whether or not the culture, business operations, and service operations have the potential to achieve the impact that would not only satisfy your passion, but do so in a way that allows you to achieve your intent and what you want for life beyond the military.

---

70. Eddie Atkins, "Survey: Charities Should Spend 23% On Overhead," *The Nonprofit Times*, August 15, 2012, https://www.thenonprofittimes.com/npt_articles/survey-charities-should-spend-23-on-overhead/#.

NONPROFIT ORGANIZATION ASSESSMENT	NAME

PART 1. MISSION IMPACT

MISSION STATEMENT	VISION (WHAT DOES SUCCESS LOOK LIKE?)

QUANTITATIVE METRICS (STATS AND NUMBERS)	QUALITATIVE METRICS (TESTIMONIALS & SURVEYS)

COMMENTS AND QUESTIONS REGARDING MISSION IMPACT

PART 2. SERVICE OPERATIONS

What accreditations does the organization have regarding its programs and/or services?

How are the people providing the program or service qualified or trained?

What control measures exist to ensure the quality of service delivery?

What are the facts regarding the effectiveness of this approach?

PART 3. BUSINESS OPERATIONS	CURRENT YEAR	PREVIOUS YEAR
REVENUE	/	/
PROGRAM COSTS/ ADMIN COSTS (RATIO)		
TOP SOURCES OF REVENUE (Choose the top 3 from the following - individual donations, grants, events, sponsorship, campaigns, paid services, public funding, or business partnership)	Number One	Number One
	Number Two	Number Two
	Number Three	Number Three
CONCERNS OR QUESTIONS ABOUT BUSINESS OPERATIONS		

NONPROFIT ORGANIZATION ASSESSMENT

NAME

PART 1. MISSION IMPACT

MISSION STATEMENT	VISION (WHAT DOES SUCCESS LOOK LIKE?)

QUANTITATIVE METRICS (STATS AND NUMBERS)	QUALITATIVE METRICS (TESTIMONIALS & SURVEYS)

COMMENTS AND QUESTIONS REGARDING MISSION IMPACT

PART 2. SERVICE OPERATIONS

What accreditations does the organization have regarding its programs and/or services?

How are the people providing the program or service qualified or trained?

What control measures exist to ensure the quality of service delivery?

What are the facts regarding the effectiveness of this approach?

PART 3. BUSINESS OPERATIONS	CURRENT YEAR	PREVIOUS YEAR
REVENUE	/	/
PROGRAM COSTS/ ADMIN COSTS (RATIO)		
TOP SOURCES OF REVENUE (Choose the top 3 from the following - individual donations, grants, events, sponsorship, campaigns, paid services, public funding, or business partnership)	Number One	Number One
	Number Two	Number Two
	Number Three	Number Three
CONCERNS OR QUESTIONS ABOUT BUSINESS OPERATIONS		

NONPROFIT ORGANIZATION ASSESSMENT	NAME

PART 1. MISSION IMPACT

MISSION STATEMENT	VISION (WHAT DOES SUCCESS LOOK LIKE?)

QUANTITATIVE METRICS (STATS AND NUMBERS)	QUALITATIVE METRICS (TESTIMONIALS & SURVEYS)

COMMENTS AND QUESTIONS REGARDING MISSION IMPACT

PART 2. SERVICE OPERATIONS

What accreditations does the organization have regarding its programs and/or services?

How are the people providing the program or service qualified or trained?

What control measures exist to ensure the quality of service delivery?

What are the facts regarding the effectiveness of this approach?

PART 3. BUSINESS OPERATIONS	CURRENT YEAR	PREVIOUS YEAR
REVENUE	/	/
PROGRAM COSTS/ ADMIN COSTS (RATIO)		
TOP SOURCES OF REVENUE (Choose the top 3 from the following - individual donations, grants, events, sponsorship, campaigns, paid services, public funding, or business partnership)	Number One / Number Two / Number Three	Number One / Number Two / Number Three
CONCERNS OR QUESTIONS ABOUT BUSINESS OPERATIONS		

3.5 SMALL BUSINESS

BACKGROUND

Small business occupies the divide between the fledgling startup and the recognizable Fortune 500 company. Specific definitions for what constitutes a small business vary by industry, but generally speaking, a small business earns an annual revenue under $100 million and has a labor force of fewer than 1,500 employees.[71] Because small businesses employ almost half of the American workforce, this sector represents a significant and important segment of our national economy.[72] Between 2000 and 2017, small businesses created two out of every three new jobs in the labor market.[73] These statistics suggest that there is a greater chance that you will find the right opportunity working in a small business environment as opposed to working for a large corporation.

DISTINCTIVE BENEFITS OF WORKING FOR A SMALL BUSINESS

Connection to Leaders and Meaningful Work. Smaller means more intimate. Leaders of small businesses are more connected with their employees, and employees have greater access to leaders and decision-makers. In a small business, you are not just another number. You will enjoy greater visibility and interaction with your leadership for the work you do. Additionally, the work you do matters more because there are fewer people doing the work. Because there are fewer people, YOU matter more to the senior leadership of the company. Employers look to hire competent people who are inspired to achieve the mission and vision of the business. Chances are that if you believe in the mission of the small business, you will be surrounded by like-minded colleagues who share in your beliefs.

Autonomy and Responsibility for Personal Development. You will typically wear many different hats working in a smaller company. If selected for a leadership position, you will likely be entrusted with a lot of responsibility, and, given the workload, you will also be afforded the autonomy and flexibility to carry out that responsibility. You will also have more exposure to different business functions with more opportunities to find a function that truly resonates with you. When it comes to professional learning and personal development, small business may provide the most challenging and rewarding experience.

Opportunity to Grow with the Company. On the path to become a successful Fortune 500 company, most small businesses go through a cycle of accelerated growth.[74] In order to

71. Flora Richards-Gustafson, "What Determines Small Business vs. Large Business?" Small Business, *The Houston Chronicle*, February 04, 2019, https://smallbusiness.chron.com/determines-small-business-vs-large-business-20302.html.
72. Jared Hecht, "Are Small Businesses Really the Backbone of the Economy?" *Inc.*, December 17, 2014, https://www.inc.com/jared-hecht/are-small-businesses-really-the-backbone-of-the-economy.html.
73. United States, Small Business Administration, *Frequently Asked Questions*, August 2018, 1, https://www.sba.gov/sites/default/files/advocacy/Frequently-Asked-Questions-Small-Business-2018.pdf.
74. "Business Life Cycle," CoVergence Group, accessed May 30, 2019, http://covergencegroup.com/business-life-cycle/.

navigate that turbulent period of transition and transformation, business owners want proven leaders to build out the structure and inspire the expanding workforce toward a common vision. Small companies hire for skills over credentials.[75] Therefore, small business might be best suited for the proven military leader looking for opportunities with significant responsibility. As an added incentive, your responsibilities may grow as the company grows. The right opportunity may have less to do with the products and services of a particular company and more to do with where that company is along the business growth cycle. Companies in periods of rapid growth and expansion may provide an optimal venue to express your full potential and leave your mark as a leader.

IMPORTANT CONSIDERATIONS FOR SUCCESS

Relationships Matter. As an outsider to the business, you will typically need to establish a trusting relationship with the founders, partners, or other senior leaders before you get the keys to their kingdom. These leaders won't have the human resources protocols of large companies, and they will likely rely upon their intuition to find their definition of the right leader to join their growing team. You may be entering the company during a period of growth, but your boss remembers what it was like to struggle through the inception and initial launch of the business. It may be hard for some business owners to release their grip on the business. Trust is essential, and building trust takes time.

Shared experiences and value alignment are important to making the connections and building the relationships essential to create small business leadership opportunities. Delegation and empowerment are essential elements to grow a business. Astute business owners seek to grow their leadership team in a way that addresses gaps in capabilities while offering distinctive skills, diversity in opinion, and alternative perspectives. A prerequisite for any addition to the leadership team is general alignment in values and a strong commitment to the strategic vision. In other words, if your values conflict with those of the owners or you simply don't believe in the vision, you might not be the right addition to that leadership team.

Place Trust in Someone Else's Vision. A great leader doesn't necessarily have a great business plan. Even the most successful CEOs in modern history have stumbled along the way. When a business owner makes a deliberate decision to expand an enterprise, they incur risk. They are taking a chance. Should you join that leadership team (or just the team in general), you also take that chance. You also incur that risk. You place a certain amount of faith in the potential of a vision that is not your own. Just as the senior leadership has to trust you, you have to trust that they have a sound plan for expansion and/or viability for the future.

---

75. "If You Truly Want The Best Career Path, You Should Be Working At Startups and Small Businesses," *Inc.*, May 16, 2017, https://www.inc.com/quora/if-you-truly-want-the-best-career-path-you-should-be-working-at-startups-and-sma.html.

Small businesses are very sensitive to market fluctuations. The first time that I left the military, I joined a large tech company before the bubble burst in 2001. A number of startups and small companies were born out of the momentum of market expansion and digitization during the late 1990s. Because the smaller companies didn't have the cash reserves or equity to absorb the tech market crash in 2001, they were the first to go. Even in the larger companies, there were new employees still coming in through the front door as laid-off workers were shuffling out the back door. The startups in the marketplace disappeared almost overnight. That's how fast and unforgiving the situation was at the time. The impact of market conditions, particularly bad market conditions, is much more pronounced on the small business. Many small businesses are created with a desire to dip into the deep pool of profitability for the next best thing, but you may want to be sure the water in that pool is deep enough before you take that leap.

EXERCISE 3.5 EXPLORING POTENTIAL SMALL BUSINESS EMPLOYMENT OPPORTUNITIES

Consider how you researched your assignment preferences as a leader in the military. The specific mission of the unit mattered. You wanted to know the reputation and leadership credentials of the commander. You probably also looked at the readiness and training plan for the organization. You wanted to know where the unit was in the deployment cycle and more importantly, when the unit was scheduled to deploy again. You did your homework before submitting your assignment wishlist to your human resources manager.

You can use the same approach when considering different small business opportunities. Start with the leadership. The culture of a small business is more intimate. You'll want to know whether or not your values and purpose align to that of the president and other founding members of the organization. As a potential leader in the organization, you'll want to understand the financial standing of the company. Revenue is to small business what readiness is to a military unit. Finally, you will want to know the business plan, it's the equivalent of the annual training guidance and training plan for a military unit. Just like in the military, you want to do your homework before you set your intentions on where you want to go.

When completing this exercise, treat the opportunity to join the leadership team of a small company like you are assuming a command. You want to know the things the unit does well and the things they don't do well. You want to appreciate opportunities for the unit to succeed, and you want to know the risks. Understanding the leadership, financial standing, and business plan are essential to making an informed decision about potential small business opportunities.

This exercise is broken down into three parts:

PART 1. LEADERSHIP INFORMATION

Joining the leadership team of a small business will require hard work. Before you make this commitment in time and effort, ensure that what you believe aligns with what the company believes. Ensure that this opportunity aligns with your values and purpose in a way that supports your intentions for life after the military.

Here is an example of a completed template for **Part 1. Leadership for a Small Business Employment Opportunity** with accompanying instructions:

Small Business Employment Opportunity	Name of Company
	Ordinary Hero Coaching, Inc.

Part 1. Leadership	

Name of Leader(s) Jason Roncoroni, Retired LTC, Former Battalion Commander, MBA, Certified Coach

Leadership Philosophy

In order to make better leaders, make better human beings. Create resilient, adaptive, and dependable leaders with the confidence and competence to anticipate, shape, and win.

Individual Values	Organizational Values
Authenticity: Have the courage and integrity to show up	Reverence: Honor and Respect each individual leader's journey as a gift
Innovation: Challenge the status quo with creativity and ambition	Integrity: Be Truthful in Word and Deed
Passion for Life: Feel Alive in the Moment	Optimism: Positive energy is a force to change the world
Faith: Let Go and Allow	Empowerment: It only takes one person to change the world
Service to Others: Improve Society One Person At a Time	

Organizational Mission

Transform Leaders who Transform the World

Personal Vision

Leaders live their passion, fulfill their purpose, and change the world.

Name of Leader(s): Identify the founder, president, and any senior leader who has been with the organization since its inception.

Leadership Philosophy: What is the overarching philosophy about leadership and management? Most military commanders publish a leadership philosophy to set the tone for their command. Many business leaders won't formally publish their philosophy, but that doesn't mean that one doesn't exist. You want to understand the core beliefs that will guide the direction of the organization to ensure that it aligns with your own leadership philosophy.

Personal Values: Smaller organizations are more intimate. You won't know if your values align with those of your boss unless you know what those values are.

Organizational Values: There should be some separation between individual and organizational values. A small business is an entity in and of itself. Small businesses are like children, they are begotten of the founder, but they grow into unique beings capable of leaving their own mark on the world.

Organizational Mission: This statement is the greater purpose (the WHY) for the organization. It represents the reason why the founders created this business in the first place.

Personal Vision: How does the founder or leader define success? Understanding the leader's vision (or lack thereof) will reveal the impact that the leader wants the business or organization to have in their specific community or across society in general. This will help you determine whether or not you can honor your purpose in working for this company in the same way the military provided a means for you to honor your purpose as a soldier.

PART 2. BUSINESS STATUS REPORT

The military assesses unit readiness through a combination of metrics related to the status of equipment, personnel readiness, and training proficiency. These metrics are combined with a commander's personal assessment based on their intuition, experience, and understanding of the mission. In the military, we call this the unit status report. In the business world, financial data provides the foundation for the business status report.

In order to gain a basic understanding of how the business is doing, you don't need a background in business or an MBA (although both will help). You only need to know how to balance a checkbook and manage your personal finances. Are you operating within a budget, or are you living paycheck to paycheck? How are you investing your earnings for the future? How much debt have you incurred, and how do you manage that debt? If you can answer these basic questions, you can complete a basic business status report.

In **Part 2** of this exercise, you want to include notes, questions, or a combination of the two as it pertains to revenue and revenue trends, investment history, and debt status. This is your assessment on the business status report for the organization.

Here is an example of a completed template for **Part 2. Business Status Report for a Small Business Employment Opportunity** with accompanying instructions:

Part 2. Business Status Report

Revenue and Revenue Trends

First year reported a loss. Second year revenue increased by $30K. Third year has seen revenue increase by almost 200%. Most revenue has come from corporate clients (70 percent in 2018). Company has almost 2 dozen total clients which represents a steady growth

Questions:

How will they maintain that growth?

How have they diversified their marketing between businesses (B2B) and direct customers (B2C)?

What is the possibility of government contracts?

What is the capacity and utilization of the business at this time?

Investment History

Company made substantial investments in employee training, website development, and marketing. These were primarily for establishing the business. Loss and low profit are a function of reinvestment of earnings back into the business, but no significant investments for expansion have been made at this time.

Questions:

What is the 'next' investment for the business?

What is the investment strategy?

What is holding you back from making investments at this time?

Debt Status

Company has no credit card balance and no debt obligations at this time.

Questions:

What is the trigger for taking out a business loan?

What has been keeping you from taking out a loan up to this point?

What was the source of capital to start the business (i.e. where did the money come from?)

What are some of the potential sources of capital for the business?

Revenue and Revenue Trends: The primary metric you want to consider in your business status report is the organization's revenue (i.e., how much money does the company make in sales). Capture the past several years of revenue data for context. Keep in mind that revenue is different from profit. Newer businesses typically incur higher expenditures and investments for expansion and growth. Even though this impacts the company's profit, this is actually a good thing. A company that responsibly invests revenue back into the company is one that is committed to growing.

Investment History: Companies have to spend money to make money. A company unwilling to make an investment may be hiring you to simply maintain the status quo. If that is the case, you have to consider whether or not that strategy aligns with your personal aspirations for growth. Furthermore, understanding how the company invests in its people will reveal how the organization does (or does not) value their people. Recognizing investments in people, future technology, and innovative programs represents a forward-looking mindset for an enterprise that intends to be profitable for the long term. Many founders and organizational leaders speak about their ambition for growth, but the investment history for the company will reveal whether or not those leaders are truly committed to that ambition.

Debt Status: You want to understand how the organization incurs and manages debt. Consider how you view debt on a personal level: If someone spends money irresponsibly, you probably wouldn't hand them your credit card. If a company doesn't effectively manage their debt and other financial obligations, how can you ensure that they will still be able to pay you in the future? If the company relies heavily on debt financing, you want to understand how and when the leaders anticipate fulfilling their financial obligations. Debt without revenue could indicate a high-risk situation for the business and for you as a potential leader in that organization.

As you make your assessment, bear in mind that the leadership may be considering adding you to their team to address some of these issues that impact revenue generation and profitability. As mentioned earlier, a company doesn't have to be profitable to be a good opportunity. A company in the red might benefit from your leadership to bring them into the black. Remember that most small businesses incur a period of loss that precedes higher rates of growth toward expansion and profitability. This could be a springboard for more significant opportunities in the future. This is why understanding the leadership philosophy, values, and vision for the organization are so important.

PART 3. BUSINESS STRATEGY

You want to have some idea of how the business is positioned to succeed moving forward. A common practice to assess the strategic potential of a business is by examining the strengths, weaknesses, opportunities, and threats—or SWOT—analysis:

- *Strengths.* You want to know what the company does well. You want to understand what makes them unique from the competition and recognize the factors that have enabled and contributed to their current success.

- *Weaknesses.* You also want to understand what the organization doesn't do well and what similar organizations in similar markets do better. Keep in mind that one of the reasons a company might be hiring you is to address one or more of these weaknesses. You need to know what the weaknesses are in order to assess whether or not you have the strengths, skills, and experience to address those weaknesses.

- *Opportunities.* Where is the potential to achieve operational and financial success for the company? Every business plan should recognize how the combination of strengths, timing, and market conditions create opportunities for growth and/or profitability.

- *Threats.* Understand the problems, vulnerabilities, and risk. Keep in mind that the company might be looking to hire leaders to help address one or more of the vulnerabilities.

Here is an example of how to complete **Part 3. Business Strategy for a Small Business Employment Opportunity**:

Part 3. Business Strategy	
Strengths	**Weaknesses**
• *Experience: 9 years of c-suite level experience, 30 years of leadership across multiple industries and market sectors* • *Credibility: Senior military leader connecting with other military leaders with a compelling personal story regarding transition* • *Business Acumen: MBA, MS in organizational psychology* • *Credentialed coach: Distinctive from transition advisors and career counselors*	• *Limited marketing: Focused on social media and personal networking* • *No Staff: Impacts capacity, revenue, and the ability to create and nurture new business leads.*
Opportunities	**Threats**
• *Creation of unique and proven programs for transition and executive development* • *Harvard Business Review – Nature of executive development is changing to a more personalized approach.* • *LinkedIn CEO stated that 'soft' skills is the greatest challenge in the workplace* • *Rise of positive psychology to promote personal self-actualization* • *Transition programs are not tailored to senior military or retirees – transform the space by becoming the example*	• *Competitors branding themselves as 'coaches' without the requisite training and education could sour the market and create a negative perception of the profession.* • *Lack of capital investment to take the program to scale* • *No GSA schedule for services to government employees* • *Growing competition in the marketplace for coaches*
Questions and Concerns about the way forward:	

This step requires some personal research into the company, market, and competition, but this is time well spent. Completing a basic SWOT analysis provides meaningful conversation pieces for the networking and interview process. It shows that you understand some of the strategic considerations that contribute to the success of the business, and because you invested the time to do this analysis, it shows your level of commitment to understanding how you could personally contribute to the business.

Small Business Employment Opportunity Number 1

Small Business Employment Opportunity	Name of Company

Part 1. Leadership

Name of Leader(s)

Leadership Philosophy

Individual Values	Organizational Values

Organizational Mission

Personal Vision

Part 2. Business Status Report

Revenue and Revenue Trends

Investment History

Debt Status

Part 3. Business Strategy	
Strengths	**Weaknesses**
Opportunities	**Threats**

Notes, Comments, or Questions

Small Business Employment Opportunity Number 2

Small Business Employment Opportunity	Name of Company

Part 1. Leadership

Name of Leader(s)

Leadership Philosophy

Individual Values	Organizational Values

Organizational Mission

Personal Vision

Part 2. Business Status Report

Revenue and Revenue Trends

Investment History

Debt Status

Part 3. Business Strategy	
Strengths	**Weaknesses**
Opportunities	**Threats**

Notes, Comments, or Questions

Small Business Employment Opportunity Number 3

Small Business Employment Opportunity	Name of Company

Part 1. Leadership

Name of Leader(s)

Leadership Philosophy

Individual Values	Organizational Values

Organizational Mission

Personal Vision

Part 2. Business Status Report

Revenue and Revenue Trends

Investment History

Debt Status

Part 3. Business Strategy	
Strengths	**Weaknesses**
Opportunities	**Threats**

Notes, Comments, or Questions

3.6 LARGE CORPORATION

BACKGROUND

We finally arrive at the most common and recognizable course of action as it pertains to post-military careers. Generally speaking, a large company is a business enterprise that has outgrown the government definition of a small business. Most large companies offer equity shares on the open market or stock exchange. Many large corporations have locations throughout the United States and around the world, and most are self-contained entities that provide their own human resources, administration, research support, and development functions in addition to business operations to produce products or provide services.

DISTINCTIVE BENEFITS OF WORKING FOR A LARGE CORPORATION

Functional Opportunities. With few exceptions, you could find a functional or technical equivalent for most military operating specialties in large corporations. If you loved a particular job or assignment in the military, chances are you can find a similar kind of opportunity in a large corporation.

Growth Opportunities. Large corporations allow—and often encourage—opportunities for employees to explore different job functions for personal and professional growth. For example, you may start with a company in logistics or operations, and after a period of time, you may have the latitude to venture into a different role in something like marketing or business development. In many cases, the company will fund your training, education, and professional development for these broadening opportunities. If you find a brand and organizational mission that connects with your values and sense of purpose, large companies are willing to support your growth under their umbrella.

Career Services Support. Most of the career services and support in the job market are geared toward the hiring needs of large corporations. Most of the recognizable tactics involved in career transition are synonymous with the hiring processes of larger companies—résumé writing, LinkedIn profile, cover letters, interview preparation, elevator pitch, etc. Given the number of resources crowded into this space, you could likely find what you are looking for in life beyond the military, provided, of course, that you know what you are looking for.

IMPORTANT CONSIDERATIONS FOR SUCCESS

Show Me the Money. The objective of every business is to make money. The need for immediate gratification causes some executives to focus on short-term metrics at the expense of long-term results. The goal is profitability, but the ways and means to achieve that end are just as important.

A myopic focus on profitability at all costs often comes at a steep price. That price may include the values, people, and even the purpose of the business. Competition in the marketplace becomes an individual fight for survival, and consequently, blame, conflict, and self-preservation can define the culture of that organization. Long hours in a high-stress work culture are some of the qualities that define many professional management opportunities. Furthermore, the preponderance of corporate scandals reveals how some companies implicitly (and sometimes explicitly) encourage unethical or illegal behavior just to meet or exceed market expectations.[76] The drive to grab the next dollar comes with toxic consequences to the culture of the organization. You have to decide whether or not such a toxic culture exists, and if so, you have to determine if you can honor your values, fulfill your purpose, and self-actualize in such a culture.

Veterans Managed as Employment Resources. Veterans are a disappearing breed across the national landscape. In 1980, veterans comprised 18 percent of the total population and 37 percent of the male population, but in 2014, veterans comprised only 8 percent of the population.[77] By 2040, the US population is expected to reach approximately 380 million people.[78] Over that same time period, the veteran population is expected to shrink to less than 13 million.[79] This means that veterans will comprise less than 4 percent of the total population in the United States. Fewer employers looking to hire veterans will have military experience, and more likely than not, they will have a hard time appreciating the full value of what veterans bring to the workplace.

As a consequence, veterans will have to work harder to translate their skills and validate the potential value of their military experience to an employer. Over the past decade, we've seen the emergence of this trend with the explosion of programs for accreditation of military experience such as PMP or Six Sigma. Veterans struggle to communicate their value in a job market that is less connected with the true value of military experience. Military service is measured against civilian standards of experience and accreditation, and the result is widespread underemployment of the veteran community.[80]

76. Chris Matthews and Matthew Heimer, "The 5 Biggest Corporate Scandals of 2016," *Fortune*, December 28, 2016, http://fortune.com/2016/12/28/biggest-corporate-scandals-2016/.
77. Gretchen Livingston, "Profile of U.S. Veterans Shifts as Their Ranks Decline," *Pew Research Center Fact Tank*, November 11, 2016, https://www.pewresearch.org/fact-tank/2016/11/11/profile-of-u-s-veterans-is-changing-dramatically-as-their-ranks-decline/.
78. United States, Census Bureau, *Projections of the Size and Composition of the U.S. Population: 2014 to 2060*, by Sandra Colby and Jennifer M. Ortman, March 2015, 2, https://www.census.gov/content/dam/Census/library/publications/2015/demo/p25-1143.pdf.
79. National Center for Veterans Analysis and Statistics, *Veteran Population Projections 2017–2037*, 1, accessed May 31, 2019, https://www.va.gov/vetdata/docs/demographics/new_vetpop_model/vetpop_infographic_final31.pdf.
80. Cathy Barerra and Phillip Carter, *Challenges on the Home Front: Underemployment Hits Veterans Hard* (Santa Monica, CA: Call of Duty Endowment, 2016), 3, https://www.callofdutyendowment.org/content/dam/atvi/callofduty/code/pdf/ZipCODE_Vet_Report_FINAL.pdf.

The evolution of the job market has even greater implications on transitioning senior leaders and military retirees. Executives are wary to hire senior leaders at a commensurate level of responsibility and compensation because of perceived inadequacies in business acumen and transferable experience. The hiring practices of large corporations are simply not calibrated to recognize the value that military leaders offer to the corporate sector.

EXERCISE 3.6 DISCOVER OPPORTUNITIES IN LARGE CORPORATIONS

The purpose of this exercise is to do an initial feasibility assessment of potential employers and possible positions in large corporations. This research will inform your Networking Collection Plan, MTRP Action Plans, and the Transition and Reintegration Timeline. Just as with the small business employment opportunities, you want to start by getting familiar with the organizational leadership. You also want to identify the vision, mission statement, and values of the organization. You may choose to go with names and brands you know and trust. The first step to finding the right employer involves identifying the WHO (values) and the WHY (purpose).

You want to understand a little bit about the performance and strategic direction of the company. How do the products and offerings for the organization fare in comparison to its competitors? Is the market expanding or contracting for this company's goods and services? What are the plans for expansion? What do the financial statements project in terms of future performance? How frequently does the organization lay off employees? It is important to understand these questions because, as a new employee, your job security depends on the performance of the organization. Given the volatility and fluctuation of today's economy, you want to ensure that the company offers a stable employment opportunity, or you risk finding another job shortly after you start working at this job.

The next step involves exploring potential positions in that company. You may search job postings on the company website, but keep in mind that those positions probably won't coincide with your timeline. You aren't applying for a job at this point. You are just conducting research into possible positions. As you conduct your research, pay attention to the qualifications for the job in terms of education, experience, credentials, and special skills. If you don't meet the requirements, don't waste your time. Recruiters and human resources specialists will immediately eliminate your application from consideration if you don't meet the published requirements for the job.

If you lack any qualification for a particular job position, you may want to look into options to meet those qualifications. This may include a certain program or software certification, particular education requirement, or a professional accreditation. You may want to look at the qualifications of similar positions from similar companies for consistency. This will shape your Professional Preparedness line of effort in your MTRP Action Plans and your Transition and Reintegration Timeline.

Detailed Instructions:

1. **NAME OF COMPANY:** Self-explanatory

2. **NAME OF LEADER(S):** Include the CEO and the senior manager or director of the department you are interested in. Find out as much as you can about their values, purpose, and why they show up to work each day for the company.

3. **CORPORATE VISION:** Most corporations will publish an aspirational vision for the company and its impact on society. Sometimes this statement is crafted as a belief statement. It is the corporate view of the world and how the company will impact society for the better. If the company publishes a vision and a belief statement, include both.

4. **MISSION STATEMENT:** Write down the mission statement for the company. Consider how your purpose aligns with that statement.

5. **CORPORATE VALUES:** Most company websites will include values and definitions of those values.

6. **CURRENT PERFORMANCE:** Make an assessment of the current performance of the company. Indicators of current performance may include:

    - Stock Price Trends

    - Earnings Reports

    - Financial Reports

    - Press Releases

7. **PROJECTED FUTURE PERFORMANCE:** Look at the projections included in the Annual Reports for the company (you should be able to find these reports on the

company website). You may also want to search for any reviews from financial analysts regarding market and financial performance expectations.

8. **WORKFORCE DATA:** You want to make several observations as it pertains to workforce data:

   - What is the veteran demographic in the company and what is the veteran turnover? A low veteran demographic could present a challenge when it comes to communicating the value of your military training and experience. A high veteran turnover could be an indicator of veteran underemployment.

   - What does career progression inside the company look like? You want to recognize and understand if and how employees progress through the ranks of the company.

   - How often does the company lay off employees? Many corporations will terminate employees based on poor financial performance or general downturns in the economy.

9. **POTENTIAL POSITION:** Identify what position(s) you would take in the company. Regarding those positions, you want to answer the following questions regarding the qualifications for that position:

   - **EDUCATION:** What is the education level of employees in that position?

   - **EXPERIENCE:** What type of experience is necessary to qualify for that position?

   - **CREDENTIALS:** What special accreditation or certifications are necessary for this particular job?

   - **SPECIAL REQUIREMENTS:** Consider the special requirements necessary for this position. This may include experience or certification with a particular software, a security clearance, language requirement, etc.

Use the templates provided on the following pages to research large corporations for potential employment opportunities. Consider up to three positions for each company to expand your potential for employment.

Large Corporation Opportunity 1

NAME OF THE COMPANY:

PART 1. LEADERSHIP

NAME OF LEADER(S):

CORPORATE VISION:

MISSION STATEMENT:

CORPORATE VALUES:

PART 2. PERFORMANCE

CURRENT PERFORMANCE:

PROJECTED FUTURE PERFORMANCE:

WORKFORCE DATA:

PART 3. POTENTIAL POSITIONS FOR EMPLOYMENT

POTENTIAL POSITION #1

EDUCATION:

EXPERIENCE:

CREDENTIALS:

SPECIAL REQUIREMENTS:

POTENTIAL POSITION #2

EDUCATION:

EXPERIENCE:

CREDENTIALS:

SPECIAL REQUIREMENTS:

POTENTIAL POSITION #3

EDUCATION:

EXPERIENCE:

CREDENTIALS:

SPECIAL REQUIREMENTS:

Large Corporation Opportunity 2

NAME OF THE COMPANY:

PART 1. LEADERSHIP
NAME OF LEADER(S):
CORPORATE VISION:
MISSION STATEMENT:
CORPORATE VALUES:

PART 2. PERFORMANCE
CURRENT PERFORMANCE:
PROJECTED FUTURE PERFORMANCE:
WORKFORCE DATA:

PART 3. POTENTIAL POSITIONS FOR EMPLOYMENT

POTENTIAL POSITION #1

EDUCATION:

EXPERIENCE:

CREDENTIALS:

SPECIAL REQUIREMENTS:

POTENTIAL POSITION #2

EDUCATION:

EXPERIENCE:

CREDENTIALS:

SPECIAL REQUIREMENTS:

POTENTIAL POSITION #3

EDUCATION:

EXPERIENCE:

CREDENTIALS:

SPECIAL REQUIREMENTS:

Large Corporation Opportunity 3

NAME OF THE COMPANY:

PART 1. LEADERSHIP

NAME OF LEADER(S):

CORPORATE VISION:

MISSION STATEMENT:

CORPORATE VALUES:

PART 2. PERFORMANCE

CURRENT PERFORMANCE:

PROJECTED FUTURE PERFORMANCE:

WORKFORCE DATA:

PART 3. POTENTIAL POSITIONS FOR EMPLOYMENT

POTENTIAL POSITION #1

EDUCATION:

EXPERIENCE:

CREDENTIALS:

SPECIAL REQUIREMENTS:

POTENTIAL POSITION #2

EDUCATION:

EXPERIENCE:

CREDENTIALS:

SPECIAL REQUIREMENTS:

POTENTIAL POSITION #3

EDUCATION:

EXPERIENCE:

CREDENTIALS:

SPECIAL REQUIREMENTS:

OPPORTUNITY ALIGNMENT

In the MDMP, courses of action are analyzed from the context of feasibility, suitability, and acceptability. Once a course of action passes a go/no-go standard based on those criteria, the staff synchronizes each course of action through the wargame process to visualize how the plan would unfold in space and time. This exercise helps optimize the plan and identify the decision points necessary to maintain the initiative and successfully accomplish the mission.

In the MTRP, Opportunity Alignment is broken down into three action items: screen, wargame, and synchronize. The intended outcome of this process is executable plans for at least one potential opportunity for each different option—Entrepreneurship, Franchising, Civil Service, Nonprofit, Small Business, and Large Corporation—with accompanying decision points for transition and reintegration that are consistent with your Identity Analysis and Statement of Intent. At the conclusion of this step, you should have a minimum of six actionable plans that can get you where you want to be when you leave the military.

4.1 SCREEN OPPORTUNITIES

The purpose of this handbook is to create an integrative strategy for civilian reintegration, continued growth, and lifelong success as a veteran leader in civilian society. The method to achieve your end state requires an opportunity that aligns to your authentic identity story. Opportunities that don't allow you to express your values (the WHO) or realize your purpose (the WHY) won't optimize your personal growth or professional potential as a veteran leader. Therefore, this action item assesses the opportunities you developed in **Step 3** against a go/no-go standard related to your values, purpose, and intent for the next chapter of your life.

Your connection and sense of fulfillment in the military was possible because the values and mission of the military aligned to your sense of identity (the WHO) and your purpose (the WHY). Values and purpose are intrinsic qualities that are revealed over the course of your life, so chances are, you didn't know (at least definitively) what your values and purpose were when you originally volunteered for military service. You learned about who you were and your greater purpose because of that connection to the military identity and sense of purpose.

The military gave you hints along your journey to discover your identity story. Through this handbook, you defined your identity story. You know who you are. You found your purpose. You clarified what you want for your life. The go/no-go criteria for what happens next are based on that foundation.

EXERCISE 4.1 SCREEN POTENTIAL OPPORTUNITIES

The purpose of this exercise is to eliminate those options that do not align with your sense of identity, purpose, and intentions for the life you want after military service. By default, you also identify viable options that will achieve what you want in life beyond the military. This is a pass-fail standard. You could have as many as eighteen different opportunities (three for each option) screen through this step of the MTRP.

Based on what you learned about different opportunities in **Step 3**, this exercise is asking you to make an assessment on two levels. The first concerns *alignment*. You have to determine whether or not the values and mission of the particular option provide a means for you to honor your values, fulfill your purpose, and achieve your end state. The second is about *credibility*. You have to have confidence and believe that the facts and assumptions concerning each option reveal a valid path. This is important because not every organization practices what they preach, and not every organization has the capacity or means to achieve their mission. If an organization has no real possibility in achieving their mission, then how would you achieve your mission by joining that team? Alignment and credibility are the means by which you will screen the opportunities you developed from **Step 3**.

Detailed Instructions:

1. **VALUES (the WHO), PURPOSE (the WHY),** and **END STATE (the WHAT).** At the top of each worksheet, input your values, purpose, and end state as a reference for comparison.

2. **DESCRIPTION OF OPPORTUNITY.** As applicable, input the details of the option

or organization that includes your projected role, assignment, or job with that organization.

3. **ORGANIZATION VALUES.** Input the stated values for the organization.

4. **ORGANIZATION PURPOSE.** Input the stated mission, vision, or both for the organization.

5. **SCREENING CRITERIA.** This is your subjective assertion about whether or not the organizational values and mission align with your values, your mission, and whether or not this opportunity can credibly move you toward your End State. Frame your assertion in the form of a belief statement. Circle or highlight PASS if you truly feel that the opportunity can honor your values, fulfill your purpose, and get you closer to your End State from your Statement of Intent (**Exercise 2.11**). If you don't believe that this particular opportunity can do all those things, then circle or highlight the FAIL box.

6. **JUSTIFICATION.** For all opportunities that FAIL, you want to capture the reasons why the opportunity doesn't PASS. Some of the justifications might include:

   • Misalignment of values and/or purpose

   • The organization doesn't authentically practice and honor their values.

   • The organization prioritizes activities that are not consistent with their stated mission or deeper purpose (e.g., focus on short-term results at the expense of long-term success).

   • Toxic work culture (poor leadership) would challenge your values or inhibit your personal and professional fulfillment.

   • The organization lacks stability or the resources to credibly achieve the mission.

   • The lack of growth opportunities will prohibit you from reaching your End State.

Once an opportunity has FAILED, it is eliminated from further consideration in the MTRP. You can always refine your options and develop different opportunities by returning to **Step 3**.

Here is an example for one opportunity:

Opportunity Alignment Screening Worksheet		
VALUES (the WHO)	**PURPOSE (the WHY)**	**END STATE (the WHAT)**
Service to Others Innovation Passion for Life Faith Authenticity	Inspire leaders to live meaningful lives in the service of others	Empower veteran leaders to improve the condition of society through their leadership example, be the example of veteran leadership, be present and grateful

DESCRIPTION OF OPPORTUNITY

President of nonprofit organization

ORGANIZATION VALUES	ORGANIZATION PURPOSE	SCREENING CRITERIA
None published. Personal values of leadership team (in practice) don't match my personal values	Alternative approach to inspire leaders	I BELIEVE that this opportunity honors my values, fulfills my purpose, and enables me to achieve end state **PASS** (**FAIL**)

JUSTIFICATION

Alignment: Seems to be alignment with the purpose. Personal values – on paper – align with those of the organization. However, personal values don't agree with those of the leadership

Credibility: Program not accredited, no quality control. No strategy to achieve the broader vision that will enable me to achieve my end state.

Now it's your turn. Use the templates provided over the next nine pages to screen the opportunities you developed from **Step 3** of the MTRP.

Opportunity Alignment Screening Worksheet		
VALUES (the WHO)	PURPOSE (the WHY)	END STATE (the WHAT)

DESCRIPTION OF OPPORTUNITY

ORGANIZATION VALUES	ORGANIZATION PURPOSE	SCREENING CRITERIA
		I BELIEVE that this opportunity honors my values, fulfills my purpose, and enables me to achieve end state PASS FAIL

JUSTIFICATION

DESCRIPTION OF OPPORTUNITY

ORGANIZATION VALUES	ORGANIZATION PURPOSE	SCREENING CRITERIA
		I BELIEVE that this opportunity honors my values, fulfills my purpose, and enables me to achieve end state PASS FAIL

JUSTIFICATION

Opportunity Alignment Screening Worksheet

VALUES (the WHO)	PURPOSE (the WHY)	END STATE (the WHAT)

DESCRIPTION OF OPPORTUNITY

ORGANIZATION VALUES	ORGANIZATION PURPOSE	SCREENING CRITERIA
		I BELIEVE that this opportunity honors my values, fulfills my purpose, and enables me to achieve end state PASS FAIL

JUSTIFICATION

DESCRIPTION OF OPPORTUNITY

ORGANIZATION VALUES	ORGANIZATION PURPOSE	SCREENING CRITERIA
		I BELIEVE that this opportunity honors my values, fulfills my purpose, and enables me to achieve end state PASS FAIL

JUSTIFICATION

Opportunity Alignment Screening Worksheet

VALUES (the WHO)	PURPOSE (the WHY)	END STATE (the WHAT)

DESCRIPTION OF OPPORTUNITY

ORGANIZATION VALUES	ORGANIZATION PURPOSE	SCREENING CRITERIA
		I BELIEVE that this opportunity honors my values, fulfills my purpose, and enables me to achieve end state PASS FAIL

JUSTIFICATION

DESCRIPTION OF OPPORTUNITY

ORGANIZATION VALUES	ORGANIZATION PURPOSE	SCREENING CRITERIA
		I BELIEVE that this opportunity honors my values, fulfills my purpose, and enables me to achieve end state PASS FAIL

JUSTIFICATION

Opportunity Alignment Screening Worksheet

VALUES (the WHO)	PURPOSE (the WHY)	END STATE (the WHAT)

DESCRIPTION OF OPPORTUNITY

ORGANIZATION VALUES	ORGANIZATION PURPOSE	SCREENING CRITERIA
		I BELIEVE that this opportunity honors my values, fulfills my purpose, and enables me to achieve end state PASS FAIL

JUSTIFICATION

DESCRIPTION OF OPPORTUNITY

ORGANIZATION VALUES	ORGANIZATION PURPOSE	SCREENING CRITERIA
		I BELIEVE that this opportunity honors my values, fulfills my purpose, and enables me to achieve end state PASS FAIL

JUSTIFICATION

Opportunity Alignment Screening Worksheet

VALUES (the WHO)	PURPOSE (the WHY)	END STATE (the WHAT)

DESCRIPTION OF OPPORTUNITY

ORGANIZATION VALUES	ORGANIZATION PURPOSE	SCREENING CRITERIA
		I BELIEVE that this opportunity honors my values, fulfills my purpose, and enables me to achieve end state PASS FAIL

JUSTIFICATION

DESCRIPTION OF OPPORTUNITY

ORGANIZATION VALUES	ORGANIZATION PURPOSE	SCREENING CRITERIA
		I BELIEVE that this opportunity honors my values, fulfills my purpose, and enables me to achieve end state PASS FAIL

JUSTIFICATION

Opportunity Alignment Screening Worksheet

VALUES (the WHO)	PURPOSE (the WHY)	END STATE (the WHAT)

DESCRIPTION OF OPPORTUNITY

ORGANIZATION VALUES	ORGANIZATION PURPOSE	SCREENING CRITERIA
		I BELIEVE that this opportunity honors my values, fulfills my purpose, and enables me to achieve end state PASS FAIL

JUSTIFICATION

DESCRIPTION OF OPPORTUNITY

ORGANIZATION VALUES	ORGANIZATION PURPOSE	SCREENING CRITERIA
		I BELIEVE that this opportunity honors my values, fulfills my purpose, and enables me to achieve end state PASS FAIL

JUSTIFICATION

Opportunity Alignment Screening Worksheet

VALUES (the WHO)	PURPOSE (the WHY)	END STATE (the WHAT)

DESCRIPTION OF OPPORTUNITY

ORGANIZATION VALUES	ORGANIZATION PURPOSE	SCREENING CRITERIA
		I BELIEVE that this opportunity honors my values, fulfills my purpose, and enables me to achieve end state PASS FAIL

JUSTIFICATION

DESCRIPTION OF OPPORTUNITY

ORGANIZATION VALUES	ORGANIZATION PURPOSE	SCREENING CRITERIA
		I BELIEVE that this opportunity honors my values, fulfills my purpose, and enables me to achieve end state PASS FAIL

JUSTIFICATION

Opportunity Alignment Screening Worksheet		
VALUES (the WHO)	**PURPOSE (the WHY)**	**END STATE (the WHAT)**

DESCRIPTION OF OPPORTUNITY		
ORGANIZATION VALUES	**ORGANIZATION PURPOSE**	**SCREENING CRITERIA**
		I BELIEVE that this opportunity honors my values, fulfills my purpose, and enables me to achieve end state PASS FAIL
JUSTIFICATION		

DESCRIPTION OF OPPORTUNITY		
ORGANIZATION VALUES	**ORGANIZATION PURPOSE**	**SCREENING CRITERIA**
		I BELIEVE that this opportunity honors my values, fulfills my purpose, and enables me to achieve end state PASS FAIL
JUSTIFICATION		

Opportunity Alignment Screening Worksheet

VALUES (the WHO)	PURPOSE (the WHY)	END STATE (the WHAT)

DESCRIPTION OF OPPORTUNITY

ORGANIZATION VALUES	ORGANIZATION PURPOSE	SCREENING CRITERIA
		I BELIEVE that this opportunity honors my values, fulfills my purpose, and enables me to achieve end state PASS FAIL

JUSTIFICATION

DESCRIPTION OF OPPORTUNITY

ORGANIZATION VALUES	ORGANIZATION PURPOSE	SCREENING CRITERIA
		I BELIEVE that this opportunity honors my values, fulfills my purpose, and enables me to achieve end state PASS FAIL

JUSTIFICATION

4.2 WARGAME

In the MDMP, the staff chooses a wargaming method based on the type of operation and time available. As it applies to the MTRP, the preferred technique is the avenue-in-depth approach that wargames different lines of effort over time, beginning with the decisive event.[81] In other words, each remaining opportunity acts as its own line of effort. The decisive event is civilian reintegration. It is the conclusion of the transition and reintegration process. It is your definition of a new steady state as a veteran leader and what life looks like once you have successfully crossed that bridge back into regular society.

EXERCISE 4.2.1 WARGAME OPPORTUNITIES

For this exercise, you require the following:

- Statement of Intent

- MTRP Action Plans

- Network Collection Plan

- Family Information Requirements

- Transition and Reintegration Timeline (one copy for each Opportunity)

- Surviving Opportunities from previous step

The wargame begins with the decisive event in the future (successful reintegration) and works back to the present. Use the backward planning checklists for the appropriate opportunity found in **Tables 4.2.1** through **4.2.4**. From top to bottom, the checklists are arranged from future action items down to the present day. Use your Transition and Reintegration Timeline to allocate time and set deadlines as necessary to complete the action items in the checklists. Starting at the top of the appropriate checklist, consider the conditions and time necessary to achieve each step as you work down the checklist to arrive at the present day. Keep in mind that not all action items in **Tables 4.2.1** through **4.2.4** will apply, and you might identify some additional steps in the process. You will need one Transition and Reintegration Timeline to wargame each opportunity.

---

81. Department of the Army, *Commander,* 9-29, 9-30.

A potential script for the wargame process is as follows:

1. Begin with the end in mind. Mark when you anticipate your reintegration will be completed at some point in the future. The standard for this handbook is six months after separation, but you can set whatever suspense you deem appropriate given your time in service, the nature of that service, and the amount of time you have prior to discharge or retirement. More time in service or combat experience may require more time for reintegration. Additionally, less than twelve months before separation may also require more time for reintegration.

2. Start at the top of the appropriate checklist for a given opportunity (**Table 4.2.1** for Entrepreneurship, **Table 4.2.2** for Franchising, **Table 4.2.3** for Civil Service, or **Table 4.2.4** for Nonprofit, Small Business, or Large Corporation) and work your way back from your targeted reintegration date.

3. Mark on your calendar when you must complete the action item to continue forward progress and meet your objective for reintegration. Allocate the time necessary to achieve that particular action item.

4. Review each of your MTRP Action Plans against that point in time and make any necessary adjustments to your SMART goals. Consider those conditions and incremental steps necessary to meet your suspense. Visualize where you want to be through the lens of each factor of the Integrative Program of Transition.

5. Review and adjust your Family Information Requirements to determine what (if any) impact this action item has on your family.

6. For any questions, concerns, or open issues, create a new information requirement as necessary. Highlight the larger concerns and potential decision points for future reference.

7. Work down the checklist to the next action item, and repeat Steps 3 through 6. Continue this process until you reach the end of the checklist. Continue walking back your transition requirements and MTRP Action Plans until you get to the present day.

8. Using another Transition and Reintegration Timeline, repeat this process for the next course of action or opportunity.

Remember, this is a backward planning exercise. You start with the decisive event in the future and sequence activities that will lead to that decisive event. Let's examine the decisive event and backward planning checklists for each opportunity.

ENTREPRENEURSHIP

Revenue generation is the decisive event for an entrepreneur. This occurs when you make the first sale and begin serving customers.

Table 4.2.1. Entrepreneurship Checklist highlights many important tasks and related action items you may want to consider in starting your own business. The time required for each of these activities varies based on the nature of your product, service, or particular industry. You may be able to complete many of these items simultaneously, and the sequencing may vary based on the nature of your business. Keep in mind that this list is not all-inclusive. The right answer is the process that enables you to generate sustainable revenue (sales). These action items generally apply to most startups, and you can gain clarity about how much time is typically required for each of these items as part of your research and networking.

Table 4.2.1. Entrepreneurship Checklist. Proposed Backward Planning Action Items for Entrepreneurship Opportunities

Entrepreneur Business Startup Activities
Decisive Action: Make the First Sale
Execute the Sales Cycle. Marketing is a lot like targeting. You have to develop a sale in the same way you develop a target. The marketing and sales cycle passes through seven different stages: prospect for leads, connect with a potential client, qualify the client, make your pitch, address questions and concerns, close the sale, and follow-up/referrals.[82] The time period between a potential client becoming aware of your offering and actually making a sale could vary between several hours to several weeks or months depending on the product, service, and the nature of your industry. You may want to allocate time for each of the seven stages. A potential networking question with other businesses in your industry would explore how long it takes to generate sales so that you can manage expectations. Too many entrepreneurs falsely assume that they will immediately generate revenue from their first advertising pitch - and that is not necessarily the case.
Register as a Veteran Owned Business. Registering as a Veteran Owned Small Business (VOSB) or as a Service Disabled Veteran Owned Business (SDVOB) requires a Dun & Bradstreet (DUNS Number) to conduct business with the federal government (https://fedgov.dnb.com/webform). The System for Award Management (sams.gov) is another government registration that is required to compete and bid for federal contracts. These steps are prerequisites to apply for special designation as a VOSB or SDVOB with the Department of Veterans Affairs. The federal government sets aside a certain percentage of contracting dollars to VOSB and SDVOB each year.

82. Wendy Connick, "Perfect These 7 Sales Cycle Stages to Improve Business," *The Balance Careers*, January 07, 2019, https://www.thebalancecareers.com/the-7-stages-of-the-sales-cycle-2917515.

Create and Package Offering. Consider the time necessary to create and/or package your value offering. You want to define what the customer will receive and the price of that product of service. For example, if you become a consultant, you may want to consider the time required to package your specific offerings for potential clients. Perhaps you want to create some handbooks, online training videos, or podcasts. These activities take time to develop, so you want to acknowledge and capture that time in your calendar.

Secure Insurance. You may consider acquiring professional or other forms of insurance. Some forms of insurance may be required based on the nature of your business or other local, state, and federal guidelines.

Establish Business Accounting Protocols. You want to have a means of tracking revenue and expenses related to the business for tax reporting purposes. You may elect to do this yourself, or you may want to allocate some time and set a suspense to find a bookkeeper or accountant to provide this service. Also, consider how you will be paid for your services (credit card, bank transfer, cash, etc.). You may need to establish an invoicing system or set up processes to receive payments and pay your bills.

Human Resources. If your business requires labor, allocate some time to build the human resources structure to ensure compliance with state and federal employment guidelines. This includes establishing a payroll and process for reporting tax withholding. You also want to take the necessary time to find and hire the best employees for your company.

Purchase Equipment and Supplies. Before you make any large purchases, obtain the necessary permits and licenses to execute your business activity. Some equipment and supplies may have lead times that you will want to take into consideration.

Build Website. Website and social media pages take time to develop. Many web design platforms are simple enough for you to create your own, but even if you have someone build a website for your business, you still need time to write content, provide images, review copy, etc.

Obtain Permits and Licenses. Given your industry and the nature of your product or service, ensure that you are in compliance with local, state, and federal guidelines for your business activity.

Create Logo and Register Domain. You can create your own logo or have someone create one for your business. You also want to register your domain name for digital communications and a business website.

Open Business Accounts. Open a business bank account separate from your personal account to simplify accounting, tax reporting, and lines of credit. Most accountants will require you to establish a separate bank account for the business entity.

Register a Federal Employer Identification Number (EIN). The EIN is to your business identity what your social security number is to your personal identity. The IRS provides a very simple process to register your business and receive an EIN. To complete an application for an EIN, visit https://irs-ein-tax.com/. The EIN is necessary for opening bank accounts, applying for a DUNS number, and registering your business as a Veteran Owned Small Business (VOSB) or a Service Disabled Veteran Owned Business (SDVOB).

Register Your Business Entity. You want to register a name for your business entity with the Secretary of State for your business location. You can search for available names with your Secretary of State at the same time that you are searching for internet domain names. Research and determine the right entity for your business (Sole Proprietor, LLC, S-Corp, etc.). You may seek legal advice on the best option for your business, and you may require some time to develop the necessary documentation to comply with state guidelines.

Secure Funding for Initial Investment. All business requires some level of startup capital. You may wish to fund this enterprise yourself, or you may wish to secure capital through borrowing or grants to cover the initial costs. Applications and approval processes may take some time, and all loan and grant applications will require a sound business plan.
Develop a Business Plan. Typically the first and arguably the most important step to creating a new business. The business plan outlines how you intend to take a good idea and turn it into a profitable enterprise. Before you start investing money (especially YOUR money), you want to know that your idea has the potential to succeed. The business plan is your strategy for how you will penetrate or shape a particular market to generate revenue. Business plans require research to determine whether a market exists for your offering and whether or not you could achieve profitability through that offering. You can pay a consultant to create a business plan, or you can complete the template provided by the U.S. Small Business Administration (https://www.sba.gov/tools/business-plan/1).

FRANCHISING

Site opening is the decisive event for owning and operating a business as a franchisee. The wargame for this opportunity involves backward planning the critical tasks and functions that are necessary to arrive at the day of your grand opening for the business.

Table 4.2.2. Franchising Checklist highlights the action items necessary to operate a franchise business. The time required for each of these activities varies based on franchisor requirements, site availability, site preparation, and financing requirements. This list is not all-inclusive, and franchise agreements will outline requirements particular to that company. These action items are general considerations for opening a business as a franchisee, and you can identify the specific requirements and time constraints as part of your research and networking.

Table 4.2.2. Franchising Checklist. Backward Planning Tasks and Functions to Own and Operate a Franchise

Tasks and Functions to Own and Operate a Franchise
Decisive Action: Site Opening
Prepare for Opening. How do you plan to generate awareness and excitement for your grand opening? Consider this a shaping operation. You may have a series of advertisements and related media appearances to create the buzz necessary for a successful grand opening.
Human Resources. If you need to hire employees and staff, you need time to review applications, conduct interviews, and complete the administrative requirements necessary to build your workforce.
Purchase Equipment and/or Inventory. If you need to purchase capital equipment, order supplies, or build inventory for your company, you want to consider the lead, setup, and any training time required that may impact your timeline for opening.
Site Preparation. You may need to construct a facility and/or renovate an existing facility for the business.

Contract Compliance. You will likely want to allocate time for the necessary inspections, insurance, and associated compliance standards commensurate with your franchise contract.
Contract Review and Signature. Give yourself time to review the agreement to ensure that you understand the terms for royalties, termination, contract renewal, quotas, compliance, standards, and particulars to the company, market, or industry. You may decide to hire an attorney to help you through this process.
Training. The company may offer training, workshops, or programs of instruction. You may want to supplement any formal training by participating in your own training and certification programs to improve your skills in marketing, human resources management, operations, compliance, or any technical specialty specific to your company.
Secure Financing. Franchise opportunities require a certain level of owner investment. Franchisors will want you to put some skin in the game. You could finance this opportunity out of pocket, but provided that you don't, it may take some time to secure financing. Many veteran specific programs for loans and grants exist, but the application process takes time. Nothing can happen to build your franchise until you secure the money to cover the initial financing requirements.
Network with Other Franchise Owners. Understand the pros and cons from other franchisees who have partnered with this company. Their challenges will be your challenges. Take time to recognize their greatest takeaways (both positive and negative) from working with the parent company.
Research the Location. Assess the profitability of opening a business at your selected location. Many companies may already have preselected sites for expansion and market penetration, but because you are making this investment, do some of your own research. Spend some time at your local chamber of commerce to understand the market and how the demographics are expected to evolve over time.
Research the Company. Before you enter any agreement, know what you are getting yourself into. You want to understand whether the company's financial performance is trending well.

CIVIL SERVICE

The decisive event for civil service employment is when you are ready to work. This occurs after you've completed the initial onboarding or training requirements for your position. Civil service includes government or public service positions at the local, state, or federal level. While local and state positions are not as easy to find as federal opportunities, you should consider them if public service is your passion. For the purpose of this analysis, we will examine some of the tasks and functions necessary to transition into the civil service sector for the federal government.

Table 4.2.3. Civil Service Checklist highlights how the civil service employment sector differs from the nonprofit and private sectors. This list is not all-inclusive, and certain positions may have longer hiring and onboarding timelines. If you are interested in civil service employment, you want to begin researching hiring requirements and qualifications as soon as possible.

Table 4.2.3. Civil Service Checklist. Backward Planning Tasks and Functions for Civil Service Employment

Tasks and Functions for Civil Service Employment
Decisive Action - Inprocessing and Onboarding Complete: Ready to Work
Onboarding. You may be required to attend a series of classes or training before you can actually begin work. The extent and nature of the onboarding activities vary depending on the position and the agency. Through networking or the Veterans Employment Program Office, you can reveal the extent of education and training that precedes you actually showing up for work.
Inprocessing. Just as in the military, most civil service jobs have a sufficient amount of administrative, badging, and other inprocessing requirements to complete before you begin work.
Relocation. Allocate sufficient time to relocate, receive household goods, and get established in your new neighborhood.
Execute the Hiring Process. If you are among the best qualified for employment, you will likely continue the hiring process. This could involve a series of interviews, surveys, and other assessments. Understand the timeline so that you can set reasonable expectations.
Submit Your Application. The application process for civil service positions can be frustrating. In most cases, you won't receive any feedback regarding your qualification status until the job closes. The nature of the position may require a sequence of reviews and approvals through different agencies and levels of bureaucracy. Find out how long the hiring process takes for your desired department or agency as part of your networking process.
Build a Federal Resume. Federal resumes are typically more involved than resumes for nonprofit and private sector opportunities. The Department of Labor has published tips for veterans preparing resumes for federal employment (https://www.dol.gov/general/jobs/tips-for-writing-a-federal-resume)
Search Eligible Positions. Federal jobs are broken down into three categories: Competitive Service, Excepted Service, and Senior Executive Service. For more information about your eligibility for these positions, visit https://www.fedshirevets.gov/job-seekers/the-federal-employment-process/#content. For most eligible positions, you can find a Job Opportunity Announcement (JOA) on the USAJOBS website (https://www.usajobs.gov/)
Gather the Tools. In addition to the DD Form 2586, you will also require a DD 214 and any determination letters for a service connected disability. You may also want to have your evaluation reports, awards certificates, and any other relevant documentation regarding your military service readily available.
Obtain Necessary Credentials. You may require certain credentials that you won't earn through military service. The PMP is one example of a credential that you can't get through the military that is a necessary qualification for many federal job opportunities. You want to research the special skills and qualifications of various positions and allocate the necessary time to complete those qualifications before you begin to apply for jobs.
Execute the Military Skills Translator. As part of the transition process, you should receive the DD Form 2586 Verification of Military Experience and Training. This validates your qualifications for civil service and many other private sector opportunities.

Determine Eligibility for Veteran's Hiring Preference. "Veterans' preference eligibility can be based on dates of active duty service, receipt of a campaign badge, receipt of a Purple Heart, or a service-connected disability. Please know that not all active duty service may qualify for veterans' preference."[83] For more information about Veteran's Preference, visit https://www.fedshirevets.gov/job-seekers/.
Contact the Veteran Employment Program Office. If you want to find out more about how to secure employment at a particular federal agency, you might want to contact the Veteran Employment Program Office (VEPO) for that agency. Each federal agency has a VEPO specifically designed to help veteran recruitment, employment, training and development, and retention. For more information, visit https://www.fedshirevets.gov/veterans-council/agency-directory/. The VEPO will let you know what veteran hiring timeline constraints or restrictions exist for that agency.
Update Your Security Clearance. If your security clearance is set to expire during the transition process, you might consider renewing your application such that your clearance covers the period of transition and reintegration. Many federal opportunities require a clearance as a prerequisite for employment.
Collect References and Letters of Recommendation. Start identifying people to write letters of recommendation or serve as potential references while you are still actively engaged in your job. Once you begin to disconnect for the purpose of transition, these may be harder to obtain. Even if you must tailor the letter or reference later on, having a collection of recommendations and associated points of contact will be extremely valuable for any background verification or personal references.
Research Civil Service Positions. As part of your networking process, you want to understand the hiring process, routines, culture, and expectations that accompany positions at different federal agencies. You also want to clarify any time restrictions for hiring veterans. Be open to the possibility that the ideal position may exist in an agency you had never considered before. Given the number of veterans who work in the civil service, you can leverage the existing network of veterans to learn more about civil service opportunities.

NONPROFIT AND PRIVATE (SMALL BUSINESS AND LARGE CORPORATION) SECTOR OPPORTUNITIES

The decisive event for employment for the remaining (nonprofit, small business, and large corporation) opportunities is the ninety-first day of employment. Many organizations have a probationary period of employment that covers the first three months on the job. Although not every organization formalizes this process, the first ninety days represents the time necessary to learn the job, assimilate into the culture, and accomplish the necessary training or onboarding requirements. You can think of the first ninety days as your Reception, Staging, and Onward Integration (RSOI) for the new job. It represents a benchmark for achieving a new state of being in life after the military. The hiring process for most nonprofit and small business organizations will likely be less formal than those for large corporations, but the methodology is the same.

Table 4.2.4. Nonprofit and Private Sector Checklist includes those activities most commonly associated with finding a new job. Most of the conventional hiring processes in the job market

---

83. "Job Seekers: Veterans Preference," *Feds Hire Vets*, accessed May 24, 2019, https://www.fedshirevets.gov/job-seekers/veterans -preference/#content.

are calibrated to these types of organizations and opportunities. Each organization will likely have some unique steps or processes used to distinguish the most competitive candidates for employment. You can discover what these processes are through your research and networking.

Table 4.2.4. Nonprofit and Private Sectors Checklist. Proposed Backward Planning Tasks and Functions to Work in the Nonprofit and Private Sectors.

Tasks and Functions for Nonprofit and Private Sector Employment
Decisive Action: The 91st Day
Complete 90 Day Review. Many employers have probationary periods for new hires that culminate after a 90 day review. An employee is considered permanent provided he or she receives a satisfactory review after the first 90 days.
Join Veteran Affinity Group. Many organizations sponsor affinity groups to help veterans integrate into a new corporate culture and help senior leaders better understand the issues and concerns of the veteran workforce.
Orientation. Most employers will allocate a certain amount of time for training, administration, on-boarding, and familiarization before you begin functioning in your intended position. Consider this the time required to inprocess your next assignment in life beyond the military.
Relocation. Allocate sufficient time to relocate, receive household goods, and get established in your new neighborhood.
Receive and Review Employment Letter. The employment letter will detail the specifics and conditions of your hire. You may have a decision point associated with a targeted window of time to receive an offer of employment.
Execute the Hiring Process. If you are among the best qualified for employment, you will continue the hiring process. This could involve a series of interviews and other assessments. Make sure you walk away from your first interview with a clear picture of the hiring process and timeline for hiring decisions. This will frame your expectations for communications and feedback through the process.
Attend Hiring Conference and/or Networking Event. Career fairs, conferences, and professional networking events are opportunities to learn about different roles and companies seeking job candidates, make connections, and move forward in the hiring process. Ensure that you attend events commensurate with your qualifications and desired intentions. For example, if you are a senior officer, it is probably not worth your time to attend a junior officer hiring event.
Develop an Elevator Pitch. Hiring conferences and events offer brief windows of time to speak with members of the company hiring team. A powerful elevator pitch that speaks to your unique value proposition can make that brief engagement a memorable one. Take some time to develop and rehearse your pitch before you start attending these conferences.
Find a Recruiter. Although not required to find a job, many companies outsource the hiring process to third parties to screen and identify candidates for job openings. Keep in mind that third party headhunters and recruiters exist to meet the needs of the companies that hire them. Their priorities may not be your priorities.
Update Your Resume or Curriculum Vitae (CV). A resume should be specific to a particular job. You want to lose the military jargon and speak in a language that someone with little or no military experience can understand. Certain employers may have preferences regarding length and format of your resume or CV. You want to ensure that you are delivering your best pitch in the format your audience wants.

Create and Update Your LinkedIn Profile. LinkedIn is the preferred social media platform for career services professionals. You want to have a professional photo and summary consistent with your personal brand. You want to ensure that the language for your experience and education is consistent across all digital and print media - including your resume or CV. As you venture into the job market, recruiters, hiring managers, and human resources specialists will almost certainly examine your LinkedIn Profile. Hiring professionals may review your profile based on the strength of your application and potential for employment. Either way, your LinkedIn Profile offers more information than the basic resume or CV, so ensure it says everything you want it to say. You may want to request some recommendations to accompany your profile as well.

Build a Personal Brand. Elements of a personal brand include authenticity (values, purpose, beliefs, and intrinsic strengths), consistent messaging, important elements of your story, expertise, visibility, value proposition, and connections - Personal branding is "about becoming conscious about what you do naturally and being more consistent and visible with it."[84]

Research Potential Jobs. Once you find a company that aligns to your values and purpose, you'll want to spend some time exploring potential jobs. You also want to identify any special requirements for any desired positions within that company. You might uncover a specific skill, software requirement, or qualification necessary to make you an ideal candidate for that job. Meeting those standards to distinguish yourself could take some time.

Research Potential Employers. This is part of the Opportunity Development phase of the MTRP that will continue throughout your search for a new career. Before you start looking at roles, positions, and salaries, you want to ensure that the organization and the leadership of that organization aligns to your authentic identity story. This will require research about the leadership and culture of the organization (See **How to Find Your New Tribe After Leaving the Military** in **Part 3** of this handbook)

At this point, you should have several draft timelines for execution. Once you have worked your way back from the decisive event from where you are today, it's time to walk through the plan from beginning to end.

4.3 SYNCHRONIZE YOUR TIMELINE

There is an art to developing your timeline for transition and reintegration. The backward planning method allows you to visualize the conditions and benchmarks in time and space beginning with the decisive event of civilian reintegration. Synchronization, the chronological walkthrough of transition and reintegration activities, turns what you placed on the calendar into an executable and manageable plan. In the military, the product that typically comes from the wargame process is the execution matrix. You can build your own execution matrix for your transition and reintegration, but that may become too cumbersome to manage. Synchronizing the schedule on the calendar and conducting periodic reviews as a running estimate is perhaps the best way to validate your plan moving forward.

After this step in the MTRP, you will have synchronized plans with decision points based on

---

84. Matt Orlic, "The 7 Key Elements of an Effective Personal Brand," *Entrepreneur*, September 12, 2016, https://www.entrepreneur.com/article/280268.

different employment opportunities. For all intents and purposes, these represent the course of action sketches and execution matrices that the staff would carry forward to complete the COA Comparison step of the MDMP.

THE IMPORTANCE OF DECISION POINTS

Recognizing the decision points along your timeline is the most difficult part of this step in the MTRP, and it is also the most important. When you populate your calendar with decision points, you assert *control* in a process that might otherwise feel very out of control. Let's face it, you don't control the hiring decisions of potential employers. You don't control the market for your small business. You don't control the employment schedules for government agencies. ***You control which line of effort you prioritize and the time in which you choose to accomplish that line of effort.*** Each opportunity will have its own decision points. By establishing these markers, you map out how you assume responsibility for your plan, your transition, and your life.

Control allows you to maintain the initiative. It is how you keep from falling victim to any number of factors outside of your control. It is how you maintain positive intention through this difficult process. It is how you persist and continue forward movement to discover your unique path—your bridge—to your intended landing point in life after military service.

IDENTIFY DECISION POINTS

The most significant decision you can make is when you decide to abandon or prioritize a different opportunity immediately before or sometime after your separation from service. At some point, you might decide to stop looking for jobs in large corporations and begin planning to open your own business. You might decide to no longer pursue that franchising opportunity and start looking for a civil service opportunity. Maybe you realize that a particular opportunity will no longer help you achieve your desired Statement of Intent. As you reflect on some potential decisions, consider what conditions would inform those decisions. Think about the actions you would take to continue forward movement along your journey to discover the life you want after the military.

The structure of a decision point includes *conditions* and *actions*. When the conditions of a particular course of action reach the point that they threaten successful achievement of your objectives, you may need to make a decision (see **Table 4.3.1** for examples of conditions and the resulting actions from decision points in the MTRP). If you approach this process with an open mind, a setback on one or more potential opportunities become learning experiences.

Table 4.3.1. Possible Conditions and Actions for Transition and Reintegration Decision Points.

Conditions That Could Signal a Possible Decision
Change in your separation date
Change that impacts a member of your family (college acceptance, graduation, spouse employment, etc.)
Change in hiring timeline for a particular job
Change in the qualifications (or timeline to achieve those qualifications) for a particular job.
Change in living conditions (lease expires, home sale, etc.)
Medical or Health Requirement
Ability to secure a corporate job by a certain date
Ability to enter into a franchising agreement by a certain date
Ability to meet qualification requirements for a particular job by a certain date

Potential Action Items
Shifting the timeline
Changing a company, position, or potential employer for consideration
Seeking an accreditation or signing up for a training course
Securing a mentor or professional coach
Reaching out to a recruiter, headhunter, or career services specialist
Relocating your family
Starting the process for a new business or franchise
Shifting your priority of effort to a different opportunity

Without decision points, you run the risk of stagnation. Think of decision points in these terms: How many job application rejections are necessary before you try something different or shift your focus? How long are you willing to wait for that business enterprise to become profitable before you shift to another opportunity? Life happens. As you go through the process of transition and reintegration, you might find that some of your assumptions are invalid. The facts and circumstances may change. Things may not work out or events may not unfold the way you had anticipated. This process opens you up to different possibilities and potentially better paths to help you achieve your Statement of Intent. If opportunities are not unfolding in the way you want, decision points are your signal to try something else.

The reason we developed multiple options through the MTRP is so that you have the latitude to shift priorities and still achieve your intentions for what you want in life beyond the military. The key is to identify the decision points so that you sustain your confidence and momentum through the transition and reintegration process. Conceptually speaking, you should be able to structure the relationship between a certain condition and the corresponding action in the format of an "if-then" statement. Some examples are included in **Figure 4.3.1.**

Figure 4.3.1. Examples of If-Then Statements that Become Decision Points in Your Plan

> *"If I don't enter into a franchising agreement by the end of September, then I will seek full-time employment options that start before the end of the year."*
>
> *"If I don't have a job offer by May 31st, then I will begin taking steps to open my own business as an entrepreneur."*
>
> *"If the hiring window for the State Department doesn't open by the end of the year, then I will begin the application process for a franchise in the coffee service industry."*
>
> *"If I don't secure full-time employment by the end of July, then I will find a headhunter."*
>
> *"If my wife secures full-time employment, then I will start my own business."*

Communicate and share these decision points with the rest of your family. You also will want to share them with your support system—mentors, recruiters, coaches, friends, and advisors. You may need their help to hold you accountable should the conditions for decision arise through this process.

EXERCISE 4.3 SYNCHRONIZE THE PLAN

During the wargame process, you walked your plan backward from the decisive point to the beginning. The purpose of this exercise is to walk through your plan chronologically from beginning to end. The outcome of this process is an executable and manageable plan that allows you to synchronize the MTRP Action Plans with your Transition and Reintegration Timeline and identify decision points throughout the process.

You can synchronize each opportunity in three steps.

STEP 1. REVIEW AND UPDATE ACTION PLANS

Your authentic identity beyond the uniform serves as the foundation for your transition and reintegration. Once you've mapped out the steps required to explore different opportunities, it's time to update your Networking Strategy and integrate your wargame results into the Transition and Reintegration Timeline. As a result of the Opportunity Alignment process, you may have adjustments to your MTRP Action Plans. You may even want to adjust your intentions across the six factors for the Integrative Program of Transition. This is normal and even expected given the research necessary and the subsequent clarity you gain through this process.

STEP 2. IDENTIFY DECISION POINTS

As you go through the timeline, recognize the conditions that would lead you to make a decision. You can reference the example in **Figure 4.3.2** to signal when it is time to take action based on what is happening through the transition and reintegration process.

Figure 4.3.2. Example of a Decision Support Template with Information Requirements

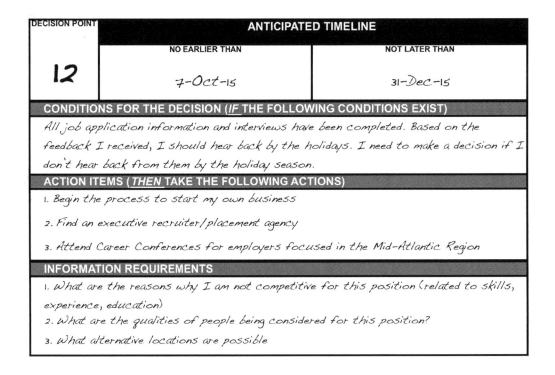

Detailed Instructions for Completing the Decision Support Template are as follows:

DECISION POINT: Identify the decision point for easy reference on your Transition and Reintegration Timeline.

ANTICIPATED TIMELINE: You may have a window of opportunity to take action and make a decision. You want to identify that window to focus your collection plan.

CONDITIONS FOR THE DECISION: Input the conditions that would necessitate a decision. These conditions should be based on your MTRP Action Plans or Family Information Requirements. They can involve any number of factors related to the Integrative Program of Transition.

ACTION ITEMS: List the actions you will take. You may want to annotate your specific action item on your Transition and Reintegration Timeline for easy reference. The two parts of every decision should take the form of an "if-then" statement.

INFORMATION REQUIREMENTS: As you conceptualize the decision points, consider the information requirements that would shape conditions necessary to take action. You can also list the information requirements by FIR number or the information requirement from your Networking Collection Plan.

STEP 3. UPDATE CALENDAR AND SYNCHRONIZE ACTION PLANS

As you identify decision points, ensure that you stay aligned with your MTRP Action Plans and Statement of Intent. Every action will likely have second- and third-order effects to your timeline, so as you walk through the calendar, take note of those branches and sequels that show up as the plan unfolds. You can even consider this final step a calendar rehearsal—analogous to a map rehearsal—to capture any outstanding issues or questions that you may want to discuss with your family, friends, coach, mentor, or transition advisor for the process.

You will want to repeat this process for each potential opportunity. Ideally, you would have at least one completed and synchronized calendar for each option—Entrepreneurship, Franchising, Civil Service, Nonprofit, Small Business, and Large Corporation—but a detailed plan for each opportunity is not necessary. The objective is to have enough executable options to achieve what you want in life after the military.

The following blank decision support templates are provided for you to map out your decision points and synchronize your timeline.

DECISION POINT	ANTICIPATED TIMELINE	
	NO EARLIER THAN	NOT LATER THAN

CONDITIONS FOR THE DECISION (*IF* THE FOLLOWING CONDITIONS EXIST)

ACTION ITEMS (*THEN* TAKE THE FOLLOWING ACTIONS)

INFORMATION REQUIREMENTS

DECISION POINT	ANTICIPATED TIMELINE	
	NO EARLIER THAN	NOT LATER THAN

CONDITIONS FOR THE DECISION (*IF* THE FOLLOWING CONDITIONS EXIST)

ACTION ITEMS (*THEN* TAKE THE FOLLOWING ACTIONS)

INFORMATION REQUIREMENTS

DECISION POINT	ANTICIPATED TIMELINE	
	NO EARLIER THAN	NOT LATER THAN

CONDITIONS FOR THE DECISION (*IF* THE FOLLOWING CONDITIONS EXIST)

ACTION ITEMS (*THEN* TAKE THE FOLLOWING ACTIONS)

INFORMATION REQUIREMENTS

DECISION POINT	ANTICIPATED TIMELINE	
	NO EARLIER THAN	NOT LATER THAN

CONDITIONS FOR THE DECISION (*IF* THE FOLLOWING CONDITIONS EXIST)

ACTION ITEMS (*THEN* TAKE THE FOLLOWING ACTIONS)

INFORMATION REQUIREMENTS

OPPORTUNITY COMPARISON

Because you have already screened and synchronized the opportunities that will allow you to honor your values, pursue your purpose, exercise your strengths, and achieve your intentions for what you want in life after military service, we are ready to take a look at some of the more recognizable factors in the process of finding a new job. We've finally arrived at the point where most transitioning service members begin. This process mirrors the Course of Action Comparison methodology from the MDMP. Just as the COA Comparison is an objective process to reveal the best option among different alternatives, the objective of this step in the MTRP is to identify your top career path from the choices you synchronized from the previous step.

The Opportunity Comparison follows the same approach from the Course of Action Comparison step in the MDMP. First, you establish criteria to evaluate the different opportunities. Next, objectively define standards for evaluating opportunities against those criteria. Just like in the MDMP, the Opportunity Comparison step of the MTRP is not a subjective comparison of one option against the other. Finally, you will develop a scoring chart or decision matrix to rank your opportunities against your criteria and standards for evaluation.

5.1 COMPARISON CRITERIA

When it comes to developing your comparison criteria, you get to decide what's important. Let's examine some possible comparison criteria in the areas of compensation, location, and job details.

1. Possible criteria in the area of *Compensation*:

Criteria	Description
Starting Salary	The value of your annual starting salary.
Salary Projection	Some opportunities may have salaries that start off on the low end, but they offer greater income potential in the future.
Hiring Bonus	Some job opportunities include a hiring bonus in the form of cash or other benefits that might be of importance to you.
Paid Time Off	The military has a generous leave and pass policy. How many days of paid vacation, sick time, and discretionary days does this particular job offer?
Health Benefits	This includes Standard Healthcare, Dental, and Vision both in the level and quality of coverage for you and your family.
Education Benefits	Many employers fully fund education benefits for their employees, and some even extend those benefits to family members.
Relocation Benefits	Some employers will pay the costs associated with selling a home, breaking a lease agreement, and moving costs. They may even connect you with a realtor in your new location.
Retirement Benefits	Some employers offer lucrative retirement plans. This is not limited to federal civil service opportunities.
Other Compensation	Employers may offer stock options, housing costs, vacation plans, and other benefits that you might find intriguing or important.

2. Possible criteria under the topic of *Location*:

Criteria	Description
Demographic	Your preference for where you work - city, suburb, small town, etc.
Climate	Your preference regarding a temperate, seasonal, or warm climate.
Culture	Your preference regarding the culture and personality of the region (country, southern, progressive, blue collar, white collar, conservative, liberal, etc.)
School District Rating	If you have school aged children, a determining factor might be the quality of public schools or the availability and cost of private education.
Tax Benefits	You may prefer to live where the state doesn't tax your retirement pay.
Spouse Employment	Your location might be influenced by the availability of opportunities for your spouse to secure employment or transfer jobs with his or her current employer.
Proximity to Military or Veteran Resources	Your desire to remain in close proximity to military installations or VA facilities

Proximity to Family	You may have a preference regarding how far away you are from your parents, children, or extended family.
Family Preference	How important is a particular location to your spouse or other members of your family?
Other Factors	Perhaps you want to live on a golf course or in a gated community. You make your criteria as specific as possible.

3. As you examine possible criteria related to *Job Details*, consider the facts concerning what led to your success in the past and the assumptions for what kinds of opportunities will lead to your success in the future (**Exercise 2.6. Common Factors and Transition Assumptions**). Possible criteria based on the *Job Details*:

Criteria	Description
Urgency	Your preference along the continuum from routine to crisis job activities.
Group Dynamics	Your preference regarding the size and composition of the team you are expected to collaborate and work with.
Schedule	How you define the qualities of when and where you show up to work. Do you prefer to work first shift, second shift, third shift, weekends, holidays, etc.?
Structure	Where this opportunity rates along the continuum of structure from low to high in terms of expectations, functions, activities, and job requirements. How much time is spent on compliance and in meetings?
Role	Your level of authority and responsibility in the organization.
Novelty	How the prospect of innovative or disruptive activities excite and inspire you.
People	Your preference(s) regarding the qualities of the people you will work for and work with.
Personal Takeaway	What you value regarding the significance, impact, difficulty, growth, or gratitude from the particular opportunity
Travel Requirements	Your preference regarding the travel included with this job
Stability	Based on the expectation of relocating after hiring. Could you expect to live in the same location for the duration of your employment, or should you expect to move in the next 2-3 years as you advance in the company?
Opportunities for Advancement	Your assessment of how attractive the career trajectory is for a particular opportunity.

You can choose any criteria or combination of criteria based on your interests or personal preferences. You are not restricted to the criteria included in this handbook. You may have other reasons why you might select one opportunity over another.

5.2 STANDARDS FOR COMPARISON

Opportunity Comparison is meant to be an objective assessment of your opportunities so that you can rank them based on the factors you deem most important through the job search process. In order to conduct an evaluation, you have to set the parameters for that evaluation. The challenge of creating standards for criteria is to remove as much subjectivity as possible. You have to consider the criteria independently and separately from any predisposed bias you might have for one opportunity or another.

One approach to defining criteria is through a Likert Scale—a rating system against parameters from one extreme to another (see **Figure 5.2.1**). The value given to a particular criterion is based on where an opportunity rates between those extremes.

Figure 5.2.1. Example of a Rating System for Opportunity Comparison

Point Value	1	2	3	4	5
Rating	Poor	Fair	Acceptable	Very Good	Excellent
Meaning	Barely achieves the minimum standard	Okay but less than desirable	Meets expectations and is neither good nor bad	Slightly exceeds expectations	Meets or exceeds the ideal scenario

The higher the point value, the higher the rating in this model. In order for this model to be effective, you have to quantify the difference between each rating level. In other words, you have to define what separates a quality from being "Acceptable" from a quality that is "Very Good." Some examples are provided in **Figure 5.2.2.** As you review some of these examples, you will notice that some criteria have only three rating levels. That's okay. In this case, the three options were considered poor, acceptable, or excellent. You may have some options where you only want to consider what is acceptable, very good, and excellent (levels 3 through 5). That is entirely up to you. This is your standard. What's important is that you set a standard before you begin to evaluate the different opportunities.

How you define your standards to compare different opportunities should be consistent and make sense based on the criteria you deem most important. Numbers may help to quantify and clarify your ratings, but numbers are not necessary. For example, under the **Role** from **Figure 5.2.2**, you may score an entrepreneur opportunity as "Excellent" because you are your own boss even though you might not have any employees other than yourself. The objective of this process is to mitigate the amount of subjective influence from the evaluation process, but eliminating any subjectivity for something as personal as your career might not be possible.

Figure 5.2.2. Example of Criteria Definitions for Opportunity Comparison

Criteria Rating	Poor 1	Fair 2	Acceptable 3	Very Good 4	Excellent 5
Starting Salary	$40K	$60K	$80K	$100K	$120K
Paid Time Off (Days / Year)	<15	20	25	30	>30
Demographic	Rural	Small Town	Large City	College Town	Suburb
Climate	Average high temperature during winter months less than 40°		Average high temperature between 40° and 60°		Average high temperature in the winter more than 60°
School District Rating	Greatschools rating of less than 7	Greatschools rating of 7	Greatschools rating of 8	Greatschools rating of 9	Greatschools rating of 10
Schedule	Off shift hours (Night, weekend, holiday work)	Standard office hours with some weekend and holiday work	5 day workweek, no weekends, office closed on holidays	Flexible work schedule based on requirements	Complete autonomy to set my own schedule
Role	Entry level manager		Director or Leader (autonomy and responsibility) of a small team (up to 10 people)		President or Leader (autonomy and responsibility) of a large team (more than 10 people)
Travel requirements	>80% Travel	50-80% Travel	25-50% Travel	10-25% Travel	No Travel
Personal Takeaway	I know I am making an impact – but the people I support don't see it		Periodic feedback from the community (Internal/external feedback)		I want to see the direct impact of my work – each and every day (high external feedback)

Once you've settled on the criteria you intend to use, it is time to build an order of precedence and rank your criteria. This allows you to weight criteria based on their relative level of importance to you and your family. Ensure you stay consistent with your standard for evaluation and comparison. In other words, if higher values are better in your rating scale, then you want your most important criteria to carry the most weight for your analysis (see **Figure 5.2.3**). Conversely, if lower values are better in your rating scale, lower values would be used in your order of precedence.

Figure 5.2.3. Weighting Criteria for Opportunity Comparison.

Priority	Criteria by Order of Precedence	Weight
1	Personal Takeaway	10
1	Role	10
3	Climate	8
3	School District	8
5	Demographic	5
6	People are described using the words: Authentic, Committed, Open-minded, Passionate	4
6	Starting Salary	4
8	Schedule	3
9	Travel Requirements	2
10	Paid Time Off	1

Notice in this example how you could have more than one top priority. You could also have two criteria that tied for second place. Ensure that you account for this when you assign weights to the remaining criteria. Think of it as scoring on a golf leaderboard. If you have two top priorities tied for first place, then the next criteria is in third place. If you have two more criteria tied for third place, then the next criterion in succession is ranked number five. This is just one way to assign weights to criteria based on their level of relative importance.

5.3 BUILD THE OPPORTUNITY DECISION MATRIX

A modified scorecard or decision matrix for the MTRP consists of two elements. The first is the score for each opportunity. The second and the final step of the Opportunity Comparison is the order of precedence for the opportunities. Let's explore these two elements in more detail.

SCORE THE OPPORTUNITIES

Once you've determined your comparison criteria, created standards for evaluating that criteria, prioritized your criteria, and assigned weights based on relative importance, you are ready to score your opportunities and build your decision matrix. Because you determine the standards before you conduct the analysis, you mitigate much of the inherent bias or preference you might have or any particular opportunity.

Evaluate and score each opportunity independently (See **Figure 5.3.1. Scoring Each Opportunity Based on Rating and Relative Importance**). The score for each criterion is

Figure 5.3.1. Scoring Each Opportunity Based on Rating and Relative Importance. This is simply the product of the rating multiplied by the weight. The sum total of the scores for the criteria gives you the total score for that particular opportunity. Repeat this process for each opportunity.

OPPORTUNITY *Entrepreneur*	*Launch my own coaching and executive consulting business*			
CRITERIA	**COMMENT**	**RATING**	**WEIGHT**	**SCORE**
Personal Takeaway	*Definitely get to see the direct impact of my work*	*5*	*10*	*50*
Role	*I am the boss! I set my own schedule*	*5*	*10*	*50*
Climate	*I have no restrictions about 'where' I do this*	*5*	*8*	*40*
School District	*My only concern is the market – Note: Need to assess the market for this business in highly rated school districts*	*4*	*8*	*32*
Demographic	*I can definitely do this in the suburbs and commute or work virtually*	*5*	*5*	*25*
People	*I get to pick and choose who I partner and do business with*	*5*	*4*	*20*

Starting Salary	I expect that it will take 2 years for the business to become profitable. Won't achieve the minimum to score this option	0	4	0
Schedule	Complete autonomy to set my own schedule	5	3	15
Travel Requirements	I don't have to travel, but some opportunities may exist	4	2	8
Paid time off	There is no paid time off with this opportunity	0	1	0
			TOTAL SCORE	240

COMPARE THE OPPORTUNITIES

The final part of **Step 5. Opportunity Comparison** requires you to tally the scores to determine your order of precedence.

Figure 5.3.2. Scorecard and Decision Matrix

TYPE OPTION	DESCRIPTION OF OPPORTUNITY	SCORE
Nonprofit	Become a Director/Operations Manager of Nonprofit X	245
Entrepreneur	Launch my own coaching and executive consulting business	240
Small Business	Director of Operations and Business Development	175
Large Corporation	Program Manager for Company Y	68

EXERCISE 5.3 OPPORTUNITY COMPARISON

Now it's your turn to establish criteria, define standards for evaluation, and develop your scorecard or decision matrix to rank your different career opportunities.

STEP 1. DETERMINE COMPARISON CRITERIA

Review **Table 5.3.1** through **5.3.3** and use the following template to define your comparison criteria:

Criteria	Description

STEP 2. ASSIGN RATINGS TO COMPARISON CRITERIA

Reference **Figure 5.2.2. Example of Criteria Definitions for Opportunity Comparison** and use the following template to assign ratings for your comparison criteria.

Criteria Rating	Poor 1	Fair 2	Acceptable 3	Very Good 4	Excellent 5

STEP 3. WEIGHT CRITERIA

Prioritize criteria based on relative importance and assign weights (see **Figure 5.2.3** for an example).

Priority	Criteria by Order of Precedence	Weight

STEP 4. SCORE OPPORTUNITIES

Use the scorecards on the following pages to tally the results from your analysis.

OPPORTUNITY				
CRITERIA	**COMMENT**	**RATING**	**WEIGHT**	**SCORE**
		TOTAL SCORE		

OPPORTUNITY				
CRITERIA	**COMMENT**	**RATING**	**WEIGHT**	**SCORE**
		TOTAL SCORE		

OPPORTUNITY				
CRITERIA	COMMENT	RATING	WEIGHT	SCORE
		TOTAL SCORE		

OPPORTUNITY				
CRITERIA	COMMENT	RATING	WEIGHT	SCORE
		TOTAL SCORE		

OPPORTUNITY				
CRITERIA	COMMENT	RATING	WEIGHT	SCORE
		TOTAL SCORE		

OPPORTUNITY				
CRITERIA	**COMMENT**	**RATING**	**WEIGHT**	**SCORE**
		TOTAL SCORE		

STEP 5. BUILD A DECISION MATRIX TO COMPARE DIFFERENT OPPORTUNITIES

TYPE OPTION	DESCRIPTION OF OPPORTUNITY	SCORE

OPPORTUNITY INTEGRATION

Congratulations!

You have successfully completed the MTRP. You have gone through a deliberate problem-solving approach that mirrors the MDMP for operations planning and management. The final two steps of the MDMP (Step 6 and Step 7) involve the Course of Action Decision and Orders Preparation. The MTRP differs from the MDMP because you are not restricted to one course of action, and you are not preparing a five-paragraph Operations Order for publication. The goal of this final step of the MTRP is to integrate your opportunities into one plan for transition and reintegration. Let's review how we got here, considerations for integrating your plans, and highlight what happens next as you cross that threshold and become a veteran leader in society.

HOW WE GOT HERE

We started by exploring your identity through the Identity Analysis to develop your Statement of Intent for life beyond the military. We also created Action Plans that incorporate an Integrative Program of Transition for a comprehensive process of transition and reintegration across six different factors including whole health, socialization, cultural assimilation, professional preparedness, economic stability, and family adjustment. You determined your values (the WHO), your purpose (the WHY), your strengths (the HOW), your beliefs, and the common factors that led to your success in your military career. You incorporated your family and built a networking strategy to facilitate your transition and subsequent steps of the MTRP.

Next, we took an open-minded approach to explore six different types of opportunities—Entrepreneurship, Franchising, Civil Service, Nonprofit, Small Business, and Large Corporations. You were challenged to develop each option separately with the intention that you would execute each opportunity. You screened these opportunities based on how well they aligned to your core identity and Statement of Intent. For those opportunities that passed that standard, you developed timelines, synchronized actions, and established decision points for execution. You ranked the opportunities based on the standards for comparison that you created. You set a positive intention to maintain your momentum toward the life you want after military service.

So, here we are. You have your results. All that is left is your follow-through on a process that has already begun. Based on your analysis, your decision regarding which opportunity you will follow should be obvious, right? Well, not necessarily.

INTEGRATION

In the operations process, the commander may choose a different option from the one that the staff recommends. The same thing could happen at the conclusion of the MTRP. Your gut may pull you in a different direction from this analysis. Your intuition is shaped by years of experience, so even if you choose a different option from the one with the highest score, the benefit you gain from having completed this analysis is perspective and awareness. The enemy gets a vote when executing a military operation, and likewise, life gets a vote when you embark upon a plan for transition and reintegration. When it does, you have this detailed analysis to fall back on. You have other options that honor your unique identity and potential to lead in society. You never have to lose momentum to step into the life you want to live.

Also, who said you had to restrict yourself to only one course of action? It is possible and even desirable to pursue multiple lines of effort simultaneously. How many and which opportunities would depend on a variety of factors that include time, resources, and the effort you are willing to commit toward a particular opportunity. For example, you may search for a job in a large company and small company simultaneously while also laying the groundwork to start your own business. Your decision points will reveal when you need to shift your focus or eliminate a particular opportunity from consideration. As time passes, you may gain clarity for one option over another. After all, the goal is to cross the divide between the two worlds, but the path you take could be one or a combination of paths that you never really considered before.

You may also choose to execute opportunities at some point in time after you've achieved successful reintegration. For example, you may choose to start your own business after the kids go away to college or when your spouse secures full-time employment. As you embark upon your new life, you have the latitude to explore different opportunities to get you where you WANT to be in life after military service. As time passes, you may discover a new opportunity beyond those considered in this process. As discussed earlier, life gets a vote. You can reference this process to analyze different opportunities to achieve the highest level of personal and professional fulfillment.

WHAT HAPPENS NEXT

Transition and reintegration are the most difficult missions of the military journey. This handbook was created and specifically designed to frame this part of the military journey using an incremental and recognizable process to inspire your confidence to achieve this mission successfully. Now it's time for you to execute your plan to achieve your intent.

Understand that the most difficult part of the transition process will typically occur sometime after you separate from the military—typically in the three to six months after you drive out the gate for the last time. You might view that time as the decisive point of the transition and reintegration process, and it is why the Transition and Reintegration Timeline extends to six months after separation from the military. Shape the conditions now to maintain your initiative through that decisive point and beyond. Identify the new, healthy habits that will fill your reservoir of personal resilience.

Part 3 of this handbook is designed to support you along that journey. It includes strategies to find your new tribe after the military and manage relationships and healthy connections through the transition process (and beyond). Remember that your potential for success begins with you. Focus on what you believe is possible in life beyond the military. Your Hero's Journey is not finished. The best is yet to come.

Remember that the prize from the Hero's Journey is not something you get. It is something you give. Once you've figured that out, you become the master of the military world you leave behind and emerge as a leader in the civilian world you are about to enter. You got this. Stay positive. Be You. It's time to step fully and confidently into the leader you were meant to be and become the hero of your own story.

CULTURE AND RELATIONSHIPS

Part 3 of this handbook explores how to find your new tribe and build meaningful relationships through the transition process and beyond. These are lifelong strategies designed to help you understand the culture of the organization and build healthy relationships for the duration of your life. Transition is a transformative experience. The final two topics of this handbook address how you can assess an organization's culture to find the right fit, and how to build and sustain meaningful relationships as you embark upon a new life as a veteran leader in society.

HOW TO FIND YOUR NEW TRIBE AFTER THE MILITARY

UNDERSTANDING CULTURE

Disconnection from the military culture is the hardest part of military transition. Likewise, connecting with a new culture in civilian society is the hardest part of reintegration. Social connection is one of our core psychological needs. According to renowned author Brené Brown, it is the reason why we are here.[85] When it comes to making connections, culture matters. So much of the urgency surrounding how to find a new job hovers around the idea of finding the right fit in a new tribe, but what does that mean? How can you assess the culture of an organization, and more importantly, how do you determine the right fit for you?

WHAT IS CULTURE AND WHY DOES IT MATTER?

> Culture is the tacit social order of an organization: It shapes attitudes and behaviors in wide-ranging and durable ways. Cultural norms define what is encouraged, discouraged, accepted, or rejected within a group. When properly aligned with personal values, drives, and needs, culture can unleash tremendous amounts of energy toward a shared purpose and foster an organization's capacity to thrive.[86]

Culture defines the explicit and implicit norms of an organization. Culture is not a tagline or a company logo. It is not a series of pictures with motivational phrases hanging on an office

85. Brené Brown, *Daring Greatly: How the Courage to Be Vulnerable Transforms the Way We Live, Love, Parent, and Lead* (London: Penguin Life, 2015), 68.
86. Boris Groysberg, Jeremiah Lee, Jesse Price, and J. Yo-Jud Cheng, "The Culture Factor," *Harvard Business Review*, August 01, 2018, https://hbr.org/2018/01/the-culture-factor.

wall. It's more than the patch on your uniform or the color of a beret. Everyone sees the order and discipline of the dress-right-dress formation from a distance, but culture describes what really happens inside the ranks of that formation. Culture is what happens on the production floor, in back office meetings, and in private communications among employees. Culture represents the living essence of an organization.

Culture is the mechanism that guides the attitudes, behaviors, and beliefs of an organization in the same way an individual's values and purpose (the WHO and the WHY) guide and influence the attitudes, behaviors, and beliefs of an individual. The benefit of understanding the WHO (your values) and the WHY (your purpose) is to align your intrinsic nature with your external intentions (what you want in life). Likewise, an organization's identity (shared values) and purpose (reason for existing) reveals the potential impact of that organization in greater service to society.

Imagine the potential of aligning your personal values with the shared values of a larger group or company. This alignment was what kept you inspired and connected in the military. There was synergy. It created a resonance that you felt through a sense of purpose, inspiration, satisfaction, and joy. When these elements do not align—as in the case of being in an organization that doesn't fit with your values or purpose—you feel lost. You crave something more because your intrinsic needs are not being met. In the simplest terms, alignment feels inspired and misalignment just feels wrong. If you imagine the potential of taking that alignment to scale, you then understand the importance of culture as it relates to organizational performance and your sense of personal fulfillment.

WHAT KIND OF CULTURE ARE YOU LOOKING FOR?

How can you leverage what you know about yourself and your military experience to assess the best cultural fit for you? Here are three questions you might ask yourself to help clarify what you are looking for.

QUESTION 1: WHAT ATTRIBUTES WOULD DEFINE THE IDEAL CULTURE IN LIFE AFTER THE MILITARY?

The first step in finding your new tribe begins by recognizing exactly what you are looking for. To answer this question, start with your values. Before you determine where you might fit, you have to know where you stand regarding the things most important to you. It's always better to know your size before you go into the dressing room to try on new clothes. As you search, pay attention to how a particular organization might honor and respect your values. Value alignment is why you fit in the military culture, so recognizing your values—the recipe that defines your unique identity—is the most important step to finding your new tribe.

QUESTION 2: WHAT ARE THE QUALITIES THAT CHARACTERIZE THE BEST UNITS FROM YOUR CAREER?

Next, reflect on your most meaningful and successful units throughout your military career. The transient nature of the military journey exposes you to some great organizations and probably some "not-so-great" ones, too. Each organization has its own traditions and nuances whether it's special operations, airborne, aviation, Marines, submariners, etc. When you think about the positive experiences, what were the qualities of that organization or team that allowed you to excel in your job and have fun while doing it?

QUESTION 3: HOW WOULD THE PEOPLE ON THE TEAM DESCRIBE THE CULTURE?

We talk about the importance of culture in finding the next job, but how many people speak with actual employees about the culture of the organization? Notice that I didn't mention the recruiter or hiring manager's opinion about the culture—even though I am sure they have one. If you get a chance to talk to the people you might work with, ask them what the company values mean to them. Ask them what they perceive to be the priorities and "non-negotiables" of the organization. Inquire what they might change about the culture. Culture is a social phenomenon that can only be understood through social interaction, so to understand the culture, you have to engage the people.

You are the only person who can recognize the right culture for you after you leave the military. In the right tribe, you will feel inspired to go to work each day. When your values align to that of the organization, you will be able to more fully express your potential and showcase your strengths to contribute to the shared success of the team. In other words, you will belong. The alternative is to make accommodations or force the square peg into a round hole as you attempt to assimilate back into society. Landing in the wrong culture comes with the bitter consequence of loneliness. By exploring the factors that determine an organization's culture—leaders, mission, people, and structure—you can set your intention to find the right tribe in the best opportunity in life after the military.

LEADERS: THE MOST IMPORTANT FACTOR TO DETERMINE THE CULTURE OF AN ORGANIZATION

"So goes the leader, so goes the culture. So goes the culture, so goes the company."[87]

—SIMON SINEK

---

87. Sinek, *Leaders*, 159, 171.

The leaders, or lack thereof, are the most important determinant of an organization's culture. Now, when I say "leader," I am not talking about titles, roles, or headlines on LinkedIn profiles. I am not talking about awards, fellowships, scholarships, or any other label of presumed expertise. Those things may give you status, a sense of entitlement, and even a healthy paycheck, but that has nothing to do with being a leader. Being in charge doesn't make you a leader. The only thing you really need to be a leader is willing followers.[88]

Leadership is a human phenomenon, not a management construct. The two indispensable characteristics of the leader-follower dyad are trust and inspiration. Think about it: If someone ordered you to trust them, would you? Of course not, it doesn't work that way. Trust is something given willingly to someone else. Inspiration is a feeling. Leaders are people who move you to action. They provide the intrinsic, emotive energy for movement along a path toward an objective. Consequently, leadership is more about what's in the heart than what comes from the head.

The two leader qualities that influence the culture of the organization are personality and authenticity. Let's explore how these qualities influence the culture of an organization and offer some leadership questions that might help you discover the right tribe in life beyond the military.

PERSONALITY MATTERS

Throughout your military career, you've heard the saying that the unit assumes the personality of the commander. By definition, personality describes the characteristics of thinking, feeling, and behaving. Given the open-loop nature of our limbic system and the existence of mirror neurons—cells and structures within the brain that essentially copy or reflect the behaviors of others in social situations—members of an organization are emotionally and biologically attuned to mimic the behavior of the leader.[89] With the stage and audience afforded through their position, authority figures—such as executives, managers, directors, and commanders—have the greatest opportunity to shape the thinking, feeling, and behaving of the organization, but that doesn't necessarily mean anyone is willingly following them.

The personality of the person in charge sets the tone or mood for the organization. Just as mood reflects a temporary state of being and feeling for an individual, climate reflects a temporary state of being and feeling for an organization. Frequency and repetition can cause qualities of mood to become hardwired into the psyche and internalized as part of

---

88. Simon Sinek, *Start with Why: How Great Leaders Inspire Everyone to Take Action* (London: Portfolio/Penguin, 2013), 85.
89. Daniel Goleman and Richard E. Boyatzis, "Social Intelligence and the Biology of Leadership," *Harvard Business Review*, October 31, 2016, https://hbr.org/2008/09/social-intelligence-and-the-biology-of-leadership.

an individual's personality. The same holds true for how qualities of organizational climate become internalized into the organization's culture. This is why climate surveys in the military are so prevalent and punitive. The institution doesn't want one commander's toxic behaviors to permanently pollute the culture of a military unit.

Why does the personality of the people in charge matter more in the civilian world? In the military, organizational leadership is transitory, we swap out the people in charge every few years. The same may not be true in the civilian workplace. The same people may work at the same location for the entirety of their career. As they ascend the corporate ladder, their personality becomes internalized as part of the culture of the organization. Understanding the personality, values, and purpose of the people in charge could be more important to finding the right fit for your next career than the published mission and values of the organization.

AUTHENTICITY MATTERS

Because leadership is a human quality, the level of authenticity from the people in charge is important. How the leader shows up is more important than what the leader does, and is significantly more important than anything the leader says. When it comes to character, team dynamics, and establishing priorities, subordinates will align their actions and behaviors based on what they see from the leader. People in the room feel the tension when a leader is angry. When the leader is inspired, people feel inspired. When there is genuine hope and optimism...well, you get the idea.

Reflect on the most impactful leaders from your career for a moment. You felt a connection. You were inspired. Because of your experience with that leader, you probably sought opportunities to serve with that person again. More than just their success, they provided an example of the kind of leader you wanted to be. They were role models. Because connection works both ways, these leaders probably saw a bit of themselves in you. These human connections set the conditions for true inspiration. You probably never compared that leader's values and purpose with your own, but I'm fairly certain that if you had, you would discover that there was alignment and synergy between you and mentors or role models you wanted to follow.

When the people in charge are not authentic, there is an inherent conflict between who they are and who they want everyone else to think they are. This conflict has a catabolic effect, and that dissonance presents itself in negative ways. From the perspective of the subordinate, you may respect the position or rank, but you don't respect the person. You might admire their achievements at the office, but you can't help but notice the genuine misery that infects every other aspect of their lives. The reason you feel disconnected from these individuals is because they are disconnected from themselves. Stated another way, if you cannot connect and inspire yourself in a positive and meaningful way, you won't be able to connect and inspire anyone else. This is why a leader's authenticity is so important.

Authenticity allows the full expression of your values, purpose, and potential in a way that invites others to be connected and inspired by your example.

WHAT KIND OF LEADER DO YOU WANT TO FOLLOW?

When assessing how the leadership of a particular organization influences the culture, you want to ask thought-provoking and insightful questions. The "yes" or "no" inquiries may not reveal whether or not the people in charge are actually anyone you might want to follow. Here are three questions to help uncover how the leaders are influencing the culture in your search for the next tribe in life beyond the military.

QUESTION 1: HOW DOES WORKING AT THIS COMPANY HONOR YOUR PERSONAL VALUES?

This is a particularly powerful question when directed at the executive and management staff of an organization. It reveals whether or not the authority figures recognize their values and how those values shape the personality of the organization. Consider how you would have answered this question about how military service honored your personal values to assess the quality of the answers you might hear from potential employers. Finding the right fit means finding a culture that honors your values, which is why this question is much deeper than simply asking someone to recite his or her values.

QUESTION 2: WHAT CAN YOU TELL ME ABOUT THE MENTOR RELATIONSHIPS AT THIS COMPANY?

This is a loaded question that presumes that mentor relationships actually exist. If nobody recognizes anyone on the organizational chart as a mentor or professional role model, it might suggest a disconnection between the workforce and upper management. Alternatively, it might suggest that nobody in the organization is setting the kind of example that anyone would want to follow. Consider how you would have answered this question in the military. Listen for the cues that characterized your mentors and professional role models from the military.

QUESTION 3: HOW WOULD YOU EXPLAIN THE TURNOVER IN THIS ORGANIZATION?

Every organization has turnover. The real question is why people choose to leave. Social connection is a basic psychological need. If people don't find it in their current organization, they will go looking for it elsewhere. Even with a great mission and an inspired workforce, the presence of a poor leader makes for a toxic organization. When you see the revolving door of management and staff, take a serious look at who's in charge. In the military, people fought hard for assignments to units with great leaders, and when those individuals were toxic, they fought hard to leave.

The most effective leaders have figured out that the people are the most important mission of any organization. When networking or interviewing with managers and staff, pay attention to how they characterize the people in the organization. Are they impressed with their business metrics or their people? Humility matters. Managers care about profit and loss, leaders care about people. Be cautious of the authority figure who characterizes their people in monetary terms. Those aren't leaders. If the people in charge don't recognize the intrinsic value of their workforce, then there is a good chance that the organization will have an unhealthy culture.

A leader who leverages their authenticity to cultivate trust and their personality to foster inspiration will always outperform the manager who sees people as a means to an end. Recognize the personality and authenticity of the kind of leaders you most wanted to follow, and remember that just because a person is in charge, that doesn't make him or her a leader. Find your inspiration and leaders you can trust, and you will likely find a culture fitting to become your new tribe.

HOW THE ORGANIZATIONAL MISSION SHAPES THE CULTURE

We honor military service for its selfless quality, but is it really? To be sure, the military life can be a hard one. Anyone who has been to combat knows the true nature of sacrifice. All that said, you volunteered. You answered the call. Hell, we all did, and given the choice, most of us would do it again. We see past the hardship and actually consider our service a privilege. It was deeper than the uniform. It wasn't just a job. It was our life. It may have been a selfless endeavor, but it satisfied an intrinsic drive to find purpose and meaning. It brought us closer to understanding our WHY.

When the mission of the organization connects with an individual's sense of purpose, the work becomes more than just a job. It becomes an expression of personal inspiration. When the members of an organization are connected to a purpose, it creates a shared sense of belonging that speaks to the attitudes, behaviors, and beliefs that shape the culture of that organization.

THE MISSION BRINGS "LIKE-HEARTED" PEOPLE TOGETHER

I've often heard service members and veterans described as "like-minded" people, but I believe a more accurate characterization is that we are "like-hearted" people. We were moved to serve, and we didn't do it alone. We were joined by thousands of other men and women who were also inspired to serve. The mission of service connected with each of us. As your career progressed, you probably noticed that the things you thought were important were often the same things your colleagues thought were important. It wasn't that your hearts were necessarily in the right place, but that they always seemed to be in the same place. When each person's unique purpose aligns with the collective mission of the group, you create a culture of connected, inspired people who believe in what they are doing.

Money probably isn't the reason why you volunteered for military service. When money becomes the main factor in the decision for what happens next, don't be surprised if it doesn't take you where you really want to be in life after the military. There is a tendency to define transition based on what we can do and what an organization does. This tendency can cause us to overlook the true purpose and reason why that organization exists in the first place. A strong mission statement communicates the value an organization brings to the rest of society. It provides a means for you to express your purpose. When it connects you to a mission, it connects you to the people of that organization. After all, they are just like you: like-hearted people searching for an opportunity to make a difference.

HOW ORGANIZATIONS GET DISCONNECTED FROM THEIR CORE MISSION

Most businesses get started with a strong vision for how they want to change the world. They normally start small and take years to become profitable. A strong belief and connection to an empowering mission sustains them when the money cannot. Entrepreneurs have to trust their intuition and rely on passion to turn a small business into a larger, more successful one. This is why you hear so many large companies searching for ways to infuse the entrepreneurial spirit back into their workforce. They want to recapture the culture of passion, creativity, and commitment. They want that direct connection to the mission—the WHY—that inspired their success in the first place.

When organizations prioritize financial metrics over the people committed to achieve those metrics, they tend to depart from that shared sense of purpose. Consequently, the people tend to look inward. They focus on their own needs. Instead of competing in the marketplace, employees compete against each other. After all, if you aren't in the game to help the team succeed, the least you can do is help yourself succeed. You squabble for incentives. You abstract the intrinsic qualities of the people into monetary metrics. You focus on revenue at the expense of things like impact, inspiration, or the very reason why the organization was created in the first place. You exist only to make money, and in the end, the "organization" exists in name only. It becomes a cluster of individuals gathered together by happenstance in a perpetual struggle for individual survival.

Nobody "wants" to create a toxic culture, but one of the ways it happens is when an organization gets disconnected from the true reason why they exist. Your challenge through the networking and interview process is to find out just how connected the workforce is to that inspirational vision. Here are three questions to help uncover whether the culture is built upon a meaningful vision in your search for the next tribe in life beyond the military.

QUESTION 1: WHAT INSPIRES YOU TO COME TO WORK EVERY DAY?

When you ask this question, pay attention to the nonverbal cues. Do they seem caught off guard by the question or do they quickly transition into a discussion about the deeper meaning of their work? You may find that some employees don't even know the core mission of their organization. Be mindful of how you might have answered this question as a leader in the military. Understanding how connected the workforce is to the reason why the organization exists could be quite revealing as to whether or not the culture is connected to a purpose that you find meaningful.

QUESTION 2: HOW DO THE QUARTERLY OBJECTIVES SUPPORT THE BROADER MISSION OF THE ORGANIZATION?

How you do anything is how you do everything. Money is important to any business, but if the top objectives for the quarter talk about everything except the core mission of the company, then that core mission is simply not a priority. For example, a hospital might trumpet high-quality, patient-centered care, but if they only ever discuss monetary instruments in their corporate meetings, don't be surprised if the patients of that hospital don't feel like the priority. How the organization sets priorities will reveal the true mission, and consequently the culture, of that organization.

QUESTION 3: WHAT ABOUT THE MISSION OF THE ORGANIZATION CONNECTS WITH YOU PERSONALLY?

This question reveals how a potential colleague's purpose aligns with that of the organization. It reveals the presence of "like-hearted" people in the organization. Given that you recognize your own purpose in life beyond the military, it allows you to see who fits in the organization so that you can make a determination as to whether or not you might fit there as well.

When you connect with like-hearted people who come together to express that purpose in a meaningful way for the benefit of society, you have a tribe. There is a greater power in community, so find an organizational mission that aligns with your WHY. That's the easy part. Your challenge in the transition and reintegration process is finding out what is truly shaping the culture of the organization: Is it the core mission, or is it something else? When "something else" shapes the culture of that organization, perhaps you need to look somewhere else to find the right fit. When you find an organization that is committed to a calling that honors your own, you may have found your new tribe in life beyond the military.

POWER OF THE PEOPLE IN SHAPING THE CULTURE

"Mr. Sims doesn't want it. He doesn't need to be labeled: 'Still worthy of being a Baird Man.' What the hell is that?...If I were the man I was five years ago, I'd take a FLAME-THROWER to this place!"[90]

—COLONEL FRANK SLADE AS PLAYED BY AL PACINO

Can you believe it's been nearly three decades since Colonel Slade talked about torching the Baird School? In the movie, *Scent of a Woman*, his caretaker and friend, Charlie Simms, didn't fit into the culture of the prestigious prep school. Charlie wasn't like the other students. He wasn't wealthy. He didn't come from a prestigious family. He may have had the grades, he may have met the admissions criteria, but Charlie wasn't a "Baird Man." Because he didn't fit with the people, he didn't fit in the school. This fictional story highlights the fact that the qualities of the people in the organization shape the culture of that organization.

WHO YOU ARE IS DETERMINED LARGELY BY WHO YOU ARE WITH

Social belonging ranks just above safety in an individual's hierarchy of needs. There is science underpinning the idiom, "Birds of a feather, flock together." Similarities in experiences, interests, talents, or values among people provide a means for connection. We develop relationships with people who are similar to us. As an application of the social identity theory, we form attachments to the shared identity of the group and differentiate ourselves from other groups across society.[91] Because our personal identity is tied to the group label, we strive to distinguish our shared prestige and collective accomplishments of our brothers and sisters. We recognize the "in-group" as something better than the "out-group." This satisfies our psychological need for esteem, the next level up from social belonging on our hierarchy of needs.

---

90. *Scent of a Woman*, dir. Martin Brest, perf. Al Pacino and Chris O'Donnell (Universal Studios, 1992).
91. Saul McLeod, "Social Identity Theory," *Simply Psychology*, October 24, 2008, https://www.simplypsychology.org/social-identity-theory.html.

Think about how this applied throughout your career. You considered yourself a part of the in-group as a soldier, and you may have had some strong opinions about civilian outsiders. Even within the military, we have subcultures and established norms for how things are done based on the groups we belong to. Paratroopers believe that they bear a standard that is distinctive from the "dirty, nasty leg." Tab-wearers tend to expect more from fellow tab-wearers. Your unit patch makes a difference, and sometimes, your combat patch does, too. We formed strong attachments to the people and the culture of our groups.

The fact that I didn't account for the kinds of people I would be working with was one of my fatal flaws in my first transition as a junior captain. My colleagues at my job were engineers, and they were exceptionally brilliant. They were never condescending, but I couldn't follow most of their conversations. They had different interests and styles of communication. Their values were rooted in science in the same way that a soldier's values are rooted in service. The things that I thought were important were not the same things they thought were important. I discovered that I fit in better with the blue-collar, union staff than I did with my "peers." I only worked there for a year, and I wasn't disappointed when I left. After all, I didn't fit into that tribe.

YOUR STARTING POINT AS A MEMBER OF THE "OUT-GROUP"

The challenge through transition and reintegration is that veterans are a shrinking minority across the country. Your life as a veteran starts as a member of the out-group. Talking end-lessly about deployments and military experiences runs the risk of reinforcing your status as an outsider. Your strategy for determining your new tribe needs to look past the purely military aspects of that culture and explore some of the more universal qualities of your experience. This is why recognizing your values, your purpose, and your intrinsic strengths are so important, they transcend the uniform and provide an opportunity to make meaningful connections with your new "in-group."

The connection point for the people who belong to successful organizations comes from the values, purpose, and vision for that organization. The military is a great example of a high-performance team that cherishes diversity in everything but the most important factors of values, purpose, and vision. These are the non-negotiable elements for assessing who belongs with the "in-group." Bringing people together who share in those intrinsic qualities is the screening criteria for any high-performance team, including your next team after the military.

ASSESSING HOW YOU FIT WITH THE PEOPLE

Assuming you recognize your values (the WHO), purpose (the WHY), intrinsic strengths (the

HOW), and your intent for life beyond the military (the WHAT), here are some questions that could help you determine whether or not you identify with the people of a potential employer.

QUESTION 1: WHAT DO YOU VALUE MOST ABOUT THE PEOPLE WHO WORK HERE?

As you listen to the answers from this question, determine whether or not the people value the same things that you value. The most dangerous answer you could hear when asking this question is "I don't know." Think about how you would answer this question about the men and women who stood next to you in formation, and it might reveal whether you would fit within the ranks of this new "formation."

QUESTION 2: WHAT THREE WORDS WOULD YOU USE TO DESCRIBE THE PEOPLE OF THIS ORGANIZATION?

This question is deeper than the more common, "Do you like working here?" Just because people like working there doesn't mean that **you** will like working there. When you are networking and interviewing, you need meaningful intelligence about the people you are going to spend at least one-third of your life with. When asked of multiple employees, this question will reveal whether or not consistency exists between how the employees identify the qualities of their "in-group."

QUESTION 3: WHAT MAKES THE PEOPLE HERE UNIQUE?

This question can be revealing when asked across different departments or echelons of management in an organization. It can uncover any cliques that could offer deeper insight into a lack of cohesion that feeds the politics of divisive corporate cultures. Alternatively, it could highlight the reasons why a particular organization might be the ideal fit for you.

FINAL NOTE ABOUT THE PEOPLE

Admittedly, it is very difficult to make an accurate assessment of the people from a handful of conversations with individuals you might be meeting for the first time. This is why the leadership and the organizational mission might be stronger indicators of the culture in the job search process. Still, these questions may help you establish whether you are more likely to fit with the people of an organization. A wide array of answers about the people may suggest a lack of cohesion or a divisive culture. Always remember that your military experience informed your intuition about people, so trust your gut.

One of the questions you will have to answer when selecting your next employer is whether or not the organization's people are *your* people. The company will do its part to make their own assessment about *you*, but it is incumbent upon you to make your assessment about *them.* Be honest with yourself regarding where you fit. Only you will know whether or not you can identify with the people. You may have all the talent necessary to succeed, you may meet all the prerequisites for the job, but from the context of the organizational culture, only you will know whether or not you are a "Baird Man."

WELCOME TO THE MACHINE: HOW STRUCTURE INFLUENCES THE CULTURE

Organizations are a lot like people. They are born out of passion. They embody a hope for the future. They start out small with great energy and innocence. Unlike people, organizations are manifested from an idea. That idea attracts others. A leader provides the energy that inspires followers. People connect with the idea or mission because it honors their values and calling to make a difference. As it matures, the organization may have the opportunity to grow. It becomes more sophisticated, refined, and complex in order to reach more people. In an effort to ensure conformity, quality, and standards throughout the organization, we create systems, rules, and procedures. The idea becomes hardwired into a machine. That machine has a name, and its name is bureaucracy.

"Bureaucracy is a system of administration distinguished by its (1) clear hierarchy of authority, (2) rigid division of labor, (3) written and inflexible rules, regulations, and procedures, and (4) impersonal relationships."[92] Given a military leader's desire to continue making an impact, recognizing how the vision for an organization can become bolted and hardwired into the impersonal processes of the bureaucracy is an important factor to determine your new tribe in life after the military.

HOW ORGANIZATIONS GIVE POWER TO THE MACHINE

Bureaucracy is born out of a desire for quality, conformity, and compliance. When the size and scope of an organization begins to outpace the leader's capacity to maintain the intimacy from the conception of the small business, the organization builds systems to fill voids and cover the blind spots. We forge structure. We mold compliance. These things are intended to augment the leaders, mission, and people that shape the culture. With the best of intentions, this structure is a good thing.

Unfortunately, the quest for short-term results tempts us to focus more on systems and processes at the expense of the people. Intimacy and trust across large or international organizations becomes more difficult, so we substitute rules for compliance in place of

---

92. "What Is Bureaucracy? Definition and Meaning," *Business Dictionary*, accessed June 20, 2019, http://www.businessdictionary .com/definition/bureaucracy.html.

inspiration through the leader. As we build this machine, the leader's identity becomes indistinguishable from the institution, and the bureaucracy becomes the master that the people serve. The mission, or the WHY for the organization, becomes a talking point, and the leaders are reduced to mere managers whose very survival is dependent upon keeping the machine running.

WHAT HAPPENS TO THE CULTURE WHEN THE MACHINE ASSUMES CONTROL?

In these organizations, the bureaucracy is the most dominant force shaping the culture. Just as a machine is cold, hard, apathetic, and impersonal, so, too, is the organization at the mercy of its bureaucracy. As the machine becomes more self-aware, it creates more bureaucracy to protect the status quo. Leaders rely on human resources instead of connection and compassion to make people-related decisions. Human beings are managed like any other asset on the balance sheet. Leaders are not empowered. Decisions are cycled through various departments for consensus. Schedules are occupied with inspections and meetings to monitor compliance to the system. The original passion, creativity, and intended impact of the organization are buried under the abstractions of business metrics that merely infer success.

This evolution leads to a phenomenon known as *passive micromanagement.* You probably recognize "traditional" micromanagement as the boss who stands over you, tells you what to do, and offers continuous monitoring and feedback as you attempt to comply with their directives. Passive micromanagement occurs when the bureaucracy ends up doing the same thing through task saturation. The bureaucracy creates an environment where employees are expected to complete more tasks than they could reasonably accomplish in the time available. One example is how the army mandates more mandatory training requirements than any unit could conceivably accomplish in a given year. Passive micromanagement creates a culture of compliance and control through task saturation.

Passive micromanagement leads to unhealthy structural and psychological control. Structural control is derived from the cycle of reviews, inspections, and surveys that force managers to spend their time focused on how to instill compliance. Psychological control comes from the fear of being labeled as inadequate or being blamed for areas of noncompliance. As managers (not leaders) become slaves to these forms of control in the bureaucracy, they become connected to the machine and disconnected from the people. Ironically enough, senior managers expect subordinate managers to "lead" even though every aspect of the culture has them scrambling for their own survival based on the next review, revenue forecast, or earnings report.

Once you abstract the human qualities from the organization, you create a culture that is toxic for human beings. Morality is framed through discussions of profit and loss. Ethics become an instrument of convenience instead of a foundation for operations. Instead of a team, the organization devolves into an aggregation of self-interested individuals who coexist in common places making transactions no different from the people in a crowded mall who exchange goods and services for their personal gain. Anxiety replaces inspiration as managers spend long hours scrambling in the Orwellian pursuit of compliance at the expense of the original mission, the individual's health, and the well-being of the people.

HOW TO DETERMINE WHO OR WHAT YOU ARE WORKING FOR

As leaders, we complain about the bureaucracy and seek a greater freedom in life beyond the military. Unfortunately, many potential employers have structure and bureaucracy that rivals any from the Department of Defense. Your challenge through the networking and interview process is to find out who or what is really driving the culture of the organization. Here are three questions to help uncover how the structure and bureaucracy frame the culture in your search for the next tribe in life beyond the military.

QUESTION 1. HOW MUCH CONTROL DO YOU HAVE OVER YOUR SCHEDULE?

This question reveals how much passive micromanagement exists in the organization. If the manager has task saturation and worries about an endless cycle of inspections, meetings, and reports, then you could reasonably expect the same lack of control and focus on out-of-tolerance conditions should you decide to work there.

QUESTION 2. HOW ARE DECISIONS MADE IN THIS ORGANIZATION?

In smaller, horizontal organizations, leaders are empowered to make decisions. Senior leaders and managers trust and back the decisions of junior leaders. This is less true for larger, vertically structured hierarchies. In a structured bureaucracy, decisions are routed through departments to attain consensus in a process that could take days, weeks, or even months. If you see yourself as someone used to taking decisive action, this could reveal a potential challenge to how you might fit in that organization. Pay attention to how people interact with their management. Is it through personal, routine engagement, or is it through meetings? This will reveal the level of connection (or lack thereof) between managers and their staff.

QUESTION 3. HOW DO YOU ENSURE COMPLIANCE TO STANDARDS AND PROCEDURES IN THIS ORGANIZATION?

Do you remember what it was like to live under the specter of the command inspection process in the military? If you didn't like it then, you probably won't like it in the corporate world either. Consider the level of fear and anxiety associated with meeting the numbers. The requirement to prepare and present metrics could consume more hours than you feasibly have in a week, and you have to decide whether or not that is the best application of your potential as a leader in life beyond the military.

WHY WOULD ANYONE WANT TO WORK FOR THE MACHINE?

The lure of bureaucratic organizations is the promise of security. For the person who worries about paying the bills, security seems worth the price of admission to join the machine. Robust compensation and retirement packages typically accompany management positions within the machine, and once you become a part of the bureaucracy, it is hard for anyone to remove you from the collective. Not all bureaucracies are bad, but it takes a dynamic visionary to wrest control from the machine and return the power to the people. The good news is that you've probably worked for some of these leaders in the military. You just need to find these kinds of leaders in the corporate sector.

Trust your intuition to recognize the leaders who seek a return to the innocence and intimacy that fuels compassion and inspiration for the organization. Some leaders are willing to establish priorities and protect the people to overcome the inertia of the machine to make meaningful connections for high-performance teams. In these cases, the leader sets the conditions for the culture, not the bureaucracy. Your challenge is to determine who is serving whom in finding your new tribe in life beyond the military.

FORGING HEALTHY RELATIONSHIPS THROUGH MILITARY TRANSITION AND BEYOND

The following portion of this handbook is included with the permission of the author, Dr. Shauna Springer, who is known as "Doc Springer" by many within the military and veteran community. This is meant to be your conversation with an expert in forging and sustaining healthy relationships from a nationally recognized professional with more than twenty years of research and practical experience working with thousands of veterans and their partners.

BACKGROUND: UNDERSTANDING THE STAKES

Based on more than two decades of focused work on close relationships and supporting successful transition from the military, it is clear to me that transitioning from the military is not simply a matter of landing your next paid gig. Successful transition requires:

1. A deep re-evaluation and rediscovery of your identity

2. The development and maintenance of a network of deeply trusted relationships, beginning with the relationship(s) of those closest to you, and

3. The intentional application of the personally held values that give life meaning and bring depth and intimacy into our closest relationships.

Transition is like a "punch in the gut" or "grey zone"[93] between two worlds. Many of you have told me that it feels as though the life you knew—and your relationships—have been suddenly

---

93. With thanks to USMC Veteran Ellliott McKenzie for sharing this phrase.

"thrown into a blender." As you discharge from the military, the loss of your military family is a relationship loss of the highest order. Many of you express feelings of sudden isolation and alienation in a society that has values that are very different from the ones that have guided your life in the military.

Many of you have described this as "feeling like a ghost" or "an empty shell inside." This experience goes beyond the personal, private transition in your military role; these feelings occur in the context of an ever-widening cultural gap between civilian citizens and warriors. Despite the rampant tendency toward "hero worship" and "thanking you for your service," it can be very challenging to establish deep and meaningful connections with those who have not served in the military. In fact, one of the interesting commonalities between the Vietnam Veterans I have served and those of you who have recently transitioned, is the theme that you often feel like strangers in a strange land. The combination of fear, social rejection, and hero worship of civilians further alienates you from meaningful connection and makes you feel invisible within society at large.

My purpose is grounded in the understanding that you, as one who has taken the oath of service, are an irreplaceable asset to society. The things that you mourn in your transition from the military are also peak life experiences that have allowed you to gain insights into things most people will never touch, the kind of love between those who would give their lives for each other, without hesitation. The deep bond of trust that cannot—and need not—be put into words. The sense of being totally and completely linked up with others and an irreplaceable part of something bigger than yourself. You have invaluable wisdom and life experience to share precisely because you have touched and witnessed things that are sacred about the nature of life and death, and the relationship bonds that define a meaningful life.

As you transition, your tribe must transform along with you. Transition is a particularly vulnerable time for romantic partnerships; there is the potential for positive growth, and, at the same time, there is heightened risk for relationships to dissolve. You must take some risks to extend your trust to those at home—your homefront tribe. With them, you must also summon the courage to stand without your armor, which may be harder than to walk into an ambush in the combat zone.

It is also critical to stay *meaningfully* connected to the tribe you served with. Your brothers-and sisters-in-arms keep you plugged in to a rich history of life experiences that have shaped you and them. They can remind you of who you are within the fog of transition. Forming a solid network of relationships with both your homefront tribe and maintaining contact with those in your military family can help you find a path of trust, meaning, and purpose in your next evolution.

We will dive into all of this more deeply in this portion of the handbook, with the overarching goal of helping you gain both insights and ways to apply them that will lead to successful relationships after the military.

A STRATEGIC, 20,000-FOOT VIEW ON SUCCESSFUL RELATIONSHIPS

The first thing to understand is that all successful long-term romantic partnerships go through three phases:[94] the "cocaine rush" phase, the "testing" phase, and the "tested romanticism" phase. In brief, the "cocaine rush" phase is the initial period of intense, highly pleasurable bonding based on the mutual fantasy that you and the other person are each other's soul mates. The "testing" phase is the period in which the strength of your relationship will be repeatedly tested by a variety of life challenges and further transitions (e.g., related to career decisions, parenting choices, etc.). The "tested romanticism" phase of successful relationships is the final stage, characterized by a rare and special form of mutual love and respect that radiates from the couple to others in their lives.

Before we delve into each of the three phases in greater detail, here is an illustration of the "20,000-foot view" of successful relationships:

Figure 3. The Evolution of Battle Tested Partnerships

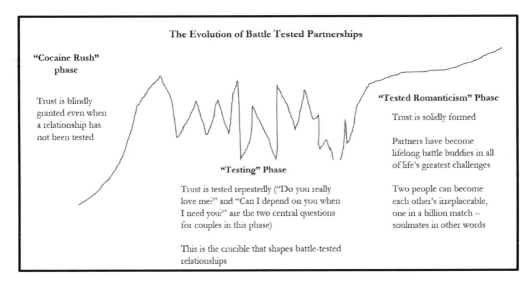

---

94. Shauna Springer, *Marriage, for Equals: The Successful Joint (ad)ventures of Well-educated Couples* (Indianapolis, IN: Dog Ear Publishing, 2012).

FALLING IN LOVE IS LIKE SMOKING CRACK COCAINE

There is a reason I named the first phase of my three-phase model of successful relationships the "cocaine rush phase."[95] It is this: There are *striking* similarities between the brain state of a person falling in love and that of a person who has just smoked crack cocaine[96]. We're not talking about the slightly buzzed feeling you might get from drinking a glass or two of wine, but rather the high-octane euphoria associated with freebasing crack cocaine. Falling in love is the best high you can get without breaking any laws. The same brain chemicals (that is, massive amounts of dopamine and norepinephrine[97]) are in play, and many of the same brain pathways and structures are active when we are falling in love and enjoying a cocaine high.

Consider for a moment the nature of the euphoric effects of smoking crack cocaine: "enhanced mood, heightened sexual interest, a feeling of increased self-confidence, greater conversational prowess and intensified consciousness. It offers the most wonderful state of consciousness, and the most intense sense of being alive [that] the user will ever enjoy."[98] If we replace the words "smoking crack cocaine" with the words "falling in love," does the sentence still make sense? *Falling in love* leads to "enhanced mood, heightened sexual interest, a feeling of increased self-confidence, greater conversational prowess and intensified consciousness...It offers the most wonderful state of consciousness, and the most intense sense of being alive that the user will ever enjoy." Yes, I'd say that fits, wouldn't you?

Users of cocaine report that it sharpens their focus and allows them to achieve an almost superhuman state of electrifying purpose. Along these lines, another common marker of both falling in love and smoking cocaine is a clear stimulatory effect. To the degree that life in the military is highly stimulating—perhaps by its very nature and the adrenaline spikes that are created through certain roles, or perhaps aided by the use of high doses of caffeine—there may be a "deficit of stimulation" after the transition out of the military. If there is, it may become especially tempting to fall in love as this rewards the brain with a stimulatory effect.

A relational hallmark of the cocaine rush phase is that *blind trust is extended between the two people in the relationship*. The cocaine rush is a period of delightful mutual delusion based on very limited information about the potential for a relationship to go the distance. Lovers in the first stage of a relationship often highlight similarities, minimize differences, and selectively filter for evidence that they are each other's "perfect match."

---

95. Ibid., "The Cocaine Rush Phase" is a copyrighted term through this book.

96. Andreas Bartels and Semir Zeki, "The Neural Basis of Romantic Love," *NeuroReport* 11, no. 17 (2000): 3829-834, https://doi:10.1097/00001756-200011270-00046.

97. Helen Fisher, "Lust, Attraction, Attachment: Biology and Evolution of the Three Primary Emotion Systems for Mating, Reproduction, and Parenting," *Journal of Sex Education and Therapy* 25, no. 1 (2000): 96–104, https://doi:10.1080/01614576.2000.11074334.

98. "In Search Of The Big Bang," *Crack Cocaine*, accessed June 24, 2019, https://www.cocaine.org/coke.html.

THE "TESTING" PHASE[99]

After the "cocaine rush" phase, we enter the "testing" phase of the relationship. The transition between the cocaine rush phase and the testing phase is marked by a "mutual fall from grace." During the testing phase, incompatibilities and differences in values surface. The private pain and shame we work to conceal from our partners during the cocaine rush phase begins to reveal itself. Violations of trust (sometimes major, sometimes minor) and attachment wounds are also common during the testing phase. Couples need to work through the suffering they bring on each other without losing the underlying trust that is the lifeblood of long-term relationships.

A driving goal of the testing phase should be to test the "seaworthiness" or conduct the rehearsal of concept "ROC" drill of a potential relationship, ideally before we legally bind ourselves to another person. In the testing phase, the main developmental tasks are to negotiate challenges and transitions while treating each other with love and respect, and to proactively invest energy in maintaining your bond when career goals or love of children could supplant our intimate connection. A number of major life transitions typically occur during the testing phase of relationships. As a result, each couple passes through several tunnels of chaos—for example, when making a major relocation, adding children to their family, finding (or losing) a job, changing a career, or launching children. There is nothing quite like these tunnels of chaos to throw the "soul mate" fantasy into question, yet it is in the very process of navigating these tunnels of chaos that two people actually begin to become soul mates.

"TESTED ROMANTICISM" PHASE[100]

Couples who effectively navigate the testing phase (which is often the longest phase in a lifelong partnership) enter the third phase of successful relationships, what I call the "tested romanticism" phase. The tested romanticism phase refers to the highly satisfying union of two people who have developed a genius for loving each other well and whose risk of divorce is virtually nonexistent. During this phase, the couple fulfills the promise of what a marriage can be: a safe and supportive base that allows each partner to flourish. At this stage of marriage, the bond of love and respect is often highly visible to others, and the couple frequently becomes generous toward others out of an abundance of love and joy they share with each other.

Partnerships in the tested romanticism phase are grounded in security and a rare and special form of earned intimacy. Effective, respectful negotiation of challenges has become habitual.

---

99. "The Testing Phase" is a term copyrighted through this book as first described in Shauna Springer, *Marriage, for Equals: The Successful Joint (ad)ventures of Well-educated Couples* (Indianapolis, IN: Dog Ear Publishing, 2012).
100. Ibid., "Tested Romanticism" is a term copyrighted through this book.

Thoughts of separation or divorce are completely alien. The partnership has become so multifaceted and the compatibilities so intricately dovetailed that one's spouse could never be replaced by anyone else. While the idea of arriving as "soul mates" is a common delusion during the cocaine rush phase, two individuals who have become perfect for, and irreplaceable to, each other have become soul mates. In other words, based on my understanding of successful relationships, soul mates are two people who have become each other's "one-in-a-billion perfect match" over time.

TRANSITION, ATTACHMENT, AND TRUST

Viewing transition from an attachment perspective helps us see why transition is such a high-stakes time for many prior service members. **Attachment is about trust**—trust that others we depend on will meet our needs. In adult relationships, attachment shows up as the fundamental element that predicts whether our relationships will be successful (or not). There are three questions that determine the health of our closest relationships, and all of them are grounded in attachment:

1. Do you really love me?

2. Is it safe to ask you for what I need?

3. Can I trust and depend on you when I need you?

A secure attachment functions like a "safe base of operations." In the combat zone, establishing a base is a critical first step that allows you to create, resource, and execute tactical operations. In the same way, in our closest relationships, having a "safe base" allows us to explore and grow, both inwardly and outwardly. If we have a solid trust that those closest to us have our back, this provides the "safe base" we need for developing our understanding of our core identity and innermost values. We can grow in myriad ways, without the paralyzing level of fear that limits growth otherwise. When those we love and trust return our love and trust in equal measure, we have the courage to overcome the fear associated with the process of life transitions.

The same safe base that helps us look inward allows us to explore the world outside of who we are—we can take on new challenges without becoming overwhelmed by anxiety. Even when we take on daunting challenges that require individual action, we are never alone, because we carry with us the strength of the tribe who has our back. Even if they are in a different ZIP code as we face a new challenge, we can tap the strength of our tribe as we think about the support they would offer us and the confidence they have in us.

This is especially true for those who are closest to us, what might be called our "inner circle[101]"—that is the three or so other people in our lives that we most deeply trust. Some of the people in our inner circle may be others we have served with, but the inner circle often includes a non-military spouse or partner, sometimes a parent or sibling, or a very longtime close friend. Regardless of where and how we met these people, they are the people that love and support us even when we fail, or when we go through times of real struggle.

Secure attachment to those closest to us is the lifeblood of achieving our full potential. These attachments give us strength and clarity as we work to exercise our personally held values. On the other hand, when we lack a "safe base" of operations, life becomes chaotic and overwhelmingly stressful. When attachment is insecure, our closest relationships become distressed and we become handicapped when it comes to fulfilling our full potential. Just as in combat operations, we need a safe base of operations to achieve success in our efforts. This insight is critical for making a successful transition out of the military.

THE MILITARY OFTEN RECONSTITUTES OUR ENTIRE ATTACHMENT SYSTEM

In the past decade, there has been a heavy focus on the military-to-civilian transition process (M-C-T). Hundreds of millions of dollars have been spent on attempts to improve this part of the transition process. What has been *overlooked* is the civilian-to-military (C-T-M) transition process. *We have to appreciate what it takes for a civilian to attach his or her identity to the uniform in order to understand the gravity of the transition process back into civilian life after the military.*

Further, the military is an attachment-creating organization. Success in the military is predicated on strong attachments to one's team. You are conditioned to recognize the value and power of the team above your own sense of individuality and personal identity. From boot camp on, the military lifestyle often forges *profound interdependence and a different level of trust than anything most of us have ever experienced before.* The military is more than just a unit or an organization, it is a band of brothers and sisters. It is a family. The situations that are orchestrated from the time of initial training through all forms of military deployment create a level of group cohesion unlike anything that many of us have previously experienced in our lives.

We explored some of the physiological underpinnings of this attachment in **Step 2.2.1 The Physiological Implications of Military Separation** as part of the Identity Analysis of the MTRP. We noted that the neurotransmission of oxytocin is a primary bonding agent in close

---

101. Other names for the same thing might be our "core unit," our "fire team", or "core team" or our "QRF" ("quick reaction force")

relationships. Oxytocin is released at the peak of orgasm and while breastfeeding newborns, but it is also released in other situations, for instance, when someone saves our lives, or when we have a deep soul-baring conversation with a trusted friend.

The military life brings not only new challenges, but also a series of peak emotional experiences of feeling deeply bonded to others. In other words, from a biochemical perspective, during your time in the military, barring certain experiences,[102] it is likely that there has been a continual flood of oxytocin in your brain that has helped develop the bonds you share with your brothers- and sisters-in-arms.

There are significant cultural factors as well that support the reconstitution of your attachment network. Even though service members may dearly love their spouses, during military service, you appreciate the delicate balance between the needs of your family and the needs of the mission. More often than not, the needs of the mission come first, particularly for military leaders, who bear responsibility for the wellness and success of their unit. Family members become support systems to their active duty service members. The lives of military families are largely shaped by the movements and needs of the military. Military spouses of deployed service members are instructed—sometimes in subtle ways, and other times in very overt ways—to handle stressful family matters on their own so that these stressors do not become distractions to the mission. You have learned the value of mission focus because, as described in the Special Forces community, "a distracted operator is a dead operator."

Even for those of you who grew up in tight-knit families, the bonds that form with other military service members are often at an entirely different level. Your survival may have depended on it. Your military unit became your family. You spent holidays together. You endured personal triumphs together, and in many cases, you faced tragedy together. You hold and share secrets that you would never reveal outside your tribe. You were with each other through the joys and horrors of life as only those within your formation could understand. Because of these relationships, you were at your best. You became something more. The unifying theme is this: *learning to be seamlessly interdependent is to reach the summit of our human potential.*

The lifeblood of your unit is the trust and love among those who would lay their lives down for each other. *This* is the protective factor that buffers against despair and disconnection in the most extreme situations, *the most challenging of which may be the period after you discharge from the military*. Transition is a uniquely challenging time, but *one that is also filled with potential*. In fact, with well-informed insights and the right support, the transition

---

102. Exceptions would include experiences of being violated or betrayed by fellow military service members or those within the chain of command.

from the military can bring you to levels of personal growth that surpass anything you have previously experienced in your life.

SHOULD WE EMPHASIZE INDIVIDUAL RESILIENCE?

The field is currently populated with interventions designed to focus on individual "resilience." Individual resilience[103] alone is *not* the model the military creates, and it is not what we should emphasize during the transition out of the military. These interventions will *not* hit their intended target because they are not based on an accurate understanding of how service members and veterans are influenced by the *attachment system* they have developed while in the military. How many times have we heard from those in transition that the hardest part was "losing connection with those they served with" or "losing the sense of purpose" that came with life in the military? As Sebastian Junger explains in the book *Tribe*, "Humans don't mind hardship, in fact they thrive on it; what they mind is not feeling necessary."[104]

We create our identities and our purpose in the context of our attachments. This is often particularly true for those of you who answered the call to military service at a young age. Others we trust are a primary source of feedback in the process of defining who we are and what we stand for. And when our own strength falters during times of struggle, it is critical that we have a functional tribe in place, from which we can draw the strength we need to persevere.

THE TRUST THAT DEFIES DESCRIPTION IS NOT BASED ON PERSONALITY COMPATIBILITY

We've all heard of the concept of "love at first sight." In the military, and other contexts, there is a flipside phenomenon that occurs which I call "hate at first sight."[105] I got isolated reports of this in my clinical chair, so I decided to confirm the existence of "hate at first sight" as soon as I got the chance. That chance soon came when I was speaking to over 200 active-duty Marines. I asked them, "How many of you hated on sight another Marine that you now love like a brother and would trust with your life?" Hands shot up all over the room—confirmation that it is not uncommon for service members who love each other like family to have hated each other at first sight. Based on the reports I heard from my patients, more often than you might think, a no-holds-barred fistfight was the first encounter of two service members or veterans who now love each other like brothers.

---

103. In fact, many service members and veterans in my circle actively dislike the term "resilience." By definition, one is "resilient" until one is not. So the term either calls to mind a kind of pride that separates peers from each other (some of us are "resilient" and some are not) and when an individual is privately struggling, there is the possibility of unintentionally creating a dangerous split within that individual ("Since I'm struggling, I must not be 'resilient'").

104. Sebastian Junger, *TRIBE: On Homecoming and Belonging* (New York, NY: Hachette Book Group, 2016), xvii.

105. This term is one I originally coined for use in the military population, but it applies to other relationships as well.

The logical conclusion to draw from this observation is that the trust formed between service members is not necessarily a result of compatible or similar personalities. If baseline personality factors do not account for the love and trust that develops, then it follows that *trust must be relatively more tied to the experiences that shape relationships* among fellow members of the tribe. In other words, the experiences associated with military service forge an indescribably deep bond of trust, creating a sense of tribe, even among cadets, midshipmen, and new recruits who have vastly different personalities and personal values upon entering the service.

Many different factors contribute to this level of trust. What we've learned is that individuals coalesce into teams through the challenge of what psychologists call a "superordinate task."[106] A superordinate task is one that requires interdependence for task completion (for example, a ropes course that cannot be navigated without cooperative behavior). You probably remember many of these types of activities throughout basic training. These conditioning exercises taught you that the team was so much more powerful than the individual. In fact, the military journey could be described as one extremely lengthy superordinate task.

The superordinate task is a powerful, proven factor in producing bonds. However, it is far from the only factor that cultivates strong, positive, secure attachments. Just as there are factors that catalyze romantic bonding, there are also powerful factors that forge deep bonds of trust between people. Before you read further, test yourself for a moment. In the following table, address the question posed by listing as many factors as you can think of. I provide one example to seed your thinking.

Now that you've had a chance to generate some insights for yourself, see if any of these insights add anything to what you came up with. To integrate these bullet points as personal insights, add them to the left side of the list and the write out in your own words *how* they facilitate the bonding process. This is not an exhaustive list, but here are ten more factors that help create the bond between you and your military family:

1. Separation of a group of individuals from the rest of society—a world that is narrowed to the people and relationships at hand. Think about what it was like when you were plucked out of the life you knew and transported to the once-foreign world of boot camp.

2. Being intentionally stripped of one's individuality in order to build toward identity

---

106. Muzafer Sherif, "Superordinate Goals in the Reduction of Intergroup Conflict," *American Journal of Sociology* 63, no. 4 (1958): 349–356.

Exercise: Identifying Trust-Building Factors

What things does the military training program or lifestyle include that help develop and sustain trust between military service members?

Trust Building Factor	How does this help build trust?
Discomfort/bonding through "embracing the suck"	Going through physical and psychological challenges with other people facilitates group bonding

aligned with a collectivist "tribe" as you earned your Eagle, Globe and Anchor, your Parachute Wings, your Trident, or your Commission.

3. Wearing the same outfit as everyone around you, and, for many of you, having the same efficient "haircut."

4. A new language—including a multitude of new words, concepts, and acronyms that align with a new cultural understanding. This language varies somewhat within each branch of service—in other words, each branch has its own "dialect"—but much of military jargon is common across all branches of service.

5. Instillation of a common set of values and a guiding ethos. For example, soldiers are instilled with the values of loyalty, duty, respect, selfless service, honor, integrity, and personal courage; and Marines are instilled with the values of honor, courage, and commitment.

6. Challenges that cannot be overcome on an individual basis, but must be done in an interdependent way (aligned with Sherif and colleagues' research on superordinate tasks, as described above).

7. A culture of being each other's "keepers."

8. Introduction of life and death stakes (using live fire in firearms training exercises which requires service members to begin to trust each other with their lives).

9. Identification of a common enemy for all involved (depending on the war of the time).

10. The requirement of sacrifice of time with one's family to be away on mission or tasks needed for military service.

EXTENDING TRUST TO THE HOMEFRONT TRIBE

The fact that military training removes you from the life you once knew, in a way that fundamentally reconstitutes your attachment system, helps us understand why the trust you developed with fellow service members doesn't automatically transfer to your loved ones at home. This also gives us insight into why you might feel closer to a military comrade that you initially hated on sight, rather than the "love of your life" that you chose because of personality compatibility.

The ability to create similarly deep bonds with family members is not only possible, but critical for life after the military. (If you go back to the exercise which catalogued factors that build trust between service members, you can adapt many of these to help you build trust with a partner and other family members. I'd suggest drawing a line though at getting the same efficient haircut as your spouse).

The inability to create a "safe base" at home lies at the root of many tragic outcomes, not just suicide deaths, but loss of potential of some of the most capable leaders who could be real assets to society. In many ways, the most powerful reintegration is the one that happens between you and your family. When trust is formed and maintained, you are well positioned to become civic leaders, artists, cultural luminaries, and exceptionally good partners and parents.

The real task of navigating transition is to reconnect with your core identity and build relationships that will allow you to fully live into your potential. A life worth having is a life in which your core values are increasingly aligned with your actions. It is an *intentional* life that calls deeply to the warrior within you, and a spirit of leadership that has always been there, from well before you entered the military. Often, you need to go through a "tunnel of chaos" to rediscover it.

CAN A PARTNERSHIP BECOME STRONGER IN THE MIDST OF CHALLENGES?

Absolutely.

This can happen for several reasons. First, when we face challenges, "autopilot" settings are traded for manual control of a relationship. Old habits are challenged and create the space for new habits—ones more attuned with our growth trajectories. Stressors of the military life often force dramatic changes in roles. If expectations are not openly discussed on an ongoing basis, though, relationships will suffer. This is particularly true during military transition when so many formed habits are challenged through the process (see **Step 2.2.2. Breaking the Habit of Being a Warrior** from **Part 2** of this handbook). In the best of circumstances, you and your partner will develop a much deeper level of communication than you have ever had previously.

Second, adapting to and overcoming stressors forges trust. The process of working through challenges together can make you and your partner a much stronger team than ever before. You can each support each other in more meaningful ways. You can develop a new level of intimacy. The "testing phase" of a relationship becomes the "crucible" that shapes battle-tested partnerships. As applied to military transition, the bond between you and your partner can grow stronger through the uncertainty and ambiguity of this transformative event.

Finally, working through challenges allows us to see that our partner *really has our back*. Many of us vow to commit to our partners no matter what may come. Those who stick it out through challenging times show their partners every single day that this was not an empty vow. Over time, this kind of process helps develop relationships characterized by a deeper, more satisfying level of love than anything that any of us encounters in the initial "cocaine rush phase" of a relationship.

In successful lifelong partnerships, we form the core of an intimate team—referred to as "command teams" or "family teams" throughout the services—with that person who has been by our side through thick and thin, who has consistently believed and invested in us. In a successful life partnership, our partner becomes our *most trusted core team member throughout life.*

THREE CATEGORIES OF RELATIONSHIPS DURING TRANSITION

Generally speaking, your current relationship situation will fall into one of three different categories: you are unattached at the time of discharge; you are dating, but not formally committed; or you are formally committed and want to sustain your relationship in life beyond the military. The sections to follow will address each category, in this order. The focus of the first section, written for those of you who are unattached to a relationship, is the personal development that is necessary to prepare yourself for a healthy attachment. The second section, primarily written for those of you who are dating, will be focused on how to evaluate the potential of a romantic attachment to be sustainable for a lifetime. The third and final section will focus on insights and relationship skills that will help you maintain a strong, mutually respectful relationship with your partner.

I recommend reading all three sections regardless of your current relationship status because each section will have some areas of applicability to deepen your insight on the inner workings of successful relationships. For instance, in the third section, which is generally geared toward those of you in committed relationships, I share guidance on "how to have a *good* fight." This content has broad applicability in all kinds of close relationships, with friends and families, as well as romantic relationship partners. I also talk about working with anger and rage in close relationships. Even if uncontrolled anger is not an issue in your relationship, it may very well be an issue for a fellow service member, a peer or those under your command. For this reason, I recommend full engagement in reading all of the material to follow, regardless of your particular circumstance.

SECTION I.

PERSONAL DEVELOPMENT: THE CORE FOCUS IF YOU ARE UNATTACHED

To be blunt, falling in love is a great way to avoid directly addressing the pain of transition from the military. Avoiding this pain unfortunately means that the opportunity to grow in ways that will lead to successful long-term relationships will also be stunted. Long-arc thinking becomes critical for those of you who are single because building and maintaining healthy relationships, like the identity development part of successful transition, requires strategic thinking.

Take note that during your transition from the military, there is a real danger of making impulsive decisions that lead to "ticking time bomb" relationships. The danger is there because of the sudden loss of your military attachment system—the band of brothers and sisters who comprise your military family. When we lose our network of support, and with it, the relational structure that gives our lives meaning, we are susceptible to attempting to replace this support with a new romantic relationship. Slow down. Take the time to assess whether or not the initial, often explosive, attraction you feel with someone has the potential to become a lifelong companionship that best honors your identity and potential for your life.

DECISIONS MADE WHILE HIGH ON COCAINE ARE OFTEN REGRETTABLE

Ultimately, the explosion of pleasurable chemicals released during the "cocaine rush phase" of new love relationships leads to some monstrously short-sighted decision-making. New lovers often interpret the supercharged emotions they feel as evidence of having found "true love." Psychologists refer to this as "emotional reasoning," which means using one's feelings in place of actual evidence of a truth. Without significant quality-control checks in place, this is a dangerous path to take because the feeling of falling in love predictably follows one of three scenarios, one of which is a bridge to nowhere and another of which is an abusive nightmare. When you find yourself saying (or even privately thinking) things like *"We just met, but it feels like we've known each other forever"* or *"I think I just met my soul mate,"* inevitably, the truth is one of three things:

1. To start out on a hopeful foot, it could be that the relationship is the real deal, the kind of love that is invigorating, freeing, and sustainable for the rest of your life.

2. Alternatively, the case may be that you and your new love are enjoying the mutually held fantasy that you are soul mates who are destined to be together (which turns out to be a heartbreaking error in judgment).

3. Or, unfortunately, what you are feeling may in fact be the echoes of former trauma in your life (which often morphs into the living nightmare of an abusive relationship).

As a population attuned to identifying and managing risk, I'm sure you can appreciate that the odds of "finding true love" when you are in a state of identity flux during the transition from the military are not in your favor. The risk of failure is high in this scenario. The state of being in love is often used to divert from, and soothe, the discomfort of doing the deeper work that is needed to make a successful transition. Authors Stanton Peele and Archie Brodsky put it well in saying, "love is an ideal vehicle for addiction because it can so exclusively claim a person's consciousness."[107] In such a state of mind, devoid of any real information about who the other person *really* is, we can make some shocking decisions that throw the rest of our lives into unnecessary and avoidable turmoil.

TURNING A WOUNDED PERSON INTO YOUR NEXT MISSION

In my work, I have often observed that for leaders in the military there seems to be a theme, a kind of gravitational pull almost, for a portion of single men and women in transition to link up with people who need to be "saved" or "fixed." The instinct to protect and support is very strong and it can lead to decisions to pair with people who will bring chaos into your life. This seems to be especially true when there is significant survivor's guilt in the mix. It's almost as though the brain and the heart are trying to actively find a way to address and "correct" things that seem fixable given the weight of hidden pain stemming from things outside of your control. If you are not aware of this pull, this can lead you to turn another person into a "project" that requires all of your time and energy.

The chaos or "drama" generated by the new relationship with a person who is actively struggling with their own issues—whether the issue is an abusive, not-quite-ex-husband or an unaddressed drinking problem—distracts and diverts (for a limited time) from the challenge of re-evaluating your own identity and your path forward. The role of protector comes naturally and efforts to save someone in distress are often done under the guise of "selfless service."

Sometimes, chaotic relationships are attractive in the way that confronting external chaos can play an "organizing role" in military life—for example, a service member who worked in EOD may be strongly pulled to a series of partners that are the human equivalent of a ticking time bomb. Almost invariably, relationships like this are not sustainable; they are characterized by a series of emotional peaks and lows, followed by a decisive (and personally devastating) crash when the relationship ends. In my suicide prevention work, it is very clear

---

107. Stanton Peele and Archie Brodsky, *Love and Addiction* (Watertown, MA: Broadrow Publications, 1975), 70.

that suicide is never caused by one single event or person. At the same time, the loss of a close relationship can be a "tipping point" associated with a suicidal spiral. So, the relationships we choose to invest in can have very high stakes.

It's not that finding the right person and creating a lasting relationship isn't a worthy goal. It's a matter really of when and from what basis you move toward this goal. Globally, there are two elements to achieving lifelong love. The first is to make sure you are in a healthy, stable place with the personal qualities and insights that will attract and sustain real love, and the second is to make sure you identify someone who is equally capable. The next section of the handbook focuses on how you can ready yourself for a relationship that will stand the test of time.

A DIVERSIFIED SOCIAL PORTFOLIO

If you were to get a lump sum of money upon discharge from the military, would you invest all of it immediately in a single company (especially one with unknown risk factors?) Would it not be wise instead to invest your money in a diversified portfolio of financial opportunities? In a similar way, rather than linking up with a new romantic relationship partner during transition out of the military, it is wise to build out a diverse array of relationships with special focus on developing the "inner circle" or "core unit" of three or so other people that are really close, and a wider group of others that you enjoy spending time with.

There are several sources that you can draw on for a "diversified" social portfolio. A primary source will be your close and extended family members. You may find that relatives you were not as close to before you entered the military—like younger siblings or cousins for instance—have since grown and developed into interesting, enjoyable people. Another source is old friendships, people you knew from before the military. In addition to shoring up relationships with people you knew before the military, it is important to invest in new friendships. A meaningful life often includes a number of "locally sourced" friends in one's neighborhood, one's kids' school or sports community (if applicable), one's church (if applicable), and other social groupings.

You can also source new friends through a wide variety of veteran service organizations and non-veteran social organizations. I emphasize non-veteran service organizations as well as VSOs because most of the society you will reintegrate into are non-veterans. There are some organizations that work to actively bridge veterans and civilians through shared efforts (i.e., superordinate tasks). For example, Team Rubicon is a national nonprofit that brings veterans and civilians together on disaster response deployments. A second example is Team Red, White, and Blue which brings veterans and supportive civilians together for athletic and social activities. There are immense benefits during the transition process for those of you who become members of organizations like Team Rubicon and Team RWB. (And if you do, perhaps I'll see you in the field).

These organizations offer a culture that feels like home in many ways, and they provide an opportunity to connect with civilians who are more accepting of the military experience than others who may have very little exposure or interaction with service members or veterans. In addition to the vital role that VSOs play, there are a multitude of social groups organized by a variety of social interests—from very mainstream interests like people who like to sample dishes made by food trucks to very nonmainstream social interests, like the work of an obscure avant-garde film director. Meetup.com and Yahoo groups as well as internet-based social networks found in local neighborhoods are great places to link up with people who share common interests.

WHY IS "SOCIAL DIVERSIFICATION" SO IMPORTANT?

Diversification is critical because it provides the "safe base" from which to evaluate a potential lifelong relationship partner. Absent this safe base of operations, in seeking meaningful relationships, you are more likely to overlook troubling patterns in a given romantic relationship. In other words, desperation—the feeling of "needing to be completed"—is not a healthy place from which to launch the search for a mate.

The best way to avoid being perceived as desperate is to not actually **be** desperate. Instead of worrying about whether you'll get left behind in life's proverbial dating game, why not use your energy to create a fulfilling life independent of your relationship status? As psychologist Harriet Lerner explains, "Without a life plan, our intimate relationships carry too much weight, and we begin to look to others to provide us with meaning or happiness, which is not their job."[108]

It begins with you. A rich and meaningful existence is entirely possible whether or not you are partnered. The smartest thing to do if you are single is to focus on populating your life with interesting people and stimulating activities in order to create a life that is aligned with your deepest values. Being your most authentic self will make you highly desirable for the person who is truly looking for the best thing you have to offer, the fullest expression of you. It will also provide the lens that allows you to see the potential in a new relationship with greater clarity. In other words, if you can view a new relationship from the stance of, "*Life is really good right now and I enjoy the freedom I have, so this person needs to be well worth it*

---

108. Harriet Goldhor Lerner, *The Dance of Intimacy* (New York: HarperCollins, 2003), 221.

for me to give up my current level of freedom," you'll be in a much better position to make the best decision for you and your intentions for life beyond the military.

People who study business practices talk about the "walk-away factor" as a core principle in effective negotiation. Robert Rubin, former US Secretary of the Treasury, described it this way, "When others sense your willingness to walk away, your hand is strengthened."[109] In a healthy, mutually satisfying relationship, both partners hold "walk-away power" throughout the premarital courtship period. The goal is not to threaten the other person with your own "walk-away power," but rather to establish a relationship in which neither person *needs* the other, but both very much *want* the other person, a true win-win outcome. And it bears repeating that when you create an exciting life for yourself regardless of your relationship status, you convey that you are someone who could be the "catch of the lifetime" for someone who connects with your most authentic self.

In fact, despite the prevalence of pop psychology books full of tips for "catching a mate," you might want to consider forgetting the spouse hunt entirely. The "hunt" mentality puts you in a mentally appetitive—and competitive—state of mind that does not often lead to good assessment of potential in others. When you create an inspired life, desirable partners present themselves with sufficient frequency even when you are not actively "hunting" for them. The best strategy is to create a full and active life for yourself and to develop relationships with others who share your values and interests. If you do, it will only be a matter of time before you attract someone who is capable of meeting you as an equal and forging an exciting life together with you.

THE RULE OF MENTAL HEALTH IN RELATIONSHIPS

If it is true that you are what you eat, then the parallel relationship metaphor is that you'll get what you are. It's well aligned with a consumerist culture to ask variations of the question, *"As I shop for a spouse, what qualities does he or she need to have to attract and hold my interest?"* There is certainly value in reflecting on the qualities you desire in a potential spouse and in being discriminating as you navigate the dating market. However, the equally important, but less frequently asked question is, "What do I have to offer to the type of person I'd like to attract and build a lifelong relationship with?" The marriage market isn't comprised of long shopping aisles which you can roam freely, laying claim to exactly what you want.

---

109. Robert Rubin, (2004), quoted in David A. Lax and James K. Sebenius, "How No-Deal Options Can Drive Great Deals: When Actions Away from the Table Eclipse Face-to-Face Negotiation," *IVEY Business Journal*, July 2004, https://iveybusinessjournal.com /publication/how-no-deal-options-can-drive-great-deals-when-actions-away-from-the-table-eclipse-face-to-face-negotiation/.

The mate you would pick must pick you back. Any effort to learn how to pick a wonderful partner without first considering whether or not that partner would be likely to pick you is missing half the picture. In some cases, you may need to actively develop certain character traits before you are even potentially capable of attracting a high-quality spouse. (The parallel in the earlier part of this handbook is the tendency for us to feel that we can "shop for our dream job" before articulating to ourselves—and our employers—what we bring to the table that will add value for them).

During the cocaine rush phase of a relationship, it may be true that opposites attract, at least initially. Most often, though, when opposites try to sustain long-term love relationships, partners who have many fundamental dissimilarities come to resent the differences in their partners that first attracted them. For instance, consider a man who is initially attracted by his partner's "social butterfly" qualities. He may initially enjoy the novelty of the relationship in terms of her ability to "draw him out" and "bring him into her social circles." His partner may be what psychologists call "extraverted," which means that she metaphorically recharges her batteries by engaging with others in social interactions.

Unfortunately, after the cocaine rush phase has passed, he may feel irritated that "she wants to constantly drag him out to social things" when he'd rather stay home and unwind, without any guests, in front of a basketball game. He may be what psychologists call "introverted," which means that he recharges his batteries by taking time by himself in a low-social environment where he can focus inward. His partner, who once told her friends that she "likes having him all to herself" is later frustrated that he prefers to stay at home when she wants to go out. She begins to resent the loss of her previous social life. With few exceptions, successful couples tend to "match" each other on levels of attractiveness, personality, moral values, spiritual beliefs, and cognitive complexity.[110]

Matching tendencies have been described in various ways by researchers and clinicians. Some refer to "the rule of mental health in relationships," which means that people usually end up paired with others at the same level of mental health. Opposites may attract initially, but like energy connects on a much deeper level. What follows next is a description of the core factors that are important to attend to in order to set yourself up for a healthy long-term relationship.

---

110. Greg James Neimeyer, "Cognitive Complexity and Marital Satisfaction," *Journal of Social and Clinical Psychology* 2, no. 3 (1984): 258–263, https://doi:10.1521/jscp.1984.2.3.258.

STRONG RELATIONSHIPS START WITH WHO YOU ARE

Understanding your core values gives you a tremendous advantage when it comes to finding, building, and sustaining a healthy close relationship. Or to put it another way, taking the time to define your values (your WHO) is another way to protect yourself from destructive relationships. Once you know what you stand for, you're much less likely to settle for relationships that don't allow you to live out your values. You completed a detailed exercise to identify your values, and you probably refined those values through the MTRP. Just as you seek value alignment in a way that honors your WHO during your search for the next job, you also want to find a companion who honors your values to build a lifelong partnership that sustains and empowers you both.

HEAL OLD WOUNDS

Before reading further, take a look at the next exercise, make a choice and describe your rationale for the choice you made. Here is the scenario:

Imagine that your car breaks down in a remote spot known to be close to dangerous criminals who have just escaped from prison. You are unarmed and badly injured from a recent fall off your roof (in other words, you can't defend yourself against a physical assault) and your cell phone isn't picking up a signal. In this scenario, would it be wiser to solicit help from another driver yourself or to sit in the car and wait for someone to notice your state of need and offer to help?

Exercise: Evaluating Choice-Making In Social Relationships	
Better to Wait or Pick Someone (note your choice below)	**Explain your Rationale**

For this scenario, one option is generally a better decision: it would generally be wiser to take an active role in picking the target of your request for help. If you decide to actively request help, you would certainly attempt to screen for certain factors that might indicate that a particular person would be relatively safe to hail—for example, a man or woman who appears to be riding with his or her young children.

Even if you picked at random, without looking for indicators of potentially safe helpers, you would be statistically less likely to pick a sociopath relative to the likelihood that a sociopath might pick you when he or she witnesses your obvious state of vulnerability. As threat expert Gavin De Becker explains, "The possibility that you'll inadvertently select a predatory criminal for whom you are the right victim type is very remote."[111] In other words, if you were to wait passively in your car for someone to help you, you would most likely attract one of two types of people—either good Samaritans or opportunistic sociopaths drawn to your state of need.

In a similar way, for many combat veterans, the mate-selection process often carries a compounded risk. That is, unhealed wounds of past trauma in your life lead to a higher likelihood that unsafe people will pick you, and if you actively pick a partner, it is much more likely that you will end up with an unsafe person. For this reason, it is vitally important that you consider whether you've suffered any previous traumas that may have "broken your picker."

A useful definition of trauma is an experience or set of experiences that has destroyed former assumptions that you are safe or that other people can generally be trusted. Further, as I've mentioned already, if you have experienced a trauma, it is often true that you will unintentionally emit certain signals and behaviors that chum the water for the psychopathic sharks (of both genders) in the dating pool. You may have a difficult time recognizing these sharks when they present themselves as suitors because somehow they "feel like home" if you have experienced certain types of past traumas.

There is also an unfortunate tendency to select partners with whom you will restage similar traumas (e.g., the son of a verbally abusive mother will often end up with a verbally abusive wife, or a service member who worked in EOD will pick partners that are metaphorical "bombs waiting to detonate"), presumably with the hope of getting a different outcome. In relationships, as in warfare strategy, if you ignore history, you will tend to repeat it, so if you have not addressed and achieved healing from your trauma experience(s), doing so in a safe relationship with a skilled and trustworthy "Doc" is recommended as a first priority. Optimizing your whole health and wellness is a priority for you and also for your ability to form healthy relationships through transition and beyond.

---

111. Gavin De Becker, *The Gift of Fear And Other Survival Signals That Protect Us from Violence* (New York: Dell, 1998), 65.

REVIEW YOUR MOTIVATIONS

In terms of motivations for committing to a romantic relationship, thus far we've been focusing mostly on delusional thinking processes caused by fantasies we create during the cocaine rush phase of relationships. For example, within the context of a short courtship, two delusional reasons for getting married are *"because it feels like I've known them forever, even though we just met"* and *"because our love story would make a great movie."* There are a number of other equally bad reasons to take the plunge. These generally fall into three categories—anxiety, inadequacy, and self-centered pragmatics. If you are contemplating marriage or are "on the hunt" for a spouse, I'd advise you to get honest with yourself and plumb the depths of your motivations. Do your motivations stem from any of the following thoughts?

Do your motivations stem from any of the following thoughts?

I want to commit to a relationship because . . .

- All my friends are doing it.

- I don't know if I'll get another chance if I take a pass on this one.

- I want to feel secure.

- I want to be spared the horrors of today's dating scene.

Entering the relationship market from a scarcity mindset leads to poor decisions. In 1986, *Newsweek* magazine asserted that a forty-year-old woman was more likely to be killed by a terrorist than to receive a proposal of marriage (and, to clarify, not more likely to be killed by a terrorist than to receive a proposal of marriage from that terrorist, but to receive a marriage proposal from any man).[112] In fact, the "terrorist" line was first written as a joke in a memo from correspondent Pamela Abramson.[113] "It's true; I am responsible for the single most irresponsible line in the history of journalism, all meant in jest," Abramson told *Newsweek* twenty years after the piece was published. This line of thinking and others like it taps into anxieties about a marriage crunch[114] and creates motivation to partner that is fear based.

Anxiety is driving the bus when we fear that we will be left behind, when we accept the premise that a full and interesting life without a romantic partner is less successful than a

---

112. "The Marriage Crunch," *Newsweek*, June 2, 1986.
113. Caryl Rivers, "Newsweek's Apology Comes 20 years too Late," *Women's News*, June 14, 2006, https://womensenews.org/2006/06/newsweeks-apology-comes-20-years-too-late/.
114. For most people, the marriage crunch hasn't really been true since the post-WWII Baby Boom era. Most people who want to get married do get married at some point.

partnered life. In a way, the person who marries for these reasons is looking to his or her partner to function as a different type of drug—not cocaine, but some type of sedative in this case. The supposed stability and security of the marital bond is sought as an antidote to the uncertainty and volatility of "life on the outside." When one looks to one's partner to be any type of drug instead of a living, breathing human being with an agenda of his or her own, the result is often a short-lived bond.

A second category of unwise motivation is coupling because of feelings of inadequacy, typified by any of the following thoughts:

I want to commit to a relationship partner because . . .

- The person I'm dating loves me and that makes me feel special and lovable

- Marriage will show everyone that I'm an adult

- Marriage will demonstrate that someone wants me

- This will bring my life into better focus

- I am lonely

The Limiting Belief of being "not good enough" doesn't just impact your ability to achieve your potential in the job market, it also infects your ability to connect with your ideal partner. If you find yourself encumbered by these thoughts of inadequacy, take special note of the next several paragraphs on self-worth.

Self-worth is, by definition, the result of your own determination of what you are worth. It is by nature a self-reflective conclusion. People often get into a lot of trouble when they give others the power to determine their sense of self-worth, endlessly seeking confirmation of their worth in the eyes of others, when it was never really others' place to determine their self-worth in the first place.

If you are single when you transition out of the military, your sense of self-worth is the greatest asset you have toward building long-term, meaningful relationships. Chronically low self-esteem and the feeling of needing to be completed are often closely linked. People with higher self-esteem are typically less likely to form relationships out of a sense of need, and are more likely to do so because they desire to enlarge their already-satisfying life experiences even further.

In addition, self-worth fuels personal growth. If you have a strong sense of self-worth, you don't take personal feedback personally. When you embrace growth as an opportunity, you have a means to grow together in a meaningful relationship. Since the only guarantee we have is that life will bring us all transitions and various tunnels of chaos, the ability to adapt and grow in your relationship becomes critical.

Self-worth is something that you and you alone create. It is a function of the alignment between what you say you value and what you actually do with your time, energy, and physical resources. An entire sub-genre of self-help books encourages readers to raise their self-esteem through repeating self-affirmations. Unfortunately, self-worth isn't something you can instill by brainwashing yourself to believe that you "are somebody" or by listening to taped self-affirmations as these kinds of books would have you believe. *The creation of self-worth is an active, energy-consuming endeavor that involves narrowing the distance between what you say are your deepest values and what you actually do with the life you've been given.* The true affirmation of self-worth is an intrinsic feeling.

To give some specific examples, if you say that you value social justice, are you living in alignment with this value? If you say you value fairness and compassion, are you regularly engaging in behaviors that allow you to live out these values? Conversely, how does engaging in private acts of unkindness affect your self-worth? If you say that you value intellectual curiosity, how does spending hours in front of the TV every day affect your sense of self-worth? If you say you value adventure and "making the most of life," how is your self-worth affected by the bondage of crippling fears?

When you have identified the ways in which you are living *out of alignment* with your deepest values and you have narrowed that gap, your self-worth will rise correspondingly. Strong self-worth is not only an antidote to desperation; it allows you to feel secure enough to live into a personal growth orientation. Secure people have a strong sense of their own values, and, at the same time, they are flexible in considering how they may be off the mark at times. Self-worth and the ability to seek and accept corrective feedback are so closely associated that one way to assess your current level of self-worth is to ask yourself whether you are able to say the following types of things *regularly and with ease*:

> *"I'm sorry."*
> *"I really messed up."*
> *"You're right; I'm wrong."*
> *"Am I missing anything? Can you see anything I can't see?"*
> *"I don't know. What do you think?"*

Finally, a third category of misguided motivation is shallow pragmatics, which boils down to thoughts such as these:

I want to commit to a partner in a relationship because . . .

- We've dated a while and this is the next logical step to take.

- I want to register for nice things and create a Pottery Barn nest for myself.

- We can save money on rent and other expenses if we do.

- Otherwise, the person I met online won't uproot their life to come move in with me.

- My taxes will be lower if I file jointly with someone else (and, as a side note, double check your facts on this, because your taxes will actually be higher)

The same line of thinking is reflected in impulsive decisions while on active duty to marry relative strangers in order to make sure that you can be stationed together during deployments. Relationships launched on this foundation don't usually lead to the outcomes that we want when we say "I do."

PRIORITIZE ONGOING PERSONAL GROWTH

If you find yourself attracted to the regular practice of self-reflection, you may already possess what I call a "personal growth orientation," which is another critical trait for creating a healthy relationship. Even if you feel that you have met your soul mate, be assured that as life unfolds, you will both change over time. How you change is in large part up to you. Will you make efforts to shape your own character and live more fully into your deepest values, or will you allow yourself to be influenced by unhealthy people and destructive thinking? *The desire to become a better person and a better partner may be the most desirable asset anyone can bring to a lifelong partnership.*

A healthy lifelong partnership calls for two people with strong personal growth orientations who are therefore open to influencing each other continuously to become perfect for, and irreplaceable to, each other. The way to achieve one-in-a-million status is not to arrive as the perfect match for each other, but to progressively become this over time. The key is how you will shape each other in the relationship over time. If you develop a personal growth orientation before you go on the marriage market, you are much more likely to attract someone with the potential and desire to work at becoming the perfect partner for you (as opposed to the perfect human being).

Exercise: Are you an emotionally safe person?		
Question	**YES**	**NO**
1. Do I admit to having some weaknesses?		
2. Would others say that I am humble?		
3. Am I defensive when others tell me that I have hurt or offended them?		
4. Do I show that I am trustworthy over time?		
5. Do I apologize, but fail to change my behavior?		
6. Do I admit it when I have problems?		
7. Do I confess when I wrong someone else (e.g. own up to it)?		
8. Do I treat others with a lack of empathy?		
9. Do I take responsibility for my own life?		
10. Do I blame other people for my problems?		

Scoring Key:

1. Score 1 point for "No"	6. Score 1 point for "No"
2. Score 1 point for "No"	7. Score 1 point for "No"
3. Score 1 point for "Yes"	8. Score 1 point for "Yes"
4. Score 1 point for "No"	9. Score 1 point for "No"
5. Score 1 point for "Yes"	10. Score 1 point for "Yes"

*Adapted by Dr. Shauna Springer, with permission, from material developed by Dr. Henry Cloud and Dr. John Townsend, as described in their book Safe People. For further information on these concepts, visit: www.cloudtownsend.com.

Ask Yourself if You Are an Emotionally Safe Person

What specific character qualities are essential for us to bring to a healthy relationship? Based on the book *Safe People*[115] by John Cloud and Henry Townsend, with permission from the

---

115. Henry Cloud and John Sims Townsend, *Safe People: How to Find Relationships That Are Good for You and Avoid Those That Aren't* (Grand Rapids, MI: Zondervan, 1996).

book's authors, I created a profile of the core qualities needed for partners in successful long-term relationships. I offer this self-assessment as your next exercise.

Scoring Your Results

2 POINTS OR LESS

This score indicates issues you may need to address in your way of relating to others. So, based on a score of 2 or less, you see yourself as an emotionally safe person. If this is true, then you will generally have long-term, healthy close relationships in your life with several other people. If true, you should also have good potential to form a solid, lasting marriage, as long as you are able to recognize these same qualities in someone you might choose to partner with for life. If you scored points on any questions, especially if your relationship history is more rocky, than stable and healthy, note these areas as possible targets for further growth.

BETWEEN 3 AND 5 POINTS

A score between 3-5 points should stimulate some pointed self-reflection on how you relate to others. It may be wise for you to use this set of questions to evaluate who may be a safe person in your life. Once you have identified someone you have known for several years who would score very low on this set of questions, you may want to privately ask for this person's feedback on how you relate to others. Character is not entirely fixed, and can be shaped by an accumulation of small decisions. Deciding that change is important and committing to working on areas where you scored points can result in positive growth over time. If you are not currently in a romantic relationship, it may be wise to actively work on areas for growth before seeking to couple up.

MORE THAN 5 POINTS

You are to be commended for taking a hard look at how you relate to others. You have identified several areas for growth. If your perception is accurate, you may have a history of cut-off or strained relationships in multiple domains of your life. You may have difficulties retaining friends and romantic partners. If your goal is to enjoy a satisfying, stable long-term love relationship, it will be critical for you to work on making some changes. There is potential for growth in character with committed effort over time. Benjamin Franklin, a known genius and globally well-regarded human being, for example, actively monitored and worked on developing certain character traits such as fairness (treating others the way he wanted to be treated) and humility (keeping his ego in check). He set a goal to work on 1 of 13 specific character traits and worked in this manner, rotating through each trait weekly, for over 50 years. If you are not currently in a committed relationship, it may be wise to work on your identified areas for growth, with the support of other safe people (including, potentially, a professional counselor) before seeking to form a romantic attachment.

AVOID THE PERFECTIONISM TRAP

Starting out as the "perfect" partner is neither possible nor desirable. In fact, strong perfectionist traits do not usually lead to healthy relationships. For those of you who have served in any leadership role in the military, perfectionism is a trap to be especially aware of. The military lifestyle comes with exacting standards—for everything from hygiene, to a code of conduct, to the exercise of planned tactical operations. Doing this "according to the manual" or "in line with mission execution standards" is a key element of being in the military. While this is necessary for the successful completion of military duties, applying this kind of thinking to one's growth through the transition process, or to the way that one manages one's relationships, can have a very serious and negative impact.

The tendency for military leaders to apply styles particular to military culture in a civilian setting are not only unproductive, but these behaviors increase the risk of social and cultural alienation in civilian society. A recurring theme throughout this handbook has been the idea that aspects of the warrior culture cannot coexist in civilian society. Unfortunately, the results aren't any better when military leaders apply this kind of behavior to their inner circle and to their interactions with their family members.

When you project the go/no-go standard of perfectionism, rather than accepting a full and healthy range of emotions, you will typically vacillate between two primary emotions, dread and relief. This frames your relationships from a pass-fail perspective instead of experiencing a full and healthy range of emotions. Consequently, you spend most of the time dreading the next potential failure, and any successes are met with a feeling of temporary relief, rather than with a feeling of satisfaction of having a thing done well.

This win-lose standard carries potentially negative impacts to your self-esteem. *Self-esteem is not built from feelings of relief, or the temporary reprieve of having succeeded at something.* Failures hit especially hard for perfectionists and may lead to long bouts of depression and withdrawal. The pattern of brief highs and deeper lows trends your overall self-perception downward over time. The rollercoaster pattern of dread and relief endlessly repeats itself in the life of a non-recovered perfectionist, and our spouses and children are often the unhappy passengers of this not-so-thrilling ride.

When you approach relationships from a perfectionist mindset, you increase the risk of hypersensitivity to perceived rejection or any possible evidence of failure. Furthermore, there is a fundamental rigidity in the relentless defense and bracing for failure. In the military, we recognize this as excessive worrying. Consequently, you fail to see the opportunity to learn from mistakes as you would otherwise with a growth orientation. You are so worried about losing that you can't see the potential for the win. The growth orientation allows you to integrate feedback in a way that will enable stronger connections and relationships in the future. Unfortunately, when we get caught up in the bondage of perfectionist strivings, we are likely to be less interested in developing healthy, mutually satisfying relationships and more interested in chasing the elusive rabbit in our own head.

CREATE AND MAINTAIN EQUAL, RESPECT-FILLED RELATIONSHIPS

If you are hoping to create a healthy lifelong partnership, you need to be able to create and sustain mutually satisfying, mutually respectful relationships. In successful lifelong partnerships, power and control give way to mutual respect. There is no sense that one person is always in the "one down" role. There is no "chain of command" or self-designated drill sergeant or commander in charge in relationships characterized by mutual respect. Energy between the two people in the relationship flows freely, and over time, those in the relationship are renewed by it in equal proportion. If this describes the kind of life partnership you want, then it makes sense to ask yourself honestly how well you've been able to maintain this kind of relationship in the past. Effective leaders are committed to taking an unflinching look at themselves to continually improve how they operate in life, and in their most important relationships. Along these lines, the following exercise provides a number of questions for self-reflection. Just as you did earlier in this handbook in looking for the patterns in the feedback you have received on your performance in military roles, look for the patterns that have guided your past relationships. As you complete this exercise, see what you learn about your past patterns.

BECOME A "TWO-MARSHMALLOW" PERSON

Making conscious choices that allow you to live in alignment with your deepest values often requires the ability to delay initial gratification. In the 1960s, Stanford University researcher Walter Mischel came up with an elegantly simple method that showed the value of the ability to delay gratification. His study subjects were a group of four-year-old children. He offered each participant a large, puffy marshmallow and told them that if they would wait for him to run a quick errand, they could have not one, but two, marshmallows. The marshmallow was an excellent choice because it had not only the taste, but also the appearance and texture of a delectable treat. The little tykes squirmed in front of their marshmallows like dogs might whimper when told to sit still with a strip of prime rib placed on their nose.

Some of the four-year-olds were able to control the impulse to snatch up and consume their marshmallows for the duration of Mischel's fifteen- to twenty-minute errand (which must have felt like several lifetimes for these four-year-olds). Others could not. Mischel followed up with his subjects many years later and found that the ability to control impulses

Exercise: Analysis of Past Relationship Patterns

1. Have your past romantic relationship(s) been ones of mutual respect and equal sharing of energy? (If you have never been involved in a romantic relationship, how do your closest friendships feel?)

2. Have you been able to sustain mutually satisfying relationships with members of your family, some collection of friends, and some of your past or current co-workers?

3. Do you give as much as you receive, or are you under-benefitted or over-benefitted in your relationships?

4. What have been your driving motivations in close relationships in the past? Have your past relationships been based in insecurity, emotional immaturity, or self-serving motives?

5. Have you paired up with others mainly because you like the way they make you feel about yourself (or because it feels good to be picked)? If not, what have been your driving reasons for partnering with people in the past?

and delay gratification was associated with success in many different areas of life as an adult. For instance, those who delayed gratification were more self-motivated and more persistent in the face of obstacles. On average, they scored 210 points higher on SAT tests. Those who had quickly consumed the first marshmallow they were offered continued to have impulse-control problems in adulthood. Mischel characterized them as more troubled, stubborn, indecisive, mistrustful, and less self-confident.[116]

As a military leader, you may already be a two-marshmallow person. Leadership requires us to keep the long arc of the mission in mind. There are also abundant opportunities in military life to delay gratification to support the mission at hand. For instance, you may have taken a difficult assignment because of the potential opportunities it created later in your career. One of the best things about those who serve in the military, at all levels of service, is that military training can actually create "two-marshmallow qualities" in people. Continuing to live with a "long-term thinking" perspective—the ability to play the long game—is important in how you find the next opportunity in life beyond the military, but it is also important to how you build lasting relationships after military service. In the relationship domain, being a two-marshmallow person pays off in many ways as you create an interesting life with a well-matched partner.

END-OF-SECTION REVIEW AND SUMMARY

The insights that you gain regarding how your values inform your relationships may lead to clear objectives regarding social opportunities in life after military service. After you complete this exercise, you may want to incorporate these practical actions into your action plans for transition and reintegration. Many of these insights are not limited to lifelong partnerships, but are also important for meaningful friendships.

To summarize then, for those of you who undergo transition as singles, key insights include:

• Building and maintaining healthy relationships, like the identity development part of successful transition, requires strategic thinking.

• When we lose our network of support, we may be especially susceptible to making a regrettable decision to commit to romantic relationships that will not be sustainable.

• Because there are striking similarities between the brain state of a person who has

---

116. Walter Mischel, Yuichi Shoda, and Monica L. Rodriguez, "Delay of Gratification in Children," *Science* 244, no. 4907 (1989): 933–938, https://doi:10.1126/science.2658056.

END OF SECTION REVIEW

Take some time and review this section on Personal Development: The Core Focus for Those of You Who are Unattached. When you are ready, go through Part 1 and Part 2 of this End of Section Review to apply the information in this handbook to your ability to forge healthy relationships through transition and beyond

PART 1 INSIGHTS

What are the 5 most important insights that you learned about relationships?

(Do this whether you are single or not - what you learn may help a friend)

EXAMPLE: When you create an inspired life that is based on your core values, it will be a matter of time before you attract someone who is capable of meeting you as an equal and forging an exciting life together with you.

PART 2 PRACTICAL ACTIONS

Identify three (3) things you plan to do to apply these insights based on the example provided

EXAMPLE: Explore volunteer opportunities in organizations like Team Rubicon and Team RWB

just smoked crack cocaine and a person who is falling in love, we need to be situationally aware of this as a risk factor for poor decision-making.

- Falling in love is a great way to avoid directly addressing the pain of transition from the military, but avoiding this pain will prevent the growth that will set you up for a healthy long-term relationship.

- The odds of "finding true love" are markedly long when you are in a state of identity flux during the transition out of the military.

- The instinct to protect and offer selfless service can lead to decisions to pair with people that will bring destruction and chaos into your life.

- Rather than immediately linking up with a romantic partner during the transition out of the military, it is wise to build out a diverse array of supportive relationships of many kinds (with civilians as well as fellow current or prior service members).

- It may be wise to forget the spouse hunt entirely since this puts you in a state of mind that often compromises good assessment of potential relationship partners.

- A stable, well-developed self-identity based on your core values gives you a safe base from which to find a healthy partnership.

- For individuals with unresolved traumas, the mate-selection process often carries a double risk—unhealed wounds of past trauma lead to a higher likelihood that unsafe people will pick you, and that you may pick an unsafe person.

- There are lots of very unwise reasons to take the plunge into marriage; they fall under categories like anxiety, inadequacy, and self-centered pragmatics.

- Taking the time to define your values is another way to protect yourself from destructive relationships. Once you know what you stand for, you are much less likely to settle for relationships that don't allow you to live out your values.

- The desire to become a better person and a better partner may be the most desirable asset you can bring to a lifelong partnership.

- Perfectionism is a barrier to healthy relationships; it also prevents growth that is needed in multiple domains for making a successful transition from the military.

- Ensure that your self-worth is healthy before you commit to a long-term relationship.

- Self-worth is a function of the alignment between your values and how you spend the time that is given to you. It does not come from self-affirmations; it is an active, energy-consuming process. You must lead yourself in the direction of your values to see gains in your self-worth.

- You may have learned in the military how to delay gratification in the service of long-term goals (or the goals of the mission at hand). Continuing to live in a "long-term thinking" mode is critical for success after the military.

SECTION II.

GUIDANCE FOR EVALUATING POTENTIAL LIFELONG PARTNERSHIPS

YOU DO NOT HAVE A 50 PERCENT CHANCE OF DIVORCE

Let's take a critical look at the frequently cited 50 percent divorce rate.[117] Often, this is translated as *"You have a 50/50 chance of divorce anytime you get married."* The general logic of the 50 percent divorce probability myth is like saying, *"Marriage is really nothing but a game of roulette. Half the numbers are black and half are red. You drop your ball in the circle and watch it spin around and around. There is a 50 percent chance that it will land on a red number, and if it does, your relationship will end in divorce."* The truth is that you do NOT have a 50 percent chance of divorce—your rate of divorce might be much higher, or lower than 50 percent, depending on several factors.

As military leaders, you pride yourselves on the ability to "own the night." The use of technology, tactics, training, and leadership create a decisive advantage over our adversaries in the dark of the night. Given this advantage, many of our organizations—such as special forces—operate at night. This concept suggests an ideal metaphor to create deep and long-lasting romantic partnerships after the military. Without the critical insights that are needed, a given couple's rate of divorce is often significantly higher than 50 percent. Those that do have the right information "own the night" and have a much lower risk of divorce. An analogy may help.

---

117. Matthew D. Bramlett and William D. Mosher, "First Marriage Dissolution, Divorce, and Remarriage: United States," *PsycEXTRA Dataset*, 2001, fig. 1, https://doi:10.1037/e609102007-001.

Let's say that you have a unit of soldiers. You divide the unit into two groups. One group receives an assignment of twelve weeks of "detail and tasking duty" (or, if you like, "kitchen patrol") while the other group is given twelve weeks of intensive tactical training and a deep understanding of how counterinsurgency tactics can be strategically deployed as an alternative to conventional warfare strategies. At the end of twelve weeks, both units are shipped out to the combat zone, where they will serve in the front lines of battle. Will their likelihood of success in a counterinsurgency environment be the same across the two groups? I'm sure we can agree that the answer is **decidedly not**, because the training and insights invested in the second group place them on an entirely different trajectory of success. The goal of this section is to provide you with insights that will greatly improve your odds of recognizing relationships with real potential and creating a foundation of success when you do find the right partner.

The content to come in this section is divided into two general categories: common pitfalls, and guidance to navigate the terrain ahead.

COMMON PITFALLS
TAKING THE PLUNGE BEFORE YOU ASSESS THE DEPTH OF THE POOL

Of all the principles of attraction, perhaps the most important thing to remember is that when we're falling in love, it's like we just smoked crack cocaine, so it might be a good idea to hold off on making any life-changing decisions in this state of mind. When I give talks on how to make wise decisions about love relationships, the burning question that someone almost always asks is, "How long do I have to wait?" The phrasing of this question illustrates the fact that waiting can feel like working against the tide of biology and the romantic rush of falling in love and making it official.

How long is it until the "cocaine rush" wears off and you can make a good decision? Some marital experts would argue that two years is a good amount of time to wait. If you are looking for a general rule of thumb, then two years is probably a good length of time for most people but remember that there are no hard-and-fast rules concerning the ideal courtship length. It depends completely on the character of the people involved, how often they see each other, in what situation(s) they spend their time dating, and how intentional they are about discovering their degree of fit. In some cases, it may be wise to wait three or more years before making a decision, and in other cases, a couple may be able to make a wise decision in less than two years.

For example, consider the case of a courtship that has played out during multiple successive military deployments. A military combat deployment is one of the most emotionally super-charged environments imaginable. The life or death stakes and the threat of sudden loss boosts attraction considerably for both partners. Lack of access to each other, paired with short-lived reunions during R & R weekends, can fuel unrealistic fantasies of the true potential of the relationship. Real compatibility is hard to assess when opportunities for interaction are limited. The fantasy script of the stateside partner incorporates the potent thought, "*My partner is a hero*," and all sorts of positive traits are then linked to this global perception. On the flip side, it's quite heady stuff to be told that you are the person a deployed service member holds in his or her heart amidst the chaos of war.

In each audience that I've spoken to about marital decision-making, there is almost always someone who raises a hand and says, "*My parents fell in love and got married a month later, and they've been blissfully happy together for the last fifty years.*" The core of this state-ment is an assertion that lifelong happy marriages are possible with very short courtships. I wouldn't disagree with this. The important point is that it's a matter of relative risk. Sure, a handful of marriages might thrive after short courtships, but for every one of these examples, a *much* greater number end in divorce. So, if we were to honestly weigh the emotional, psychological, and financial costs of a bad decision, wouldn't wisdom in all cases suggest a relatively long courtship?

Instead of trying to fix a target courtship length that applies to all relationships, it makes more sense to gauge whether and when the relationship has transitioned from the cocaine rush phase to the testing phase. How would you know if this has happened? If the cocaine rush phase is essentially about untested idealization of each other, then during the testing phase, you begin to notice some of the less-than-wonderful qualities in each other. Your sleep patterns return to normal and you start to see the rise of some conflicts in the relationship. Differences of opinion start to surface once you both stop trying to demonstrate how similar and "made to be together" you are. All of these changes are normal, healthy, and vitally important in the process of assessing true relationship potential.

COMMUNICATING THAT YOU ARE A LOW-VALUE TARGET

Ever watch the Disney movie *The Little Mermaid*? It's a kid's movie about a mermaid who falls madly in love with a guy she doesn't know at all and then puts her entire family and future at stake in her pursuit of his love. She literally gives up her voice to gain his affection. Sadly, in real life, there are plenty of "Ariels" (both men and women, some of them highly ranked members of the armed forces) who commit themselves in radical ways to people they barely know. Real-life Ariels fly off to a faraway city to meet up with someone in person that they've just barely met over the internet.

Real-life Ariels make cross-country moves to live with someone they've only ever known through internet correspondence. Real-life Ariels quit their jobs and leave their network of support, captivated by cocaine rush feelings for an attractive stranger. When you are willing to make this kind of commitment with limited knowledge of the other person, what message do you think this sends about your self-worth? What does your behavior teach the other person about your value as a mate, when you are willing to make a huge investment without any evidence that it is a wise one to make?

Another part of holding your value high is to listen very carefully to the other person's reasons for pursuing you. What is their WHY? Do their primary reasons for committing to the relationship align with any of the ill-advised reasons for marrying that were presented earlier in the handbook? Are they shallow reasons? Is their love for you based on how *you* make *them* feel? Are their reasons linked to cocaine rush feelings or are they based on reasons that are more likely to lead to a lifelong commitment?

Linking Up with Someone with an Untreated Personality Disorder

A personality disorder is a clinically diagnosable condition with a very poor prognosis. Personality disorders are "ego syntonic," as opposed to "ego dystonic." That is, an individual with the personality disorder tends to feel, "*This is just the way I am*" and does not see his or her own behavior as problematic. In fact, from this person's perspective, if others were not such complete asses, there would be no problem at all.

In therapy, treating patients with personality disorders can be very challenging. A personality-disordered patient is often urged by others to seek treatment but may not stay in treatment because he or she often lacks intrinsic motivation to make changes. He or she may be temporarily motivated by acute distress, but typically, when the distress subsides, it's back to business as usual.

In the book, *Emotional Vampires: Dealing with People Who Drain You Dry*, Dr. Albert Bernstein describes an array of diagnosable personality disorders using everyday language and concepts. For instance, in reference to individuals with narcissistic personality disorder, he says, "Just as sharks must continuously swim to keep from drowning, narcissists must consistently demonstrate that they are special, or they will sink like stones to the depths of depression...Narcissistic vampires' greatest fear is of being ordinary."[118] People with narcissistic personality disorder are extremely challenged when it comes to creating sustainable relationships because a relationship implies reciprocity, and for a narcissist, it is always all

---

118. Albert J. Bernstein, *Emotional Vampires: Dealing with People Who Drain You Dry* (New York: McGraw-Hill, 2001), 130-131.

about him- or herself. Your ability to assess others' characters will be immeasurably improved by a close read of Bernstein's book.

LEGALLY COMMITTING TO A GLUM (NOT A MILITARY ACRONYM) OR A PRINCESS

GLUM stands for a "good looking, under-functioning male." It's not a military acronym, it's a term I came up with in conversation with my little sister back when we were in high school. In the world of a GLUM, all that ought to be required of him is to radiate his obvious "studliness." Charming and smooth, with beguiling looks, the GLUM is least likely to be found in any place where chores are actively being completed. When it's time to do the dishes, he backs out of the kitchen with a boyish smile while saying, "I know better than to get between a woman and her kitchen!" GLUMS look to the women in their lives to do not only the chores but also the mental work of managing the family's needs. The result for their wives is that the GLUMs begin to feel like an additional child to manage and tend, which is a far cry from participating in a marriage of equals.

The female counterpart of a GLUM is a "Princess."[119] From the perspective of a princess, all that ought to be required of her is that she continues to look fabulous. A princess doesn't mind being patted on the head by someone from time to time as long as that someone continues to pay her shopping bills. A princess doesn't hold down an unrewarding job or contribute substantially to the work of running a household. Marry a princess at your own peril. Less an adult than an overgrown child, she is a play-at-home wife who spends all day frolicking in the garden with her golden ball (or getting her hair done, chatting with friends at Starbucks, and doing the downward dog before the admiring eyes of the creepy guy in the back row of her yoga class) while your own butt gets bigger from all the hours you log in the office, supporting her self-indulgent lifestyle. It's always a shame to see a good person get duped by a princess.

GUIDANCE TO HELP YOU NAVIGATE THE TERRAIN AHEAD

FYSA: SOME RELATIONSHIPS ARE ESPECIALLY PRONE TO POOR DECISION-MAKING

It might be tempting to see separation from the military as a good time to formalize your relationship, either legally, financially, or otherwise. But even if you've been dating someone for four years, you can still be in the "cocaine rush phase" of the relationship if that relationship has been mostly long-distance or interspaced with several long deployments. With the

---

119. I didn't coin the term "Princess" in this context, but I did develop an assessment to profile this concept. You can access this free of charge via this link: https://www.psychologytoday.com/intl/blog/the-joint-adventures-well-educated-couples/201208/marry-princess-or-glum-your-own-risk.

distance and lack of time together, it's easy to maintain the fantasy that you've both found your "soul mate."

Before you make a significant commitment to any relationship, it is critical to view your leading man or woman in multiple lights. Long-distance relationships and internet-mediated relationships are two types of courtships that are especially vulnerable to poor decision-making based on relatively little information over a potentially lengthy period of time. In a long-distance relationship, when you visit your partner, you get to leave your normal life behind to immerse yourself in their world, far from the stress and routine of your own life. You can be assured of a warm, loving reception. As such, this type of relationship may be especially protected from the intrusion of mundane, stressful elements of day-to-day life.

With the distance and the lack of face time, it is relatively easy to maintain illusions of mutual perfection, thereby extending the time during which each of you project and perceive unrealistic fantasies. Because the limited time you spend together can feel so magical (remember, the scarcity principle intensifies your hunger to see each other), you may quickly begin to feel certain that you have found "the One." It is important to bear this in mind, because people in love often overestimate the actual potential of a succession of steamy phone conversations and weekend dalliances to translate into a successful life partnership. Almost anyone can be accommodating, flexible, and attentive for a long weekend, but this says very little about how accommodating, flexible, and attentive that person will be when you see them every day, year after year.

ASSESS CORE CHARACTER OF POTENTIAL PARTNERS

It is also wise to evaluate how a potential partner behaves under stress. Does he lash out at others, or can he generally control his aggressive impulses? Does she treat others with respect even when she doesn't see things the same way, or even when she doesn't have to be respectful? It is also a good idea to note how a potential partner behaves when he or she has messed up. Does she become defensive and immediately make a case for how whatever happened is actually someone else's fault? Does he accept a fair share of the blame, and does he take responsibility for making things right?

As previously mentioned, Drs. Scott Cloud and John Townsend wrote a helpful little book titled *Safe People*.[120] They write that "safe" people admit their weaknesses, are humble, confront-able, and are able to prove their trustworthiness over time.[121] Unsafe people have some clearly identifiable negative characteristics that are best avoided. To help you make

---

120. Cloud and Townsend, *Safe People*.
121. Ibid., 28.

accurate distinctions between "safe" and "unsafe" people, I've converted several distinguishing personality characteristics into a brief ten-question assessment, as follows. This is a very important and practical tool to help you assess the core character of potential partners.

Exercise: Are you Dating an Emotionally Safe Person?		
Question	YES	NO
1. Does this person admit to having some weaknesses?		
2. Would others say that this person is humble?		
3. Is this person defensive when others tell them that they have hurt or offended them?		
4. Does this person show that he or she is trustworthy over time?		
5. Does this person apologize, but fail to change his or her behavior?		
6. Does this person admit it when he or she has problems?		
7. Does this person confess when he or she wrongs someone else (e.g. own up to it)?		
8. Does this person treat others with a lack of empathy?		
9. Does this person take responsibility for his or her own life?		
10. Does this person blame other people for his or her problems?		

Scoring Key:

1. Score 1 point for "No"	6. Score 1 point for "No"
2. Score 1 point for "No"	7. Score 1 point for "No"
3. Score 1 point for "Yes"	8. Score 1 point for "Yes"
4. Score 1 point for "No"	9. Score 1 point for "No"
5. Score 1 point for "Yes"	10. Score 1 point for "Yes"

(More than 2 points and you begin to wonder…more than 4 points and red flags should go up)

*Adapted by Dr. Shauna Springer, with permission, from material developed by Dr. Henry Cloud and Dr. John Townsend, as described in their book Safe People (1996: Zondervan Press). For further information on these concepts, visit: www.cloudtownsend.com

If I had to pick the five most important character qualities of people with lifelong partnership potential, I would select trustworthiness, dependability, emotional maturity, sense of fairness, and openness to influence. Let's zoom in on each of these qualities.

Trustworthiness

I previously mentioned that self-worth is a function of the alignment between what you say you value and what you actually do with your time, energy, and physical resources. In a parallel way, trust in a relationship is a function of the alignment between what you say you will do and what you actually do. Trust builds when we show others that we are safe people. Building trust requires you and your partner to take some risks in sharing things that are uncomfortable to talk about. The level of risk you take should be on pace with the level of trust you have already earned with each other. Over time, as we progressively disclose the nature of our experiences to each other and we respond to each other in "emotionally safe" and respectful ways, trust builds. To put it another way, trust forms as a function of how you handle each other's vulnerabilities.

Dependability

Dependability is closely related to trustworthiness. We live in a society of increasingly flaky people. Have you noticed that people nowadays do not like to be pinned down by specific plans and are often quick to change social plans when a more exciting invitation comes their way (or when they just don't feel like going out)? If the self-esteem movement prioritizes self-love and self-interest above all else, then it naturally follows that the stock of values like dependability would decline correspondingly.

Dependability is a consistently desired end state for military leaders. Some people in our (seems-to-me increasingly flaky society) may view dependability as an outdated value aligned with an "old school" or "active duty military" way of behaving. As a military leader, you appreciate the value of dependability when the stakes are highest, so how could you imagine forming a successful life partnership with someone who isn't dependable?

In the context of close relationships (or even working relationships with colleagues), dependability communicates respect. Dependability builds trust and a sense of safety. Dependability allows you to rely on others and lets others know that they can rely on you. Imagine the impact on your unit if your team didn't develop a pattern of being dependable, and imagine what storms lie ahead for a lifelong partnership absent the quality of dependability. What storms lie ahead during the transition to parenting for those who have not developed a pattern of being dependable?

Emotional Maturity

Another important dimension of character to assess has been labeled with various related terms like emotional intelligence, emotional maturity, or theory of mind development. Emotional intelligence (sometimes called EQ[122]) refers to an individual's ability to understand his or her own, and others', goals, intentions, responses, feelings, and behaviors. EQ is related to emotional maturity, which some people have at an early age, some develop at a later age, and some fail to develop, ever. The key here is a person's capacity for self-reflection, empathy, and insight.

How do you assess emotional maturity? There is no substitute for a large number of conversations about how each of you thinks and feels about various topics. If you think about a primary lifelong partnership as a really long conversation, you should ask yourself during the exploratory phase if this is the person with whom you would want to have the conversation of a lifetime. See if you can correctly perceive and demonstrate that you understand each other's points of view, especially when you disagree.

Additionally, the way that people talk about and make sense of failed relationships is a critical source of data on emotional maturity. Does the person you are dating take responsibility for their part in the challenges of that relationship? Alternatively, if, for example, he or she says that all of their exes are "total psychos," what does this say about them? These trends might indicate a deeper psychological issue at play that might become your issue as the relationship develops. Alternatively, they may be projecting their own deficiencies onto their past partners. This kind of statement might signal an inability to take ownership for their part in past relationship problems and may predict that someday, they will regale their friends with stories of how you are the latest in a long line of "psychos" that they somehow keep picking.

Sense of Fairness

Assess your partner's sense of fairness before you get married. Full stop. Does your partner have a sense of justice, and is he or she moved to correct injustices that are in his or her control? Does your partner consider men and women equal? If so, how does this value show up in how your partner treats the opposite sex? Does your partner have a good work ethic, and does he or she make efforts to do a fair share of the chores and the most boring tasks you have to manage together while dating? If your partner does not place a high value on fairness, you may be much more likely to end up cleaning all the toilets in the house for the rest of your life.

---

122. Daniel Goleman, *Emotional Intelligence: Why It Can Matter More than IQ* (New York, NY: Bantam Books, 1995).

Openness to Influence

In my opinion, one of the most important character traits to assess is openness to positive influence. Openness to positive influence is highly associated with the value of respecting others. Openness to positive influence goes hand in hand with a personal growth orientation and the emotional flexibility that allows us to create wonderful, mutually satisfying relationships. People can and do change, and the formative period in a relationship is the time to assess a potential partner's ability to make and sustain positive changes.

There are a few ways to assess openness to influence. The most direct way is to give your partner some difficult feedback and see what happens. (Obviously, don't do this just for sport, do it when something arises that calls for feedback). When you do point out a problem you have with their behavior, do they make statements like, *"Well, that's just the way I am"* or *"I'm sorry that you feel that way,"* suggesting that they do not want to change? Another way is to ask your partner this question: *"Would you be willing to go through premarital counseling with me?"*

You could arrange to do this with a professional counselor, or perhaps with a minister in your church, or even informally with a successfully married older couple who can then mentor you through the tough patches in the future. Your partner's answer to this question communicates information you would be wise to note. If a person is willing to engage in a course of some form of premarital counseling and actively participates in the process that follows, this would demonstrate openness to influence and a personal growth orientation. If the answer is *"I don't think we really need to"* or *"I'd rather not talk to a stranger about our problems,"* this may not bode well for the future you may have together.

Past Trauma Shapes Character, Sometimes in Really Great Ways

When you are assessing the character of a potential partner who has had past trauma of any kind—whether combat exposure, sexual trauma, childhood trauma, or other forms of trauma—do so with an open mind. It goes without saying that civilians often have misperceptions of those who serve in the military, to the degree that they have little exposure to those who have served in the military. Some of the best people I've known have been exposed to unimaginable traumas or have grown up in terrible family situations.

Traumas shape people in powerful ways. Take, for example, someone who was raised by an alcoholic parent. Research tells us that people who were raised by an alcoholic parent are more likely to become alcoholics themselves. So, at first blush, we might consider alcoholism in the family of origin to be a huge red flag. What is also true, however, is that people who grew up in an alcoholic environment are also more likely to avoid alcohol entirely for fear of repeating the dysfunction they experienced in childhood.

Likewise, statistical figures might suggest that a person with divorced parents may be more likely to end up divorced him- or herself. If this person has insight and a personal growth orientation, however, he or she may become capable of creating a truly beautiful union if he or she is determined to forge a new path. As a general rule, trauma often pushes people to the extreme ends of the behavioral spectrum. Those who lack the capacity for insight and the motivation to change the pattern in place often blindly play out the same script. Others reflect on their family of origin experiences and tell themselves, *"There is no way on earth I'm going to do my family the way family was done to me!"*

With this character-defining stance in place, these individuals actively work to become much better partners and parents to their children, despite having had very poor role models when they were young. This goes for all kinds of human behaviors and predicts all kinds of decision-making in the areas of life planning, mate selection, and parenting style. The key here is to make sure that the person you are dating has insight into the destructive patterns in his or her past and can articulate a clear vision for how to do things differently going forward.

Conduct Your ROC Drill Before You Deploy for a Lifetime of Missions

While you are dating, it is helpful to simulate some elements of how you might handle challenges together. For example, see if you can be two-marshmallow people together by jointly saving up enough money to do something really special. Or decide to do something really challenging together and see how you handle it as a team. When my husband and I were dating, I don't think we consciously thought, *Let's challenge ourselves in order to test our relationship's potential,* yet that is exactly what we did.

When we began to talk about getting serious, we decided to apply for a grant to help lead a community service initiative in Chile, South America. We cowrote the grant application and funded our travels with the money we were jointly awarded. With a team of eight people, we traveled to Pachica, Chile, to live within a community of Aymaran Indians in the Atacama Desert, where it has never rained. We lived in fairly primitive conditions, bathing in a freezing aqueduct and coping with ongoing (and very unsexy) gastrointestinal issues. We integrated into the life of the Kusayapan community for a time and shared in their festivals of celebration. We formed bonds with our team members. We shimmied along a shale-stone cliff and saw the remains of someone who had fallen there previously. We waited for help on a dark highway in the middle of nowhere when we punctured a tire. We shoveled loads of rocks and sand, poured and mixed concrete, and helped build the foundation for a laundry facility for the Kusayapans. We also built the foundation of our future marriage. If handled well, these kinds of experiences, like combat deployments, can help develop a strong working trust.

This experience has often led me to wonder whether a two-month rustic adventure like this would tell people more about their compatibility than two years of dating would. After all, we cannot tell where future cracks will appear unless our relationship is significantly stressed. Instead of avoiding challenges and sources of discomfort, consider accelerating directly into it. It is good to be stressed together during the exploratory phase of your relationship so you can see how you would negotiate and work through things together. Remember, we strengthen our muscles by first ripping them.

Ensure You're Clear and Secure BEFORE You Occupy

This piece of guidance is probably the most important of anything I have to share for those who are dating, but not yet formally committed: As suggested above, a major reason to wait out the "cocaine rush phase" of a relationship is to date for long enough to see if you can weather a few storms before you take the plunge together. In fact, it is highly beneficial during the exploratory phase of your relationship to proactively move through "minefields" of tough questions and areas of disagreement before you bind yourself in marriage. Of course, you need to learn how to have a safe and constructive fight first (which we will cover later in this handbook), but once you are armed with this understanding, by all means accelerate into conflict when it arises.

Tripping off landmines helps you see through the haze that comes from the high of the cocaine rush phase of the relationship. It gives you a sudden jolt of objectivity and awareness, not unlike splashing cold water on your face. Couples that set off some landmines up front benefit from some of the protection that comes from the way we idealize each other in the cocaine rush phase. That is, motivation to overcome barriers and find common ground is typically at peak levels before we are legally bound to each other. Two people who go into their marriage knowing that they can stay connected, despite conflict, have a much better chance of staying together in the long run. Clear the space for your relationship to build security before you make a legally binding commitment.

On the other hand, if differences do not come to light before you commit, the risk for post-marital disillusionment (and dissolution) is higher. In an interesting way, conflict becomes *critical* to trust formation—provided that conflict is addressed in a respectful, healthy way. In combat and in close relationships, trust forms "in the trenches" of conflict: it is *conflict* that allows us to evaluate whether another person is fundamentally trustworthy. Hardship strengthens the bonds of trust. Even a slight rupture, followed by a repair of the relationship, often heals to form a much stronger relationship. The true nature and strength of the relationship is revealed during tough times. Ruptures and repairs give us critical sources of information about how much we can trust each other to stay connected, show respect, and stick it out when the going is rough—things we would not know otherwise.

If sources of incompatibility and disagreement can come up before marriage, then each partner will have an opportunity to decide whether incompatible values and behaviors are ones he or she can live with or not. In the midst of conflict, *how* we work through problems is often more important than the actual issue(s) we resolve. Couples need to approach, rather than avoid, challenges and areas of struggle while staying intact as a functional team. Partners in successful marriages show core respect, recognize the validity of each other's thoughts and feelings, and make generous attributions for each other's behavior.[123] Conflict allows us to ask ourselves if we feel heard and respected despite a squall of negative emotions. Only in the context of conflict will you be able to see whether each of you can do things like...

- Manage and de-escalate your own negative emotions

- Understand each other's perspective even when you don't agree

- Treat each other with respect while in the heat of conflict

- Strengthen your bond through the process of post-conflict insight and repair

When it comes to strengthening the bonds of your relationship, you have to experience what it is like to lose together in order to know that you can win together.

Questions for Starting a Good Fight

To end on a practical note, when you are beginning to form a strong attachment to someone, don't avoid asking the hard questions up front. This is not an exhaustive list, but here are some hard questions to get these types of conversations moving (of course, don't ask these questions until you are both seriously considering a long-term commitment—this isn't first date material):

---

123. Paul Koren, Kathe Carlton, and David Shaw, "Marital Conflict: Relations among Behaviors, Outcomes, and Distress," *Journal of Consulting and Clinical Psychology* 48, no. 4 (1980): 460–468, https://doi:10.1037/0022-006x.48.4.460.

Exercise: Discussion of Roles, Goals, and Past and Potential Future Challenges
1. How were chores split up between your parents when you were growing up? How would we do chores? How would we split up roles if we were to get married in the future?
2. Do you believe that women are just naturally better at some things and men should do other things? If so, in what areas do you believe this is true?
3. What is your credit score and how much debt do you have (if any)? What is your plan for paying down this debt?
4. How do you feel about having children? How might this expand or limit the experience of a life without children? What do you imagine are the biggest challenges in the phase right after having a child?
5. What is one model of good parenting that you've seen, and what role would you see yourself playing as a parent? How would you like to be involved on a consistent basis in childcare?
6. How do you handle failures? What have been some of your greatest failures and disappointments in life so far?
7. How do you make sense of why your previous romantic relationships have ended? What role did you play in past relationships that have not worked out? What did you learn from these experiences?
8. What are some of your most ambitious goals in life? What kind of support do you see yourself needing from a life partner to help you achieve these goals?

END-OF-SECTION REVIEW AND SUMMARY

This section has provided you with essential insights to help you assess a potential life partnership and build a strong foundation for a long-lasting relationship. After you complete this exercise, you may want to incorporate these practical actions into your action plans for transition and reintegration.

Many of these insights are not limited to lifelong partnerships but are also important for meaningful friendships and other relationships. For example, in the earlier part of the handbook, we talked about assessing the organizational "culture" of places where you might find employment. You can think of organizations as having a "personality" in the same way that people do. So many of the insights you gain from this section may help you get clarity on other domains of your life—like whether you would want to work for an organization that is characterized by institutional narcissism or other toxic cultures.

END OF SECTION REVIEW

Take some time and review this section on Guidance for Evaluating Potential Lifelong Partnerships. When you are ready, go through Part 1 and Part 2 of this End of Section Review to apply the information in this handbook to your ability to forge healthy relationships through transition and beyond

PART 1 INSIGHTS

What are the 5 most important insights that you learned about relationships?

(Do this regardless of your relationship status - what you learn may help you help a friend)

EXAMPLE: Your odds of divorce are not 50% - they may be much higher, or lower than 50%, based on your understanding of how to build and maintain a successful lifelong partnership. Happy relationships are more a matter of choice than of chance.

PART 2 PRACTICAL ACTIONS

Identify three (3) things you plan to do to apply these insights based on the example provided

EXAMPLE: When I am seriously considering committing to someone, I will engage them in difficult conversations intended to identify our areas of incompatibility so that we can see how we deal with the tension that arises from conflict and value differences.

To summarize, then, for those of you who undergo transition while exploring a potential romantic partnership, key insights include:

- Your odds of divorce are not 50 percent—your particular risk of divorce may be much higher or lower than 50 percent—depending on the degree to which you "own the night." In other words, your odds of divorce are related to the depth of your understanding on how to build and maintain a relationship that can last a lifetime.

- It's not wise to make binding life decisions while you are high on cocaine. Engage in a proactive process for determining goodness of fit and give yourself time to assess the potential of a future relationship.

- A sufficient length of time to make a good decision varies. It depends on how intentional you are about assessing compatibility and how much time you have spent working through conflicts and challenges.

- Rather than fixing a "target" courtship length, focus instead on ensuring that your relationship is well out of the "cocaine rush phase" and is well into the testing phase before you make a legal commitment.

- Be aware that some relationships, such as those formed during lengthy deployments or other long-distance relationships, may have extra risk factors in terms of poor decision-making.

- Don't communicate that you don't value yourself that highly when you are dating (and the best way to communicate high self-worth is to actually build and maintain solid self-worth by making decisions that are aligned with your values).

- Be careful with people who have personality disorders—by their nature, these conditions are fairly well entrenched. Even though GLUMs and Princesses are not part of the formal psychological canon of personality disorders, perhaps these personality types should be. The theme is to be careful about people that are well entrenched in a way of operating with limited motivation to change their behavioral pattern.

- Assess the character of any potential life partner before making a legally binding commitment. In addition to using the profile I developed to help you assess the qualities of emotionally safe people, five key personality traits to assess are trustworthiness, dependability, emotional maturity, sense of fairness, and openness to influence.

- Past trauma doesn't doom us, it shapes us, often in powerful ways. Sometimes, past trauma shapes us to be exceptionally good partners or parents.

- Conflict is essential to getting clarity and building a strong relationship. Have a number of good fights before you get married. Otherwise, you'll miss important learning opportunities and your marriage will be at higher risk of divorce.

SECTION III.
GUIDANCE FOR MAINTAINING STRONG, HAPPY PARTNERSHIPS

This final section of the relationship-focused portion of the handbook is divided into a series of insights to help you see what right looks like, followed by guidance for managing conflicts and challenges in relationships.

GOT YOUR 6: SIX ELEMENTS TO SHOW WHAT RIGHT LOOKS LIKE

In brief, there are six elements to fill out a good picture of what right looks like. Strong, happy, lifelong partnerships are characterized by intentional love, intentional respect, and intentional support for new freedoms. In addition, partners in healthy relationships shoulder each other's burdens, assert their needs directly and maintain good boundaries, and protect each other's vulnerable places.

1. INTENTIONAL LOVE

One of my favorite books on learning how to express love with intention is *The Five Love Languages*[124] by Gary Chapman. In the book, Chapman outlines some unspoken principles for how we learn to express love in our closest relationships. First, he points out that **we often repeat patterns we learned in our family of origin.** This is a well-established tendency, generally referred to as "social learning" or "modeling" in the field of psychology. If, for example, your parents were in the habit of referring to each other constantly with various terms of endearment, you are more likely to repeat this behavior in your marriage.

Second, Chapman also points out that **we often crave forms of love we did not get in our early years.** So, if we were raised by parents who did not provide much verbal praise, we might be strongly attracted to partners who provide a lot of praise. As I've stated before, family of origin experiences often result in repetition of previous patterns or in intentional rebellion against them.

---

124. Gary Chapman, *The Five Love Languages: How to Express Heartfelt Commitment to Your Mate* (Chicago: Northfield Publishing, 1992).

A third principle is a variation of the "Golden Rule" that doesn't always work out as well as the Golden Rule should: **We do unto others as we would have done unto us** (even when the form of love we offer misses the mark for the other person). For example, we might keep writing our partners love notes because this is what we would want from them even if this doesn't hit the target for how they feel loved. This isn't necessarily a selfish act; in fact, in my observation, it's often as unconscious as speaking in our native language (and then feeling increasingly frustrated when other people do not respond in kind).

There are two additional principles that I would add to Chapman's analysis. First, **we base our expressions of love on what we see in the media**. The media has such a powerful shaping effect that I decided to lead off my first book, *Marriage, for Equals*, with an effort to shed some light on the manipulations inherent in the script for how to fall in love as played out on the ABC television show *The Bachelor*. (For those of you who might poo-poo the show's influence, consider this: the **twenty-three seasons** of *The Bachelor* have captured a viewing audience of an estimated 190 million people, and the show has launched multiple spin-offs in America and abroad).

Finally, a further principle I would add, in addition to Chapman's theory, is that **we offer whatever causes us the least anxiety to offer**. In some cases, it's not that we don't know what our partners would like to receive; rather, we may know what they want, but continue to show love in ways that are *easier for us to provide*. If we are uncomfortable saying, "*I love you*," writing notes to express our affection, or making regular sexual connection a priority, we make nice meals and buy them little gifts. I see this pattern *frequently* in my sessions with couples. And when I do, I have to find a way to ask whether loving someone in the way that feels most comfortable to us (once we realize we're doing this) is actually love at all.

If you would like to love your partner more intentionally, the first thing to do is to find out whether your understanding of how he or she most wants to be loved is on target—and if it is not, then adjust fire and meet your partner's actual needs. I recommend Chapman's book as a further resource for expressing love in a more intentional way.

2. INTENTIONAL RESPECT

A healthy lifelong partnership is one in which two people become each other's closest battle buddy. Inherent in this concept is the presence of mutual respect. In these partnerships, there are continual efforts to recognize imbalances of power and then to renegotiate and shift power in order to maintain a respectful balance. Such relationships offer frequent checks against one partner having too much power over the other in a way that preserves and strengthens the core of equal respect in the partnership. Healthy self-esteem and openness to influence allows equally matched partners to share power, to admit wrongs, and change course as needed. For example:

> **As an example of *Intentional Respect*, consider this interaction between two equally powerful partners who were working for different departments in the same company:**
>
> ***Partner A:*** *I'm really worried about this new policy statement put out by the company—do you think it's going to lead to anything I should worry about?*
>
> ***Partner B:*** *There are a lot of things to worry about today, but I don't think this is one of them.*
>
> ***Partner A:*** *Whoa—that felt condescending!*
>
> ***Partner B:*** *You're right, sorry. I see that—I did just sound like a pompous ass—I just came from a staff meeting in which my boss praised me in front of the entire staff and my head was temporarily swollen. What I meant to say is that my read on the situation is that this isn't going to lead to anything bad for you and I hope you won't worry about it.*

3. INTENTIONAL SUPPORT FOR NEW FREEDOMS

When I was a young woman looking at the types of marriage represented among my friends' parents, I didn't know if I would ever be able to establish a truly satisfying marriage. On a few occasions, I remember thinking, *If that is what marriage is like, I might be better off without a husband.* I had a strong independent streak and have always craved what I think of as *Walden Pond interludes*—that is, lengths of time when I can meet life on my own terms, often in solitude, and sometimes in various new social settings. At various times in my life, I have strongly identified with Henry Thoreau, who once said, *"To be in company, even with the best, is soon wearisome and dissipating. I love to be alone. I never found the companion that was so companionable as solitude."*[125]

I think it might be helpful to share an example or two that illustrate my version of the "time to think" guidance preached to military commanders as part of the "develop self" leadership competency: My dissertation on the effects of stress on marriage won one of four University dissertation awards, which came with a few thousand dollars. I decided to spend the money on a two-week walking tour through Tuscany to unwind from graduate school and prepare for the next chapter in my life. Most of the touring companies I contacted had a policy that every female must be accompanied by at least one other person, but eventually I found a representative in one company who saw that I could manage myself capably.

---

125. Henry Thoreau, "Solitude," *Life in the Woods* (1854), included in *Norton Anthology of American Literature*, 4th ed., vol. 1 (New York, NY: W.W. Norton and Company, 1994), 1789.

Exercise: Construct a Vision for A Relationship That is Freeing

What kind of marriage would you create if you were assured of your partner's commitment to helping you live into your full potential? What kinds of needs would you support for each other's well-being and growth?

Describe 1-2 important INDIVIDUAL short-term growth goals for the next 6 months (for example, "I want to join a local pick-up basketball team and play at least once a week"):

Describe very specifically how you need your partner to support you in your identified short- term goals (i.e. "I need you to cover the kids on Tuesday nights after work")

Describe 1-2 important INDIVIDUAL long-term growth goals for the next 5 years (for example, "I want to complete an MBA at the local university"):

Describe very specifically how you need your partner to support you in these identified long-term goals (i.e. "I'll do my best to get my graduate school assignments done during the day, but when that isn't possible, I'll need you to support me while I work on them in the evenings")

Exercise: Construct a Vision for A Relationship That is Freeing (continued)

Describe 1-2 ways that you need to detach from your primary relationship in order to recharge your batteries (i.e. "I need to take a weekend with my friends from college soon").

Describe 1-2 ways that your partner can help meet your need to detach at times ("I need 30 minutes to myself when I get home from work - after that, I'll be ready to talk about my day and have fun with you"):

CRITICAL - DON'T MISS THIS!
Now, ask your partner to do the same and tell you how you can meet his or her needs in the same way as you would ask them to meet yours.

He moved my luggage from inn to inn, leaving me free to walk from hill town to hill town on the *Strada Bianca*, the ancient pilgrimage trail in Tuscany, with only a daypack filled with a few thick slices of bread, a wedge of good pecorino cheese, a bottle of water, some maps, and a journal. I had no cell phone and didn't miss it. For that two-week period, I lived entirely at my own whim, off the grid, pursuing whatever interesting adventures I might discover along the way. After a few days of unwinding, my mind began to explode with new ideas and insights. I wrote more than a hundred pages in my journal, and to this day, I am still renewed when I remember this golden solitary interlude in my life.

A few years later, when I was feeling somewhat burned out, I pursued another Walden Pond interlude, this time a week in a cabin in the backwoods of a small town in North Carolina. Once again, my senses came alive during this trip, as I faced both new and anxiety-provoking situations. On this trip as well as my trip to Italy, I had to navigate new challenges on my own. This process brought moments of pure exhilaration and renewal, in a way that is *different* from the renewal I experience on adventures with my family (which is also good, just different).

Finding a life partner should not be a reason to stop growing individually. In addition to learning how to be interdependent, moments of self-reliance are also a vital part of a successful partnership. The intentional investment of both love and respect creates the safe base that we need to live into an expansive freedom. It is this freedom that lets us fill our full potential as individuals and partners.

4. HEALTHY PARTNERS SHOULDER EACH OTHER'S BURDENS

There is a funny irony about bearing each other's emotional burdens: helping carry the emotional burdens of our partners often means doing absolutely nothing...but listening with love and acceptance. And the irony is that this is often the **harder thing to do than to take action to try to solve our partners' stressors.** People of action—which is the case for many military leaders—want to DO something when someone they love is suffering. However, even the act of advising a course of action, let alone managing another person's challenges, disrupts the healthiest form of relationship between you and your partner.

Why? Because advising, counseling, and giving advice quickly shifts the relationship from one between a family team to a "one-up, one-down" kind of relationship. The recipient of advice may feel disrespected because, while not intended, their partner has essentially communicated: *"You can't handle your own challenges. I can manage them better than you can. From my place of superior wisdom, here is what you ought to do."* That is why scores of women for many centuries have repeatedly told their husbands, *"Look dude, I don't need you to solve my problems. I just want you to listen to me."*

Ultimately, creating the core of an effective command team at home means trusting in the competence of your partner (or their ability to develop their competence) while letting them know that you have their back. This allows them to draw from your strength to discover their own strength from within. Remember, vulnerability is a gift. Sometimes the hardest and most valuable thing you can do is be present, hold the space, and receive the vulnerability your partner is willing to share.

5. HEALTHY PARTNERS ASSERT NEEDS DIRECTLY AND MAINTAIN GOOD BOUNDARIES

One of the most common things I have observed in working with military couples is the tendency for partners to assume that the other person will read their minds. I have a theory that the basis for this comes in part from military training. Let me tell you a quick story. For the last few years, I have been working closely with a circle of Marines in units that have been highly impacted by losses of their brothers in arms, to combat and to suicide. Many of these Marines have become like family to me.

In the context of one reunion, I decided to show, rather than tell them, the power of drawing from the strength of those we love and respect. I set a challenge for myself, a twelve-week fitness challenge that felt impossible to me. I put out an email to a group of twelve of these Marines letting them know about the challenge I set for myself. I talked openly, with great vulnerability, about how this issue has led to some ongoing feelings of personal shame. I asked for their help and support in the following specific way: *"Can I call each of you, one per week, and ask you to tell me stories about how you have "embraced the suck" and overcome challenges in your own life that once felt insurmountable? This will help me put my own suffering in perspective and will give me strength to persist with the challenge I have set for myself."* I got exactly one supportive response—otherwise, it was crickets.

My first reaction was to go deeper into a place of shame, asking myself questions like *"Maybe they really don't feel the same bond with me that I do with them?"* and other things along the same lines. But I had the advantage of lots of very sacred moments with these Marines and I knew from these experiences that our bond is real and that they DO have my back, even if they don't put that into words. I was still scared to reach out that first week, but I did, asking the first of them if he would spend some time on the phone to encourage me with some of his stories. His response to my text was immediate: "Of course, Doc. Anytime, call me anytime." So, I did, and we had a wonderful conversation. He was more vulnerable and open with me than he has ever been and the encouragement he gave me that day put wind beneath my wings for the hardest initial part of my challenge.

Through this experience, I gained an important insight. In military training, actions are repeatedly drilled to the point where verbal communication becomes unnecessary and is discouraged under the pretense of noise and radio discipline. Tactical operations are conducted in a way that minimizes—if not altogether excludes—verbal communication. Actions and expectations are understood as briefed or as part of a routine battle drill. You have been conditioned to communicate, understand, and take action without saying very much, but this aspect of the military culture may prove unproductive in life outside the military, particularly as it applies to your intimate relationships. The verbal expression, in words that loved ones can hear, of feelings and intentions is critical for maintaining a healthy relationship. It's a matter of remembering to take that next step and then having the guts to take your armor off with those you love.

6. HEALTHY PARTNERS PROTECT EACH OTHER'S VULNERABLE PLACES

A colleague of mine in the Dr. Ben Karney lab, Dr. Lisa Neff, brought clarity and wisdom to the ongoing debate: *In their close relationships, do people want to be known for who they are, warts and all, and loved despite their flaws* OR *do people want to perceived by their partners in a slightly idealized way?*[126] For many years, this debate filled the pages of a slew of academic journals until Lisa came along and pointed out that people want ***both***.[127] In other words, we want to be seen and known for who we are, flaws included, AND we want to be slightly idealized (seen through a tint of rose-colored glasses) by our partners.

In translating this research into practice, I have observed that relationships occur at two levels: the "Global" (G) (actions that have strategic implications) and "Specific" (actions that have tactical implications). The Global (G) level refers to the overarching sense we have of our partners—things like whether they are a desirable partner or not and things that capture their character as a whole. On the "S" (Specific) level of relationships are all the behaviors that happen in relationships—some good, some bad, some not bad or good, just incompatible between partners. The essence of being a "battle buddy" in one's closest relationship is to maintain a solid, positive "G." To frame this from the perspective of the strategic corporal, actions on the tactical level have strategic implications.

When we first meet our partners, "G" is rock solid—in fact, it is "pathologically secure," as we idealize our partners in the first flush of love, overlooking all kinds of specific behaviors that are negative or incompatible. As we transition from the cocaine rush phase to the testing phase of our relationships, we start to notice a whole range of negative and incompatible "S" behaviors, which can create a shaky "G." In other words, we may start to wonder if our partner really is a desirable "catch" or not. During the testing phase, we start to engage in conflict, and if we can accelerate into conflict, and navigate it skillfully, we will emerge with a positive "G" that is based on real data (rather than the idealization and wishful thinking of the cocaine rush phase).

Essential to navigating this skillfully is the ability to ask for changes in a way that protects our partner at the level of "G." If we can do this, we can transform all kinds of negative interactive behaviors at the level of "S." For comparison, here are some examples of approaches that

126. Sandra L. Murray, John G. Holmes, and Dale W. Griffin, "The Benefits of Positive Illusions: Idealization and the Construction of Satisfaction in Close Relationships," *Journal of Personality and Social Psychology* 70, no. 1 (1996): 79, https://doi:10.1037//0022 -3514.70.1.79.
127. Lisa A. Neff and Benjamin R. Karney, "Judgments of a Relationship Partner: Specific Accuracy but Global Enhancement," *Journal of Personality* 70, no. 6 (2002): 1079-1112, https://doi:10.1111/1467-6494.05032.

fail to protect the vulnerability of our partners, statements which are nearly guaranteed to set off a primitive panic at the level of G(lobal) identity:

"You always [insert any undesirable behavior]."

"You're such a loser [or another term that indicates broad-sweeping character assassination]."

"I can't take it anymore! I'm done with you!"

"What's the point—why don't we just get a divorce?"

"I don't have the same feelings for you anymore."

Now compare these kinds of statements with an example of what right looks like. Let's say that a chronic stressor in our relationship is excessive spending from a joint checking account without agreement by both parties. Asking for change while protecting our partner at the level of "G" might look like this:

"I love you and I'm proud of how we're handling (give specific examples of challenges already overcome). We are becoming a stronger team and I know that you have my back. When you spend more than $100 from our joint account without checking with me first, I start to get ulcers when I look at our checking account balance. Can we please agree to check with each other before making any purchases of over $100? Thank you for looking out for me in this way."

By doing this, one has effectively shored up one's partner at the level of "G" while asking for changes at the level of "S." This kind of approach is much less likely to generate unproductive, rage-state conflict. Managers of successful companies use a variant of this technique when giving corrective feedback to their employees. They start with a positive statement, give corrective feedback, and end with a positive statement. It's the classic "turd sandwich." Successful managers are skilled turd sandwich artists. They do it because it works, and it can help us ask for change in our close relationships as well. Doing this well takes more work upfront, but the payoff is well worth the effort—your partner will feel loved and respected, and you will be able to work through conflicts without getting stuck in needlessly destructive cycles of attack and counterattack.

It bears repeating that there is wisdom and growth to be gained by advancing into productive conflict. As I mentioned earlier, trust within combat units and close relationships is theoretical until the first (fire)fight. However, what I've observed is that many of you are extremely reluctant to engage in conflict with your partners. Avoiding conflict—whatever the reason—has hidden costs. These hidden costs do not often register for many years (not unlike other lifestyle decisions that build to a head over many years). When a couple habitually avoids conflict, they create a potential "sinkhole" issue in the relationship.

Sinkholes are common in states like Florida, where the topsoil sits over layers of fine sand. Over time, hidden streams of water—sometimes just trickles—erode the sand layers under the surface. What looks solid on top looks like Uncle Milton's ant farm underneath, until one day, the bottom drops out. In Florida, sinkholes were known to drop below houses, semi-trucks, sometimes even an unlucky solitary jogger. Avoiding conflict erodes intimacy and trust and places a relationship on unstable ground. In conflict-avoidant relationships, it is often just a matter of time before the bottom drops out. This part of the handbook will give you a clear understanding of what healthy conflict looks like.

A Different Kind of Courage than the Courage Required in Battle

> *"Honestly Doc, I would rather walk into the kill zone of an ambush than tell my wife how much I need her."*

When an airborne ranger looks straight at you with a face full of fear and dread, it gets your attention. That is how Joe (not his real name) looked at me in the middle of a therapy session. I had just shared some counsel on how to repair his badly strained marriage.

During the first few therapy sessions, Joe presented as someone with a serious anger management problem. He enjoyed fighting and felt a sense of release after physical conflicts. He was spoiling for a fight, coiled up and hoping someone would provoke him to violence. He scored high on some of the supplemental questions I asked in my assessments, like, "*Missing the adrenaline rush of combat and frequently wishing you were back in the combat zone*" and "*Wishing someone would pick a physical fight with you because it would feel good to fight.*" The first story he told me to explain his anger was that "*People who haven't served have no respect for the military.*" Joe's personal mission was to "re-educate the ignorant" by way of brute force.

As we built trust, though, another story emerged. Joe had always been particularly close to his wife. He described her as "his rock." In attachment terms, this means that she was the "stable base" who created his sense of security as he went through life. After his last deployment, their marriage had become seriously strained. In one session, he told me that he had tried reaching out to his wife, but she had walked away. Joe said, *"It felt like I was reaching my arms out to her and she just cut them off and let me bleed out."* In attachment terms, by turning away from him at a time of vulnerability and need, his wife was effectively saying, "You're dead to me." This attachment wound was setting off what master therapist Dr. Sue Johnson refers to as a "primal panic."[128]

As Johnson, the founder of Emotionally Focused Therapy, explains: "Our loved one is our shelter in life. When this person is unavailable and unresponsive we are assailed by a tsunami of emotions—sadness, anger, hurt and above all, fear. This fear is wired in. Being able to rely on a loved one, to know that he or she will answer our call is our innate survival code. Research is clear, when we sense that a primary love relationship is threatened, we go into a primal panic."[129]

While Joe had sufficient restraint not to take his anger out on his wife, he was taking it out on a growing number of other people. Frankly, the situation was quickly becoming very dangerous. In this case, the work involved coaching him in how to address the loss of trust and intimacy in his marriage. This was what caused him to look at me with such fear and dread. Clearly, repairing his relationship called for a different kind of courage than the kind required to operate in the combat zone.

But Joe dug deep and took the risk of standing before her, without armor, in the way that I had suggested. Joe's wife then responded by taking a risk and opening up to him in return. She shared that while he was deployed, she found a letter confirming that he had volunteered to redeploy. They were due to have a second child and he had told her that he had no choice but to return to combat. She explained that when she found the letter she felt like he had abandoned her and their children. Her rage grew and grew during the time he was away, and she was alone, with their toddler and a newborn. This was the original attachment wound that had catalyzed the negative spiral in their relationship. So, there were two layers of stories behind the original story he initially told me. Both Joe and his wife were suffering because of the attachment wounds they had inflicted on each other.

Happily, with the right insights and the risks they took to act on those insights, they were

---

128. Sue Johnson, *Hold Me Tight: Seven Conversations for a Lifetime of Love* (New York, NY: Little, Brown & Company, 2008). Johnson explains that a "primal panic" is set off when our primary attachment bond is perceived to be insecure.
129. "Where Does Love Go Wrong?" Dr. Sue Johnson, accessed June 24, 2019, http://www.drsuejohnson.com/where-does-love -go-wrong/.

able to turn their relationship around completely and had a second round of "falling in love" once they took their armor off with each other. However, if I had failed to learn these truths, and treated this as a standard anger management case, the outcome would have been very different.

Understanding Why We Keep Our Armor On

As I said earlier, it is common for many of you to feel that no one will ever be closer than your military brothers and sisters. This mindset often leaves your wives and other loved ones feeling like outsiders. Failure to develop the kind of deep trust we're talking about in close relationships—to learn how to really have each other's back—undermines relationships. Of course, none of us marry someone expecting to get divorced someday. We generally marry each other "in good faith" with the intention of being each other's battle buddy for the years to come.

But, as we've discussed, building trust and deepening intimacy is not a passive process. Relationships don't get better as a function of time alone. They get better as a function of two people being able to stand without armor in each other's presence, especially during times of high stress. In my observation, many of you (and perhaps people in general?) keep your armor on with your partners for three main reasons, all of which can be traced to a kind of protective instinct.

The most common reason you keep your armor on can be summed up in a statement like, *"I am just trying to protect him or her from worrying about me."* That is, you restrict what you share with your loved ones because you are afraid that it will cause them to feel more anxious about your military experiences. So, the intention here is a good one but this doesn't achieve the intended effect. To put this in military language, it's an example of *"good initiative, bad judgment."* As a rule, the anxiety we hold is **often directly related to what we don't know**.

When we have a vague sense that something is wrong, but we lack any details to help us understand what the problem is, our anxiety goes way up. In military marriages, it is often the case that a spouse pushes for more disclosure in order to better understand the hidden pain of his or her military partner. Without a good understanding of the problem, he or she is left with a chronically high level of anxiety. So, rather than protecting them, you are unintentionally exposing your partner to chronic anxiety.

Sometimes I get pushback on this point in the following way: *"I don't want my partner to live with the images I have in my head."* There are ways to talk about problems without revealing specific details. For instance, rather than saying something like, *"I was put in a situation where*

I had to shoot a little kid and I can't forget the way he looked, lying on the ground with his insides spilling out," one could say, *"I had to make some terrible choices that no one should have to make. I made those choices to protect my brothers- and sisters-in-arms, but I am haunted by the memories of what happened. I know I had to protect my fellow soldiers, but the guilt is eating me alive. It makes me feel like I have done things for which I can't be forgiven."* **This is what it sounds like to stand without armor with your partner.** Details of what you saw and you did aren't necessary for your loved one to understand the hidden emotional pain of your traumatic experiences. And without understanding the emotional impact of your experiences, a supportive spouse is powerless to be an effective partner—during and after the transition from the military.

A second reason why we keep our armor on is to protect ourselves. This motivation can be summed up in a statement like, *"If my spouse really knew who I am, she would think I'm a monster."* When we do this, we pay two very high costs—we lose out on the chance to build deep trust, and we lose the chance to feel unconditionally loved by our partner. Our choice to keep our pain hidden introduces a split into the relationship where our partner is denied the opportunity to support us in our suffering. Again, a statement like the one above that shares the impact of past experiences without any details can help bring hidden pain out into the open. This can be tricky though. Disclosure can transform pain into healing very quickly, but only in cases where our partner is an emotionally safe and supportive person.

I had the advantage of being able to assess the partners of the veterans I saw in my couples' clinic in order to determine whether this intervention would be helpful or harmful. I only did this intervention when I encountered what I call "warrior wives" (or husbands with the same qualities). A "warrior wife" was someone who I knew would be able and willing to listen without any judgment, whose opinion of their partner would not change no matter what was shared.

I can recall these sessions with particular clarity because the healing effect was so powerful, and so immediate. The veteran's face changed as he or she released a thousand-ton burden of shame, and the relationship went to a much deeper level of trust than ever before. In these sessions, the veteran's warrior wife would say something like, *"I'm so sorry you've carried this on your own for so long. If I'd been in your shoes, I would've done the same thing you did. You did what you had to do to protect your fellow Marines and do your job. I know you're a good man and I love you even more for sharing this with me."*

These warrior partners were mature enough and safe enough to draw from their own hidden pain to connect with their veteran partner in a critically vulnerable time of need. They are their partner's "rock." I definitely wouldn't recommend this as a general strategy without some thoughtful assessment of how this interaction would play out in a given relationship. Because the stakes are so high, I would recommend that this kind of conversation be facilitated by a skilled therapist.

The third reason we keep our armor on is that we want to protect our loved ones from our rage...which takes us to the next topic.

Working with Uncontrolled Rage: How to Have a Good Fight

I include the following section on uncontrolled rage for three reasons:

1. As a psychologist who has worked with veterans and their partners for many years, I've been in a unique position to see what happens behind closed doors. People in general, including leaders in the military and civilian sectors, often have issues in their close relationships that no one would guess from the outside. Uncontrolled anger is an issue that is common in the couples I've treated, both in civilian and military settings. (Rage was no greater an issue for military couples than for civilian couples—in fact, as I'll point out later, military service members have some specific skills they can draw on to protect their partners from their own rage).

2. In confirmation of what I just said, when I would host groups in the VA, my group on "How to Have a Good Fight" was often "standing room only"—sometimes drawing up to thirty people for that particular group. This confirms for me that, as a society, we need some help navigating anger and conflict in our closest relationships.

3. If uncontrolled anger is not a problem in your relationship, what you may learn in the following section may help you to help someone you care about—whether a civilian friend or a fellow service member or veteran in your life.

Aggressive Behavior Comes from Different Sources[130]

First, a helpful distinction to draw is whether anger is more impulsive/reactive or intentional/premeditated. People whose anger is intentional and premeditated don't necessarily have "anger control issues"—some people like dominating others and feel the right to be aggressive. You have known people who enlisted in the military because they had always enjoyed

---

130. In fact, one of the "stories behind the story" was that in some cases, wives were the much more violent partner. I had several cases where veterans were battered by their wives. Often, they were terrified to respond because they were afraid of very seriously hurting their partners.

violence, and military training only further honed their capabilities for aggressive responding. In domestic violence scenarios, such individuals treat their partners like property. They show little genuine remorse.

However, the vast majority of veterans I have treated are **not this way**. Far and away, the common pattern I saw was impulsive/reactive anger. With this kind of anger, you feel helpless and ashamed when you lose control of yourself (*"This rage comes over me and it's like I turn into a monster...I see my wife's face and she is so scared...I hate it"*). Some of you isolate yourselves out of a fear of being triggered and suffering consequences as a result of losing control (*"I don't want to end up in jail because some jerk triggers me"*). Rather than being **predatory** by nature, you are **protective** by nature, and want to protect your loved ones from your rage. After your anger subsides, deep shame often sets in. When thinking about the possibility of future anger episodes, you may feel dread.

Sometimes, in couples' therapy sessions, the partner of someone with reactive/impulsive anger withholds disclosing what happened because they do not want their veteran partner (who is generally loving) to be perceived by the therapist to be an "abuser." In such cases, it is often the case that the veteran's baseline personality is not characterized by strong narcissistic or antisocial elements. Instead, such behavior represents the temporary hijacking of higher values when a primitive drive arises. If this has happened to you, perhaps you felt psychologically flooded or cornered in some way, and said something horrible, or shoved or slapped your partner, and then expressed genuine horror for having done so.

In cases like this, it is very important to avoid inducing further shame, since shame can be related to the emergence or sharp escalation of suicidal ideation for some of you (*"It's like I turn into a monster"* can quickly become the thought, *"I am the problem that needs to be eliminated"*). Is it possible to deepen the understanding of the impact of violence on safety and trust in the relationship without inducing shame? Yes.

Here is how I did it with my patients:

> I want to imagine that we've been meeting for nearly a year and we've had really good sessions every time we've met. You've always felt safe here. In fact, you've actually told me in the past that my office and our therapeutic relationship is the only place you've felt safe since getting out from the military. But then one day, without any warning, you come into my office and I suddenly throat punch you. So, you tell my boss that you want to be reassigned to a new therapist and I react with shock. I ask you why would you feel unsafe with me now? We've been meeting for well over

a year. The past thirty sessions were all completely safe. I only throat punched you once, so you really ought to get over it.

Through this analogy, we can see that any violent behavior—even impulsive, unplanned acts—have a long-term negative impact on our partner's sense of safety and security.

Do Veterans Have More Issues with Rage than Civilians?

Not in my experience. In fact, I find it odd when people share what to me is a misperception that veterans are "ticking time bombs." Sometimes people cite news stories about an individual service member who perpetrated a mass casualty. Mass casualties are perpetrated by civilians and veterans alike, but if you do a comparison of who will do more damage when engaged in aggressive actions, logically it follows that someone with advanced weapons training will cause a greater impact.

Far from seeing veterans in this way, I have generally observed that those who serve in the military are intensely *protective* of others—including civilians—as a rule. Many of you see yourselves as "sheepdogs" who are looking out for the "wolves" in society on behalf of all of us. In the past few years, I have fairly often found myself as the only woman in large circles of combat warfighters in off-the-grid locations. At times, some of my civilian friends have registered concerns: *"Shauna, is that really a good idea?"* This question betrays the fear that civilians with relatively little exposure to warfighters may carry based on a widely held misperception.

My response is to laugh and inform them that being in the woods with twenty or thirty Marines is in fact the *safest possible place that I could be*. As their trusted "Doc" and an adopted member of their tribe, I pity the person who might lay a hand on me given the group of warfighters in my life that I know have my back.

Here's the thing: *due to your military training, you typically have an incredible ability to restrain your aggressive impulses in situations that would lead most of us to react impulsively*. Combat training does not develop aggression without any restraint—quite the opposite. The *undesirable* state that military combat training seeks to avoid developing has been referred to as the "berserk" state by psychiatrist Jonathan Shay[131]. As he explains, "'Berserk' comes from the Norse word for the frenzied warriors who went into battle naked, or at least without armor, in a godlike or god-possessed, but also beast-like fury." The best warfighters and operators are those who stay clear of the "berserk" state, instead using focused aggression in strategic and tactically sound ways. This requires you to stay in control of yourself, to hold

---

131. Jonathan Shay, *Achilles in Vietnam: Combat Trauma and the Undoing of Character* (New York: Scribner, 1994), 77–79.

your center in incredibly dangerous and chaotic (or, as you might say "kinetic'") environments. In the book *What It Is Like to Go to War* (one of my favorite books of all time—I highly recommend it), author and combat Marine Corps Veteran Karl Marlantes gives a clear picture of what right looks like: *"When I was fighting…I was usually in a white heat of total rationality, completely devoid of passion. I had a single overwhelming concern, to get the job done with minimal casualties to my side and stay alive in doing it."*[132]

Moreover, combat training requires you to regulate your physiological state in order to hit targets with good accuracy. People who are unfamiliar with firearms fail to understand that for many of us who enjoy shooting, a day at the range can bring almost a meditative state of focused concentration. Skillful marksmanship is about regulating your body and your breath so that the firearm can do the work. Squeezing a trigger very gently, without anticipating recoil, and relaxing with the recoil, is an act of physical self-mastery. As a result, because of this training and these experiences, you are, in fact, unusually skilled at downregulation of your bodies.

Making these links for some of my patients has been game-changing for them. These insights have created immensely positive change for many of my patients as they have stopped seeing themselves as someone "with an anger problem." Instead, they have started to map existing abilities to restrain themselves and down-regulate their bodies onto the way they interact with their loved ones. It is my hope that if you are carrying a burden of shame or fear about your ability to protect your loved ones from your own rage, you may achieve the same shift in your thinking and the same positive outcome as many of my patients.

Moving Toward Emotional Self-Mastery

The good news is that when anger is impulsive/reactive, rather than coldly premeditated without remorse, there is hope for a good outcome. The goal becomes helping you develop a sense of control and power so you can deploy skills to protect your loved ones from uncontrolled anger. The end state for both partners is to develop emotional self-mastery and meta-awareness of their habitual patterns.

Emotional self-mastery is a skill, and it can be developed, just as you are trained in the military to balance aggressive responding with self-control. Awareness is always the first component of skill building. Well over a decade ago, when primitive watches with heart rate monitors were just coming onto the market, I used this tool to help my patients develop emotional self-mastery.

---

132. Karl Marlantes, *What It Is like to Go to War* (New York: Grove/Atlantic, 2011), 96.

The intervention is quite simple. First, you need to get two weeks of individual baseline data under four conditions: your heart rate upon waking from a peaceful sleep, your heart rate when awakening after a nightmare, your heart rate when relaxed, and your heart rate when angered. An important observation was that for some of my veteran patients, a lower, not higher, heart rate is most associated with destructive rage.

So, the key was to measure the heart rate values that were reliably associated with various mind states. This allows you to immediately feel a sense of control and predictability as you move into "estimating" your heart rate in light of your level of irritability/anger. Then you can fold in experiments to help yourself down-regulate.

The ways and means of downregulation are as varied as people are themselves, so you must lead yourself in discovering what works for you. For some, it may be vigorous physical exertion (but NOT "venting" your rage on a punching bag while thinking of the violent ways you might like to engage your partner). For others, it might be deep breathing, listening to certain kinds of music, calling a friend to get an outside perspective, etc.

Once you have cracked the code for what helps you down-regulate, you are well positioned to access the "meta" mental state that is required for emotional self-mastery. It then becomes possible to use even a crude biofeedback tool—a primitive heart rate monitor—to give you biologically based data on when you can productively engage in conflict with your partner. If your heart rate is too high (or too low), this can help you see that protecting your partner from your rage means making a tactical withdrawal for a space of time. I'll explain the "tactical withdrawal" process shortly.

Understanding the Alligator Brain Mode

Another building block to better understanding starts with the story of an alligator I once met named "Mojo." Mojo was a bull gator—the barrel-chested alpha (i.e., dominant) alligator—within a famous family of alligators that lived two miles from my home in Florida. Visitors came in throngs to the Kanapaha Botanical Garden to see Mojo and his growing family. Like other bull gators, Mojo grew about a foot a year and spent his days lazily sunning himself on the banks of the lily pad pond.

I happened to meet Mojo two weeks before he made the local news. With no barrier between us, I walked on the path five feet away from where he had settled down for a midday siesta. Two weeks later, he was dragged up from the bottom of the pond and killed. His stomach was cut open to retrieve the arm of the park's lead custodian, Don Goodman, which was so badly digested that it could not be re-attached.[133] To his credit, the custodian was philosophical about losing his arm. He reflected on how Mojo's act of aggression was not premeditated—it was based on the animal instinct to react defensively to a perceived threat. So it is with many human relationships.

At the time, I was studying human emotion and the Mojo attack helped me see this: We all have an alligator brain in our skulls. Stacked on top of our alligator brain—what scientists actually call the "reptilian brain stem"—is the part of our brain that makes us fully human. The upper part of our brain, the "Executive Functioning Center," is meant to control our behavior in most circumstances. This part of our brain allows us to plan, strategize, and critically evaluate how to go after what we want without damaging those we love. What follows is not a scientifically accurate description, but rather a narrative that illuminates how rage works. It is an explanation that has helped many of my patients.

First, divide the brain into just two parts for a moment, the alligator brain and the executive functioning center. Now imagine that there is a very thick, solid iron gate on thick hinges between the two parts of the brain. When we are consumed by rage, a wave of chemicals pushes the gate between the two parts closed. We are hijacked by our alligator brain—the same one that controlled Mojo when he literally bit off the hand that had fed him.

In "Mojo mode," we see red, our vision tunnels and the feeling of threat compels us to see our partner as a hostile combatant, rather than the person whom we committed to honor and love for the rest of our lives. We say things that later burn us with shame, cruel things that our partners often remember for many years. We inflict attachment wounds and hack away at the roots of security in our relationship. In this state of mind, we cannot access our executive functioning center, the part that allows us to consider options for responding. We are overrun by rage and feel compelled to annihilate the perceived threat.

However, if we can build awareness that we are in "Mojo mode," we can make a tactical withdrawal to regain our emotional self-mastery. Even if we do nothing fancy—no soothing relaxation exercises, no guided meditation, no thought-stopping sheets—and we simply just wait with the goal of regulating our emotional state, we would see the iron gate swing back open again. There are several detectable signs to tell us when our gate is open again, for instance:

- Our field of vision expands back to baseline

- We see clearly with a range of colors (not just red or grey fuzz)

---

133. "Alligator Bites Off Man's Arm at Garden in Florida," *Los Angeles Times*, September 25, 2002, https://www.latimes.com /archives/la-xpm-2002-sep-25-na-gator25-story.html.

- We begin to think of options for creatively responding to the situation at hand

- Our muscles unclench

- Our heart rate returns to baseline (or a calm state)

The Art of Making a "Tactical Withdrawal"

When we are in "Mojo mode" the wisest course of action is to detach from conflict for a space of time. To emphasize the difference between passive submission (undesirable), conflict avoidance (undesirable), and protecting loved ones from our own rage (desirable), I developed the concept of "tactical withdrawal."[134] Tactical withdrawal is fundamentally honorable. It is what we do when we want to develop emotional self-mastery. In order to be effective, however, detachment must be done in a way that creates a stronger attachment.

As I have mentioned in an earlier section of the handbook, the withdrawal of a primary attachment figure can create what Dr. Sue Johnson has called a "primal panic." This is what happens by default, unless care is taken to explain the detachment in a way that deepens trust. An example may help. Imagine you are in the middle of a heated conflict and your partner says, "*I am getting too angry and I need to calm myself down before I say or do something that I don't intend. I need to calm down because I love you and I don't want to hurt you, or us. I will come back when I am calm and we can continue this then.*" Or here is another way to get to the same end, "*We are doing this again. I don't want us to hurt each other in this way. I'm going to go calm down. Let's try again when we're both calmer.*"

It can be hard to touch our partners in a loving way when we are angry, but it can be the most powerful thing you can do during conflict. Gentle, loving physical touch, even a hand placed on an arm, can help us re-regulate and may communicate love and trust more deeply than words can. This can be especially powerful in combination with explicit verbal statements of your intentions as shown in the examples given above.

Tactical withdrawal must never, ever be used as a tactic for continually avoiding conflict. The partner who initiates a tactical withdrawal must re-engage when he or she is in a more productive state of mind. Otherwise, trust is broken. A tactical withdrawal is, by definition, one that is temporary. The time apart allows for a shift to a more productive state of mind, followed by a strategic re-engagement. Some of my patients have found it helpful to lead themselves through a simple thought exercise, presented here.

---

134. Springer, *Marriage.*

Exercise: Self-reflection to Support "Tactical Withdrawal"
(Do this when you are NOT angry)

What made that feel so hurtful to me?

Is this about the thing we're fighting about now, or older stuff that is still impacting me? If so, what?

What do I want? What is my end state?

Can I think of *3 creative options* for responding that won't escalate this conflict?[135]

How can I explain what I want to my partner in a way that is respectful – that treats her or him like my closest team member?

---

135. For example, I remember a time when I *really* wanted my husband to help me clean up the house but he needed rest. He drew a picture that was hilarious and the caption said, "How I feel about housework right now." It immediately converted tension to humor—I laughed and got it, and he got the rest he needed.

Use Tools Learned in the Military to Generate a Good Plan

It is common for roles in the home to shift dramatically during the process of military transition. As I mentioned earlier, military partners are often socialized to make independent decisions about a range of family matters while their active duty spouse is focused on training or mission objectives. Military families often learn to create interdependent networks to fill in the gaps and gain mutual support, especially during times when military loved ones are deployed for an extended period of time. Structuring roles in a way that supports the requirements of the military is simply part of military life. With transition, after an active duty military leader separates, there is often a need to re-negotiate roles in the family. Approaching this process with an open mind and making a commitment to shifting roles in

---

Example: Applying OSMEAC to Social Growth Goals

ORIENTATION: *When I think about how we make non-military friends, my kids sports teams seem to be where we have the most engagement and we're able to build relationships with people who do not have associations with the military.*

SITUATION: *We're moving to a new location and we have to get the kids registered for school and extracurricular activities.*

MISSION: *To get the kids involved in sports, but in addition to this, to have my wife and I involved so that we can build out new friendships with others in our community.*

EXECUTION:

1) We need to find out what kinds of teams are available based on my son's skill level

2) We have to find out what kinds of coaching/volunteer opportunities exist for the team

3) We have to get signed up for sports and volunteering roles, respectively

4) We need to attend the volunteer/team meet and greets and make a good effort to introduce ourselves

ADMIN/LOGISTICS: *We've got travel schedules, equipment requirements, fees related to the team, fund-raising responsibilities that we need to account for, paperwork to be submitted, and our son may need a physical as part of the registration*

COMMAND/CONTROL: *My son is going to research the equipment requirements, I am going to take care of reaching out to the coach, my partner is going to take care of reaching out to learn about other volunteer opportunities, and we will get all this done by the end of July.*

a fair-minded, transparent way is critical for maintaining a culture of mutual respect within a partnership.

To support this process, Jason provided a family planning tool earlier in the handbook, **Section 2.8, Determine Family Information Requirements (FIR)**. For some military couples, another helpful tool, one that many of my patients have learned in the military, is the "five paragraph order"—Situation, Mission, Execution, Administration and Logistics, and Command and Signal (SMEAC)—from the MDMP. During the session where this first emerged as a tool, I was with a Marine Corps veteran with approximately ten combat deployments. The strain in his relationship was overwhelming and he was becoming emotionally disregulated during one very difficult session. I asked him, "*Is there any tool you learned during the military that can help you organize the chaos in your mind right now? What did you use to organize the chaotic variables of fluid situations during combat operations?*"

His eyes focused and his head cleared—his face changed. He said, "Yes, of course! SMEAC."

In the same way we applied the Military Decision-Making Process as a model for the Military Transition and Reintegration Process, you can apply the SMEAC to develop your plan for sustaining healthy relationships through military transition and beyond. A familiar process may help provide clarity during an otherwise unfamiliar period of your life. Using tools like this that may already be very familiar to you can provide clarity and a way forward, with respect to a range of necessary adjustments, including shifts in roles within the family, or the pursuit of other goals, such as building a new community of support after military discharge.

Asserting Your Needs Respectfully and Maintaining Good Boundaries

OK, let's say that you have used either the "tactical withdrawal" exercise or one of the military planning tools described above and you are clear on your objectives. The next step is to learn how to communicate these effectively and respectfully to your partner. However, in my observation, many people in society can't explain the difference between being aggressive, being passive, and being assertive, let alone deploy these insights. Let's see if we can derive some helpful distinctions from an example of each of these types of behaviors. Imagine that you are in the midst of a long and stressful week and your partner tells you that she has committed you both to attend the birthday party of one of her friends on Friday night. Here are three possible ways you could respond:

1. "This Friday night, really? You've already RVSP-ed for us? I guess it's too late and I'll have to go, but as I've told you many times before, I really wish you'd check with me first before committing me to social plans."

2. "Crap! That's about the last thing I want to be doing after the week I've had—I don't even like your friend that much! You'll just have to un-RSVP, because we're not going!"

3. "This Friday night? I know that she is one of your best friends. If you had asked if I could go before the week started, and if I knew it was important to you that we both go, I might have been able to shuffle some of my other commitments, but this week has been a wild and wooly one and I'm going to be exhausted on Friday, so I won't be able to go with you. If you want to go without me, of course that would be fine and I'd love to meet up with you for a movie later on if you'd like, once I've had a chance to unwind."

The second response, which is the aggressive example, would obviously be inconsistent with the goal of maintaining a respectful, loving relationship. This response bears the clear markings of an alligator brain hijacking—if Mojo could talk, this is what he might say to his partner. On the other end of the spectrum, it might seem that the kindest way to go is the first response. This response appears gentle and accommodating. If this type of passive response is a pattern, however, in the long run, this breeds resentment in the relationship. In the short run, being assertive almost always takes more energy than being passive, but in the long run, less energy is drained off by chronic resentment.

There are a number of people whom others view as "great givers" whom I would not classify as givers at all. If your giving is based on a lack of boundaries and you give because you can't say no, then what you are doing is not really giving—it's a compulsive behavior. What you do does not come from a position of love or generosity, but stems instead from a sense of fear or a feeling of obligation (*"I can't say no...they won't understand...it will hurt their feelings"*). The profile of a passive person is a person who feels resentful but does things for others anyway, who approaches a good portion of the things he or she does with a feeling of dread or irritation (often covered up by a veneer of "selfless service"), and who begins to use avoidance and social withdrawal as a way of getting out of having to say no. Passivity as a lifestyle makes us feel undefended and at the whim of everyone else's agendas.

To be a "lover," you must not engage in acts of love compulsively. You must feel free to say yes and equally free to say no in accordance with your values and priorities. This doesn't mean that you always do what is best for you. Some books on assertiveness may suggest that being assertive is not only the best, but also the only healthy response to all situations. I do not believe this to be true. There are times, even in a healthy relationship, to be passive and times when an aggressive approach may be warranted. In a good relationship, you will often take a hit out of love and may choose, in this scenario, to attend the birthday party of your partner's friend after an exhausting week. The point I'm making, however, is that when you do this, it should be a choice you are making, not the result of your inability to take a different path.

A way to understand the difference between aggressive and assertive approaches is that aggressive responses favor your rights more than the rights of others, while assertive responses value your own and others' rights equally. In being assertive, you would state your thoughts and feelings openly, boldly telling someone else what you want while also accounting for the fact that the other person has an equal right to pursue what he or she wants. The picture of two people who use the assertive style as a pattern in their relationship is one that involves continuous negotiation and compromise. As you may have noticed, the third response from the previous set of examples is the longest and most skillfully worded of the three options. The responder is in full possession of his or her "best brain" and has considered how to respond in a loving, yet assertive, way.

Although it's relatively easy to be passive or aggressive, it requires energy and thought to practice assertiveness, especially if you are learning to do so for the first time. Assertiveness is a skill, however, and like any skill, it can become routine over time.

Practice Direct Communication

I mentioned in an earlier part of the handbook the observation that sometimes those who serve in the military do not put into explicit words what they need from their partners. My theory is that this pattern is borne from all the training you get that converts explicit verbal communication into more subtle forms of communication (body language signaling, having a shared understanding of the mission, etc.). Regardless, expecting your partner or other civilian friends and family to decipher your needs without your having to put them into words will harm your relationships.

This behavior is quite common among lots of couples—civilian and otherwise. Some have called this the expectation that your partner will read your mind and know what you need. In fact, I've had a pushback more times than I can remember on partners who say things like, "*If he* really *loved me, he or she would* know *what I need.*" This isn't fair to your partner, and it's not the way to build and maintain a strong positive bond. It is your responsibility to speak up and tell your partner what you need.

Here are a couple very common examples of issues that come up in relationships. Let's say that you get home from a long day of work, and your partner immediately wants to engage you in a deep conversation. Your partner has missed you all day and is looking to reconnect with you. The problem is that you need some time to unwind before you are ready to reconnect with your partner. If you try to take the time you need without putting this into words, it's almost a guarantee that your partner will feel that you are avoiding him or her, which will damage the bond you have.

If, on the other hand, you are able to say, "*Babe, I love you and I want to reconnect with you at the end of the day. Before we reconnect, what I've realized is that I need a period of time—maybe just thirty minutes or an hour—to unwind on my own. Having this time to myself allows me to fully let go of the stress of the day and transition to our time together in the evening. What I need from you is to give me this space of time. When I've had the opportunity to unwind a bit, I'll find you and we'll enjoy the rest of the evening together.*"

Here is another common issue. Let's say that for whatever reason—maybe it is the anniversary of the loss of someone you cared about in the military—you are hit hard by strong emotions. Your partner sees your distress and wants to help, but doesn't know how to help. In these cases, clear guidance from you is essential to preserving your good bond of trust with each other.

Rather than rejecting your partner's well-intentioned efforts to support you (*You look sad, let's talk about what's going on for you*), it is best if you lead yourself and your partner toward a plan to best support you. Your needs may vary according to the situation at hand, but being able to say things like, *I know you have my back. I love you and you are my rock. What I really need from you is...*

- To spend a day with you and the kids fishing off the dock, just having fun and focusing on enjoying some time together.

- To get your support for going to visit my friend from the military this weekend.

- To have some time to myself this afternoon.

- For you to cover the kids so I can get some rest.

- To talk this out with you later today once I've had some time to think.

To return to the very start of this part of the handbook, to the concept of secure attachment, the hallmark of secure attachment is the ability to directly express our needs to our partner with confidence that they will do their best to meet our needs because they love us. This is the core goal and the essence of what "right looks like" over the long arc of a strong partnership.

Taking a Strategic Point of View

I have also noticed that couples who are good at conflict have an ability to do what I call "zooming out." I have seen a related concept referred to as meta-cognitive processing, more simply defined as "thinking about thinking." When we meta-cognate, we lead ourselves. We pull back from the immediacy of an interaction and think about the *process* of how we are interacting with someone else. We become more mindful of our emotional state and can slow our rate of emotional response. If you like, think of yourself as Neo from the movie *The Matrix* when he pulls back from a spray of bullets and slows time so he can avoid getting damaged. After zooming out, we can assist our partner in shifting gears by using humor or providing reassurance that although a part of us is really pissed off right now, a much bigger part of us loves them very deeply.

We begin to observe our behavior differently from this zoomed-out perspective and we start to notice new elements of our partners' behavior and consistent patterns across conflict situations. Of course, we deploy these meta-cognitive skills from the executive functioning center of the brain, *not* the part where Mojo lives.

In therapy, I often find it productive to help couples alternate between zooming out from the emotional themes in their repeated conflicts and zooming in on some core emotions they are experiencing in the moment. This practice strengthens their ability to apply a wide range of strategies in managing conflicts. The practice of pulling out and engaging the executive functioning center of the brain also converts animosity into curiosity, which leads to individual and collective growth.

One-up, One-down Relationships

It is also important to mention a subject that can be touchy, which is this: all too often in military partnerships, I have observed a tendency for an imbalanced relationship, where one person is consistently the caregiver for the other. I am not referring to the noble calling of military spouses who step up to support their injured partners as needed, but a more nuanced pattern that some couples fall into, to their detriment.

Sometimes this pattern is an extension of the ethos shared by active-duty warrior families, where the homefront tribe often cultivates a life that is centered on being supportive of their deployed warrior. As I mentioned earlier, military families may be told to handle all the stress at home so that their deployed loved one is not "distracted" by stressors at home. And this may indeed be necessary during seasons of deployment, as a distracted warrior can be an impaired warrior.

However, if this pattern continues, it will create a parent-child relationship rather than a partnership of two equal partners. In the long run, this pattern of emotional caretaking depletes the inner resources of the caregiver and atrophies the inner strength of the care-receiver, who would be better served by exercising the muscles of self-mastery and self-leadership.

This creates a "one-up, one-down" relationship that isn't satisfying to either partner and it absolutely impacts the capacity to enjoy a healthy sex life. To break this pattern, partners must become battle buddies who support each other in reciprocal ways. To put it another way, there can be no "identified patient" in the relationship, but rather two individuals who have come together to have each other's back through the storms that life brings. That's the difference with a team. Changing this often requires one partner to become vulnerable, to disclose their struggles, to start a new pattern where both partners will help shoulder each other's emotional burdens in a reciprocal way.

END-OF-SECTION REVIEW AND SUMMARY

The insights that you gain regarding how to grow and maintain a strong committed relationship will help you when this is your central goal, or when this becomes your goal in the future. After you complete this exercise, you may want to incorporate these practical actions into your action plans for transition and reintegration.

To summarize, then, for those of you who are formally committed with a desire to maintain a strong relationship as you undergo transition from the military, key insights include:

- We often express love to others according to unspoken, and unacknowledged, rules of behavior—whether from what we learned in childhood, didn't receive, see on TV, etc.). Taking the way we love each other off "auto-pilot" and becoming intentional in how we love each other is critical.

- Healthy partners balance, and constantly rebalance, respect in the relationship so that no one consistently feels "one down."

- Good self-esteem and openness to influence allow us to share power, admit wrongs, and change course as needed.

END OF SECTION REVIEW

Take some time and review this section on Guidance for Maintaining Strong, Happy Lifelong Partnerships. When you are ready, go through Part 1 and Part 2 of this End of Section Review to apply the information in this handbook to your ability to forge healthy relationships through transition and beyond

PART 1 INSIGHTS

What are the 5 most important insights that you learned about relationships?

(do this whether you are single or not, because what you learn might help support a single friend, colleague, or subordinate who is in transition).

EXAMPLE: Healthy partners extend each other support for new freedoms - fulfillment of both individual and relationship potential are both viewed as important.

PART 2 PRACTICAL ACTIONS

Identify three (3) things you plan to do to apply these insights based on the example provided

EXAMPLE: If I have a need to detach for awhile, I will directly express this in a loving way to my partner. When my partner meets this need, I will sincerely thank him or her for loving me well.

- Healthy partners extend each other support for new freedoms. Fulfillment of individual and relationship potential are both seen as important goals.

- Some of us may need times of detachment to recharge our batteries. If we do, then we need to express this directly to our partners. When they meet this need, it is a gift from them that builds secure attachment.

- Helping to shoulder our partner's emotional burdens may require us to do nothing at all except hold the space for their vulnerability.

- Explicit expression of needs and intentions to meet our partner's needs may not come easily for some of us. If so, this is a growth area since our partners can't read our minds (and should not be expected to do so).

- Rather than being idealized by our partners, we want to be known for who we are, warts and all, and still be seen as a great person and a great partner.

- We can give our partners lots of constructive feedback if we protect them well at the level of global perception (if we make sure they are in no doubt that we see them as great people and great partners).

- Avoiding conflict is easy in the short run, but creates a relationship that is built on an unstable foundation—it is a matter of time before the bottom drops out.

- Intimate conflict requires a different form of courage than the kind of courage required in battle.

- We often avoid being vulnerable for protective reasons; still, we must learn to stand without armor if we want to build a relationship that will stand the test of time.

- Not all aggressive behavior comes from the same source, reactive/impulsive anger often has a much better prognosis than premeditated/cold anger.

- If uncontrolled anger is an issue in your life, remember that you can draw on skills learned during the military to gain greater emotional control.

- Understanding the alligator brain and the role of the executive functioning center can help you gain greater emotional self-mastery.

- Using tools from the military can help us generate a good plan for our growth goals.

- Since our partners can't read our minds (and this isn't a fair expectation), it is up to us to practice direct communication. Remember that directly expressing what we need is the hallmark of secure attachment.

- Taking a strategic point of view by "zooming out" during a given fight can help de-escalate unproductive conflict.

- One-up, one-down relationships will not be sustainable in the long run. Changing this pattern is possible and requires the mutual expression of vulnerability and reciprocal meeting of needs in the relationship.

LIFE IS FULL OF CHALLENGING TRANSITIONS

In wrapping up this portion of the handbook, I would note that the transition from the military is **one of many future transitions**. Tunnels of chaos are the chorus of our lives, and they can bring an explosion of positive growth to us, individually and collectively. Take, for example, the transition some couples undergo if they decide to bring children into their family. Consider the words of a close friend of mine, a combat Marine, who once said, *"I'm a Marine. I am proficient at suffering. But the newborn phase of raising kids is a whole new level of suffering that I wasn't prepared for."*

A number of major life transitions occur during the testing phase of our close relationships as we forge careers, set down geographic roots, and, in some cases, become parents. As a result, we pass through several tunnels of chaos—for example, when making a major relocation, adding children to our families, losing a job, changing a career, or sending a child to college. Within each tunnel of chaos, the previous rules and assumptions of our partnership get shaken up and potentially realigned.

Rather than being surprised by the turbulence that transition brings, it is helpful to remember that transitions are a normal part of life for all of us. No one gets a pass. As you go through periods of transition, recall that three questions are central to relationship satisfaction or distress in adult relationships:

- "Do you really love me?"

- "Is it safe to ask you for what I need?"

- "Can I depend on you when I need you?"

Times of transition, or any other times of very high stress, are particularly susceptible to attachment wounds (translate this as the feeling of *"I needed you and you were not there for me"*). Attachment wounds are dangerous because they are often used as a touchstone for the degree of trust and closeness in the relationship going forward.

What we've missed in the relationship field, however, is that the opposite is also true—times of transition also carry unique potential to greatly deepen our trust and bring us closer together. There are lots of references in the field of couples therapy to "attachment wounds" but we have no term that captures the opposite state, so allow me to suggest one: "attachment gifts." The essence of an "attachment gift" is the feeling of, *"I was broken down and you were there for me, even when others were not. You are my rock and my safe harbor, and you and I have earned a rare level of trust and built this beautiful relationship together."*

It is in the very process of navigating tunnels of chaos in life that two people become soul mates. If humans can develop finely honed skills in music, athletics, and language arts, wouldn't it be equally possible for them to become perfectly suited and *completely irreplaceable* to their partners? A virtuoso develops perfect pitch and can instantly play complex musical patterns after listening to them just once. The best soccer players combine incredible footwork skills with a holistic awareness of the playing field; at the highest levels of play, soccer becomes a game of angles, similar to billiards. Someone who becomes fluent in a language "thinks" in that language—there is no effortful retrieval once the language becomes second nature.

Along these lines, successful couples are able to stay connected within the chaos, protect their partner's vulnerable places, and adapt to new roles that meet the demands of new stressors. In the best lifelong partnerships, we take off our armor and express our attachment needs directly. As we do this, the partnership becomes so multifaceted and the compatibilities so intricately dovetailed that our partner could never be replaced by anyone else.

Relationships (and careers, and lives in general) don't get better as a function of time alone. Transformation in any domain of our lives requires us to actively invest our time and energy, and to take uncomfortable risks. Relationships transform as a function of two people continuing to treat each other with love and respect, despite the challenges life brings. We can all be assured that life will continue to bring us new challenges, but with the right support from the people we love and trust, we can become *stronger* over time by weathering the storms we encounter.

As life unfolds beyond the military, engage the warrior within yourself, keep your tribe close, extend trust to those in your homefront tribe, embrace the suck, accelerate into experiences that challenge you, continue to act on your most sacred values, and fully commit to traversing the crucible of transitional cycles in life. This is the path of the warrior, and continuing to walk the warrior's path will renew your strength and lead to a life that is full of hope and meaning.

—DOC SPRINGER

ACKNOWLEDGMENTS

From Jason Roncoroni

I'd like to thank my wife, partner, and best friend, Jill, for her continuous support and love over the twelve months it took to complete this project. This would not have been possible without you. I would also like to thank Aidan and Everett for providing me with the inspiration to make a difference in this world. To my parents, Linda and Ed, thank you for the continuous support through my military journey and beyond. I want to thank the people who took the time to provide feedback for this work including Ian Fuller, Lance Calvert, Machim McHargue, Heather Glinski, Mike Kuypers, Sara McNamara, and Zebrina Warner. To Kathleen O'Grady, Laura Reichert, and the Raleigh Coaching Academy, thank you for providing me with clarity and confidence for this project. I'd like to thank all the men and women whom I've had the pleasure to serve with through my military journey—may you find passion, purpose, and happiness as veteran leaders in society. I'd also like to thank the team at Lioncrest for believing in us and supporting our vision to change the condition of the veteran community. Finally, I'd like to thank my co-author in this work, Dr. Shauna Springer, for her collaboration, friendship, and commitment to improving the wellness of the veteran community.

From Doc Springer

I have two families, my homefront tribe (the family I am related to by blood and marriage) and the tribe of military service members and veterans who have brought me into their circle as a trusted Doc. My homefront tribe has made many sacrifices to allow me to walk with those who have served in our military. I especially want to thank my husband, Utaka, and my children, Terran and Tea, for their steadfast support. Those who serve in the military tribe have made many personal sacrifices to protect and defend all of us. I especially want to honor Zachary Neil Phillips and all those who take the oath of military service. The best way to really honor these sacrifices is to do our part to bring our service members *home*, not just into new jobs after the military. We must bring them all the way home, into lives that are filled with continued purpose and meaning, and deep connection with both their military tribe and their homefront tribe.

I am grateful for the contributions and thoughtful critiques of early drafts of this work from those in my circle, military leaders of all ranks who have earned the trust of their peers. They have asked for no public acknowledgment, telling me that "it's enough to be able to contribute to something that could help a lot of my brothers and sisters." Still, I'm grateful, and I acknowledge the insights and lived experience of those who have shaped this effort. It is my hope that together, we might disrupt the current transition process to allow more of those who serve to find their place as civic assets and exceptionally skilled leaders in life beyond the military. I also want to acknowledge the team at Lioncrest who have had our back since the first conversation we had about this project. And finally, I want to thank my co-author, Jason Roncoroni, for inviting me to contribute to this game-changing effort. Jason is one of the smartest people I know and I'm fortunate to count him as both a friend and valued colleague.

Made in the USA
San Bernardino, CA
02 December 2019